# FAILING THE ORDINARY CHILD?

## The theory and practice of working-class secondary education

GARY McCULLOCH

OPEN UNIVERSITY PRESS
Buckingham · Philadelphia

For Edward

Open University Press
Celtic Court
22 Ballmoor
Buckingham MK18 1XW

email: enquiries@openup.co.uk
world wide web: http://www.openup.co.uk

and

325 Chestnut Street
Philadelphia, PA 19106, USA

First published 1998

A catalogue record of this book is available from the British Library

ISBN    0 335 19788 4 (hb)      0 335 19787 6 (pb)

**Library of Congress Cataloging-in-Publication Data**
McCulloch, Gary.
Failing the ordinary child? : the theory and practice of working-class secondary education / Gary McCulloch.
p.      cm.
Includes bibliographical references (p.   ) and index.
ISBN 0-335-19788-4 (hardbound). — ISBN 0-335-19787-6 (pbk.)
1. Working class—Education (Secondary)—England—History—20th century.   2. Working Class—Education (Secondary)—Wales—History—20th century.   I. Title.
LC5056.G7M33   1998
373.1826'23'0942—dc21                                        97-39367
CIP

Typeset by Graphicraft Typesetters Limited, Hong Kong
Printed in Great Britain by St Edmundsbury Press, Bury St Edmunds, Suffolk

# Contents

# Acknowledgements

This book brings to a conclusion a research project that I have developed over the last ten years to consider the different forms of provision of secondary education in twentieth century England and Wales: the 'liberal' education associated with the grammar and public schools, the 'technical' and 'vocational' education represented in the technical schools, and the mass provision of the secondary modern and comprehensive schools. The earlier works in this series are *The Secondary Technical School: A Usable Past?* (1989) and *Philosophers and Kings: Education for Leadership in Modern England* (1991). I should like to take this opportunity to thank everyone who has helped me to sustain this project.

I am pleased to acknowledge the Leverhulme Trust for its support for the research project 'Education and the working class: history, theory, policy and practice' (F118AB) on which the present book is based, and also my research associate during this project, Liz Sobell.

I am grateful to members of the conferences and seminars where I have developed issues relating to the current work, and in particular to Richard Aldrich, Ivor Goodson, Peter Gosden, Roy Lowe and Brian Simon for their support and advice. My colleagues and students at the University of Sheffield have also provided invaluable support. The library staff at the University of Sheffield have been unfailingly helpful during my research, as have the staff at all the various libraries and archives that have been involved. I should also like to thank everyone who allowed me to interview them for the purposes of the current work. As always, my wife Sarah has been unstinting in her support. This book is dedicated to Edward, my son.

*Gary McCulloch*

# Abbreviations

| | |
|---|---|
| ACEO | Association of Chief Education Officers |
| AEC | Association of Education Committees |
| A level | Advanced level examinations |
| AMC | Association of Municipal Corporations |
| ATDS | Association of Teachers of Domestic Subjects |
| ATTI | Association of Teachers in Technical Institutions |
| BEC | British Employers' Confederation |
| CAC | Central Advisory Council |
| CCA | County Councils Association |
| CEO | chief education officer |
| CSE | Certificate of Secondary Education |
| CTC | city technology college |
| DES | Department of Education and Science |
| DfEE | Department for Education and Employment |
| GCE | General Certificate of Education |
| GCSE | General Certificate of Secondary Education |
| HMI | Her (His) Majesty's Inspector(ate) |
| LCC | London County Council |
| LEA | local education authority |
| MP | Member of Parliament |
| NAHT | National Association of Head Teachers |
| NAS | National Association of Schoolmasters |
| NCB | National Coal Board |
| NUT | National Union of Teachers |
| O level | Ordinary level examinations |
| SMS | secondary modern school |
| SSEC | Secondary Schools Examinations Council |
| *TES* | *Times Educational Supplement* |

TVEI      Technical and Vocational Education Initiative
WEA       Workers' Educational Association

# 1

# Introduction

Secondary education in England and Wales has systematically failed the ordinary child over the past hundred years, in the obvious sense that most children have emerged into adult life branded as failures from its processes of classification and grading. In the late nineteenth century the 'ordinary child' was not included in secondary education at all, since secondary education was defined exclusively in terms of a social and educational elite. During the twentieth century, access to secondary education has broadened to the extent that since 1944 all children have been entitled and indeed obliged to attend secondary school, at least up to a statutory school leaving age. Despite this major development of first mass and then universal secondary education, the majority of pupils have failed to traverse the obstacles that have been erected to judge their performance and potential.

These processes of discrimination have promoted a language of 'sheep' and 'goats' that is employed on an everyday basis to describe the basic tendency of secondary education to mark off the superior from the inferior, the first rate from the second rate. This is avowedly an educational divide, but it is also a social distinction, because there has been a consistent tendency for the failures in the system to be in the main working-class children. Its successes, on the other hand, have generally either been middle class in origin, or have been assimilated during their education into a middle-class system of values and rewards.

There is therefore a second vital sense in which secondary education might be said to have failed the ordinary child: that the system has a basic responsibility for such failure in that it has undermined the potential of the majority of children, partly in the very act of classifying them as failures, and partly by negating a wide range of abilities and interests in favour of a narrow emphasis on a particular form of ability expressed in academic examinations. This is the basis of a profound unease that has been experienced at different times during the twentieth century, but with particular resonance in the 1990s, that secondary education has failed to promote the interests of ordinary children as well as it has catered for the interests of a small elite group. In the late 1950s, for example, C.P. Snow complained that 'Somehow we have set ourselves the task of producing a tiny *elite* – far smaller proportionately than in any comparable country – educated in one academic skill.'[1] In the 1990s, the Paul Hamlyn National Commission on Education was acutely aware that the education system had 'concentrated for too long on the needs of the academically able at the expense of the rest'.[2] The public and political debates over the future of secondary education during the 1990s have drawn much of their fervour from a shared, though diffuse and confused, sense of failure.

These specific problems are explicitly recognized and addressed in the White Paper *Excellence in Schools*, the first White Paper produced by the incoming Labour administration, in July 1997. This White Paper acknowledges a need to 'put in place policies that benefit the many, not just the few',[3] and claims:

> The problem with our education system is easily stated. Excellence at the top is not matched by high standards for the majority of our children. We have some first-class schools and our best students compare with the best in the world. But by comparison with other industrialised countries, achievement by the average student is just not good enough.[4]

It argues, indeed, that these problems have what it calls 'deep and historic roots', in that unlike in many other nations, the importance of mass education was neglected at the end of the nineteenth century and has been only slowly recognized during the twentieth century.[5]

The contemporary debates of the 1990s, then, are based largely on historical issues that have been fought over for at least the past century but that remain contested and unresolved. At their most obvious level, they revolve around the experience of the comprehensive schools, which since the 1960s have been the major institutional form of state secondary school in England and Wales. Appraising the future of comprehensive schools, and whether they need to be maintained, improved, or abandoned, necessarily involves taking a view with regard to their record of achievement since the mid-1960s. On the one hand, many critics have argued that the comprehensive schools have failed. Most strikingly, David Blunkett, then the shadow spokesperson on education and employment for the opposition Labour Party, argued in a lecture to the Social Market Foundation in February 1996 that comprehensive schools had failed successive generations of children over the previous 30 years and would need to change, and claimed: 'In spite of more than fifty years of universal state secondary education and thirty years of comprehensive education, the pattern of excellence at the top and chronic underperformance at the bottom persists.'[6] Other commentators have echoed this general view.[7] According to Bernie Grant, the left wing Labour MP for Tottenham, north London, the comprehensive schools in inner city areas of London were 'very bad indeed', and were 'failing our children'.[8] On the other hand, there were many who defended the record of the comprehensive schools and sought to maintain their role.[9]

Also evident in the debates of the 1990s are the echoes of arguments that were played out earlier in the century, which in many cases had long since seemed to be settled but now found new life in a rapidly changing social and political context. Disputes over previously discredited ideas such as 'parity of esteem', and over abandoned and burned out vehicles like the 11-plus examination, were again fiercely pursued. The institutional forms of the 1940s and 1950s were also revived to play a morbid role in national debate, as the Conservative government harked back to the ideals and traditions of the grammar schools, while its opponents warned of the threat of a return to secondary modern schools. Thus, for example, Tony Blair, as leader of the opposition Labour Party, could claim that

> To return to the 11-plus, as the Prime Minister wants us to do, would be a mistake of monumental proportions. Who can really justify settling a child's fate by one exam at 11? Do we really want the majority of children going to secondary moderns? But, equally, the comprehensive system is not working as well as it should and we want to refine and redefine it.[10]

Such issues were usually evoked to stir memories, either to promote nostalgia for a 'golden age' in the case of grammar schools, or as a reminder of the inequalities of the past.[11]

At a still more profound level, the debate over secondary education during the 1990s has been about basic and enduring social distinctions between 'two nations' symbolized on the one hand by private (called public) schools such as Eton and Winchester, and on the other hand by state schools designed for the majority of the population. Such social antagonisms were unpredictable in their impact. They were clearly evident in the controversy that arose in early 1996 over the decision of Harriet Harman, a front bench Labour Member of Parliament (MP), to send her child to a (state) grammar school, avoiding the local comprehensive school. This episode, occurring shortly after Tony Blair had chosen to send his son to a grant-maintained school, led the Conservative government to portray 'the smart, young Labour leadership' as 'elitist, chattering classes who are all too ready to whisk their kids off to posh schools leaving you, the ordinary voter, exactly where you were'.[12] The deep seated nature of this social divide was acknowledged in a more thoughtful way by a Conservative MP, George Walden, who proclaimed the existence of an 'internal frontier' between the state and private sectors of education that embodied a 'two-nation education system' as 'an insurmountable reality, the division too deeply embedded – in our culture, in our politics, in our sclerotic British bones – to be changed'.[13]

At the same time, these social distinctions also reflected the longer term resilience of three different forms of education and schooling that have each been associated with the needs of different groups in society. First, and foremost in the prestige attached to it, has been 'liberal' education for a small elite group. Based principally in the public schools in the Victorian era, the grammar schools also assumed this mantle during the twentieth century, and many other educational institutions attempted to imitate its characteristic forms.[14] Second has been technical and vocational education designed for skilled workers, whether for particular trades and industries as with the junior technical schools of the 1920s and 1930s, or for a broader relationship with industry and commerce in general as was the case with the secondary technical schools in the 1940s and 1950s. This kind of institution, and the curriculum aligned with it, have suffered from a lack of social status, especially when compared with more liberal forms of education.[15] Last, there has also developed a banausic form of education considered especially suitable for the mass of the population. The terminology related to such provision has varied from the frank descriptions of the 'working class' that were characteristic of Victorian debates, to the euphemisms coined during the twentieth century such as the 'less able', the 'average and less than average', and the 'ordinary child'. These three different forms of educational provision, often described as a 'tripartite' arrangement, have survived the many changes and reforms in the structure of schooling virtually unscathed, to form a strong underlying cultural influence even at the end of the twentieth century.[16]

Many initiatives have been promoted over the past century to develop the most effective approach to the mass provision of secondary education. These might be described most accurately as 'experiments', and indeed have often been proudly claimed to be such on the part of their supporters. Their effects on the pupils involved and on the wider society have been observed in minute detail during that time. They have also tended to be carried out on other people's children, since nearly all of the leading educational policy makers and officials have been the products of the liberal and 'elite' form of provision. As R.H. Tawney, the highly influential social reformer, noted in the 1930s, English educational policy had been carried out in the main 'by men few, if any, of whom have themselves attended the schools principally affected by it, or would dream of allowing their children to attend them'.[17] In relation to working-class education in particular, Tawney complained privately, the 'classes who determine educational policy' and the 'nice officials' at what was then the Board of Education had no direct experience or real understanding of the problems involved, 'as do those who have friends who, themselves and their children, have been under the harrow'. Some of them might have some vague knowledge, Tawney continued, but 'they do not think it matters', and this was reflected in their own preferences:

> After all, if they really believe that the best thing for young people is to cease schooling at 14 and then enter a factory, they can prove the sincerity of their convictions by applying that regimen to their own children. How many of them do?[18]

Most of the theorists of educational change were also educated at elite institutions, including Tawney himself, a product of Rugby School and Balliol College, Oxford. In this important sense, the mass provision of secondary education since the nineteenth century might well be seen as a succession of experiments conducted *de haut en bas* on other people's children. They have been inherently paternalistic in nature, and essentially speculative as to their effects, derived as they have been from imagining what would be best for the children of other people who inhabited in the main a different social world.

Broadly speaking, there have been two major types of approach in these initiatives designed to promote the mass provision of secondary education. The first has been generalist in nature, with the aim of catering equally for children of all abilities and aptitudes, regardless of their social background. The key institutional example of this approach during the twentieth century has been the comprehensive school. A great deal of attention has been given to the development of the ideals associated with the comprehensives,[19] to their social composition,[20] and to the problems that they have encountered.[21] In the 1990s, fresh challenges to the existence of comprehensive schools have encouraged reappraisals of their development and further potential for the future.[22]

In such studies there has often been a tendency to regard the comprehensive ideal as the dominant tradition in English secondary education, towards which provision has gradually evolved despite setbacks and opposition. The leading historian of the period, Brian Simon, emphasizes that although the system of comprehensive schools 'has suffered almost continuous attack and negative criticism from leading politicians, including the Prime Minister', it had survived and would continue to do so because they 'embody ideals and practices which stretch back into the past and which retain their predominance in the minds and hearts of local populations'.[23] Caroline Benn declares that comprehensive education today 'is the culmination of that drive for secondary education for all – that has occupied the whole of the twentieth century in the same way elementary education for all occupied the nineteenth'.[24] Yet another, alternative tradition has been at least as powerful, no less resilient, and a key factor in the drive for secondary education for all as it worked itself out in the earlier part of the century, and its consequences need still to be remembered and confronted as part of our understanding of alternatives for the future.

This other major approach to mass provision has been separatist or tripartite in nature, with the aim of differentiating between different social groups and classes in such a way as to distinguish suitable provision for the 'mass' of the population, or the 'working class', from that designed for the 'able', or the 'middle class', or the 'elite'. The idea of creating a distinctive form of 'working-class secondary education' has been a pivotal aspect of this general project. The key institutional example of this approach during the twentieth century has been the secondary modern school (SMS), which served to demonstrate both the strength and the inbuilt contradictions of working class secondary education. These schools catered in their time, only a generation ago, for the large majority of the 11 to 15 age group. In the early 1960s, there were nearly 4000 SMSs in England and Wales, with over 1.5 million pupils. Their decline after that time was precipitate. However, little detailed attention has been given either to the long term development of this approach, or to the SMSs themselves. The standard account of the SMS remains that of William Taylor, published as long ago as 1963.[25] Taylor's study is naturally reliant on published observations by contemporaries on the problems and possibilities of such schools. It remains useful as a well informed interim discussion of their characteristics and prospects, rather than as a history. In essence, it constitutes a preliminary account of the development of the SMSs which are long overdue for reappraisal.

In contrast with Taylor's work, David Hargreaves's *Social Relations in a Secondary School* (1967) is very much an internal and particularized account that is set in a specific SMS in a 'highly industrialised and densely populated town in the North of England'.[26] Lumley Secondary Modern School, as Hargreaves calls it, is examined in great detail to discern the 'structure of social relations' within the school.[27] However, Hargreaves's study is of only partial value in terms of an understanding of SMSs in general, because of its internalist focus. It does not attempt to develop a wider account of the schools as they related to policy and political issues, although there is some very interesting material on the relationship between families and the SMSs. Nor does it reveal anything about the development over time of the 'social relations' that it documents so fully.

In general, while both Taylor and Hargreaves provide important accounts of differing types, there is one important aspect that is missing from them both. It is the social history of the SMSs that constitutes the neglected dimension of these studies; the relationship between the secondary moderns and their wider social, political and cultural configurations. Such a social history should be crucial in helping to explain the reasons for the emergence of SMSs in the 1940s, their characteristics, successes and problems as educational institutions, and the reasons for their early demise. It should also enable us to assess their longer term historical significance, and their influence in relation to subsequent historical change, conceived in terms that will permit a critical engagement with the problems and policies of today.[28]

The current work is therefore concerned to understand the development of the differentiated form of 'working-class secondary education' in England and Wales over the past century, with the secondary modern schools as a major case study. Part 1 explores general social and historical issues related to the tradition, and the emergence of the idea of working-class secondary education in the late nineteenth and early twentieth centuries. In Part 2, the secondary modern schools are examined in detail in order to appraise the reasons for their rise, their successes and failures, and their ultimate failure. Part 3 then pursues the underlying theme of differentiation in secondary education since the 1960s, and suggests that it has remained influential despite the spread of comprehensive schools in that time and forms a key to understanding the educational and social debates of the 1990s. The principal themes in the first two major sections highlight the distinction between the 'theory' and the 'practice' of working-class secondary education, as the theory developed in the decades prior to 1944 was tested out in practice in the experiment of the secondary modern schools. The nature of its 'legacy' is the focus of Part 3.

The overall argument of this book is, first, that differentiation is at least as deeply ingrained in the English social tradition of education as the generalist aims of the comprehensive school. In the early 1950s, Harold Dent, editor of the *Times Educational Supplement* (*TES*) and a leading historian of the principle of 'secondary education for all', could insist that tripartism was 'a natural result of the historical evolution of post-primary education in England and Wales'.[29] It was not, 'as many people appear to imagine, the result of a modern passion for administrative tidiness, nor, as even more seem to believe, a sinister plot to deprive "working-class" children of the educational opportunities which are theirs by right'. Dent argued that it was, rather, 'a manifestation of the "tradition of the society", with long and deep historical roots, and should be treated as such'.[30] A major purpose of the current work is to examine the basis for such a claim.

Second, it is suggested that the application of this principle to the mass provision of secondary education has been wasteful and contradictory, with the practical outcomes belying the generally well meaning and idealized hopes that were entertained for 'working-class secondary education', and that it was tested to destruction in the experiment of the secondary modern schools. This book sets out to demonstrate both the inherent strength and resilience of this tradition, and its no less inherent weaknesses, confusions and dangers.

# PART 1

## The theory

The half-conscious striving of a highly industrialised society to evolve a
type of school analogous to and yet distinct from the secondary school,
and providing an education designed to fit boys and girls to enter the
various branches of industry, commerce, and agriculture at the age of 15.

(Hadow Report, 1926: 35)

# 2

# Working-class secondary
# education

In the nineteenth century, the orthodox view was that working-class education should be 'elementary' rather than 'secondary' in nature. In the twentieth century, it became common to argue that secondary education should cater for all, regardless of their social background. Within this historical framework of development, the notion of 'working-class secondary education' seems at first sight to be a contradiction in terms. Yet the class based nature of educational provision as it became organized during the nineteenth century actually served to encourage a debate over the possibilities of secondary education in relation to the working class, and this had a major bearing on the structures of secondary education and the assumptions that underlay them. This debate involved thinking about how to cater for those children of the working classes for whom elementary instruction would be insufficient.

## Secondary education for the working class?

Secondary education in nineteenth century England and Wales was organized privately and based on differentiation along lines of social class. It was separate and indeed entirely remote from elementary provision for the working classes, which the state began grudgingly to support in the second half of the century.[1] The Newcastle commission in the 1860s and the Cross commission in the 1880s were concerned specifically with the development of working-class elementary instruction.[2] Secondary education was intended, explicitly and consciously, for the middle classes. There was also differentiation within secondary education, also broadly along class lines. The so called 'public schools' such as Eton and Winchester catered for the elite,[3] and the Clarendon commission of the 1860s was established solely for the purpose of reporting on the nine leading public schools of this type.[4]

There also existed a wide range of local secondary schools, with different kinds of characteristics depending on their clientele. The Taunton commission of the 1860s identified three general categories of such schools. The first grade catered for the sons of 'men with considerable incomes independent of their own exertions, or professional men, and men in business, whose profits put them on the same level', together with 'the great majority of professional men'.[5] It was classical in its emphasis, although some parents were anxious to add other subjects such as mathematics, and it continued to the age of 18 or more. The second grade included the classics but was broader in its general curriculum, and continued to the age of 16. According to the Taunton Report,

> The education of the first grade which continues till 18 or past, and that of the second grade which stops at about 16, seem to meet the demands of all the wealthier part of the community, including not only the gentry and professional men, but all the larger shopkeepers, rising men of business, and the larger tenant farmers.[6]

The third grade of education, up to the age of about 14, was for a large group 'distinctly lower in the scale', made up of smaller tenant farmers, small tradesmen and superior artisans.[7] These differing forms of provision amounted in practice to a complex and elaborate system based explicitly on social gradations among the middle and upper classes.[8] In this hierarchical system, the schools of the first grade constituted what has been described as the 'defining institutions' of the 'emerging system of secondary education',[9] that is, those that schools which sought elite status must seek to emulate and indeed to imitate.

Class based provision formed an iron logic that confined working-class children to elementary instruction. This logic was powerfully reflected in nineteenth century discussions about the proper nature and role of a state education system designed for the mass of the population. The majority view of the Newcastle Report in the early 1860s favoured increasing state aid for elementary instruction of the working class, but strongly opposed the idea of a compulsory or universal system or any advanced instruction for working-class children.[10] Robert Lowe, vice-president of the Committee of the Privy Council on Education and head of the education department, went further than this as he acknowledged that the 'education of the poor' was 'not a matter to be left wholly or entirely to private enterprise, but is a duty of the State'.[11] He concluded that it should therefore be compulsory so that 'those people should be able properly and intelligently to discharge the duties devolving on them'.[12] However, Lowe drew a rigid distinction between the kind of instruction that was appropriate for the 'lower classes' and the education that was required for the 'higher classes', and concluded that

The lower classes ought to be educated to discharge the duties cast upon them. They should also be educated that they may appreciate and defer to a higher cultivation when they meet it; and the higher classes ought to be educated in a very different manner, in order that they may exhibit to the lower classes that higher education to which, if it were shown to them, they would bow down and defer.[13]

Such views continued to be influential during the remainder of the nineteenth century.

Yet this kind of argument appeared increasingly inadequate as a response to the challenge of mass education. A complete denial of the possibility of secondary education for the children of the 'lower classes' might be the most convenient and straightforward solution, but it would be unable to accommodate the hopes and ambitions of many working-class people. In this situation, it became of paramount importance to try to reconcile social class structures and divisions with a clear means of pursuing such ambitions. Broadly, two distinct kinds of response to this issue began to emerge in the late nineteenth and early twentieth centuries. First, the idea of a 'ladder' for able children from a working-class background gave some prospect of providing secondary education for the working class on a selective basis. It was this idea that underlay the system of state secondary education following the Education Act (1902). Second, the notion of a distinctive form of secondary education that would be especially suitable for working-class children offered the promise of a purpose-built working-class secondary education. This latter idea gave rise to a number of educational initiatives in the late nineteenth century, but remained a largely unrealized ideal until well into the twentieth century.

The first of these alternative strategies, designed to allow access to secondary education for a selected number of working-class children on the basis of their individual 'merit', had a number of factors in its favour. It would leave the existing social order relatively unscathed in that the large majority of the 'lower classes' would remain in elementary schools. Indeed, it had the potential for strengthening the social order still further as the 'higher classes' would be buttressed by able recruits from the working class. Such a solution had the added advantage that it left largely unchallenged the existing values, structures and traditions of 'secondary education'. In particular, it tended to reassert the liberal values associated with the secondary school curriculum, as distinct from the technical, vocational and other kinds of curriculum that would continue to be undermined and downgraded. Even so, although such goals already appeared highly attractive in the late nineteenth century, the means by which to establish such a 'ladder' and the apparatus required to confer 'merit' still remained contentious and open to debate.

As has already been seen, the Taunton commission in the 1860s was acutely aware of the social class basis of the provision of secondary education, relating this kind of education explicitly to the needs of the middle class. During its investigations, it heard evidence from a wide range of witnesses who discussed these social distinctions in intimate detail. Some were strongly in favour of mixing the social classes. For example, Revd J.C. Bruce claimed that it was 'an injustice' and 'an unchristian thing' to reject the son of an artisan 'simply because his father is a workman'. No less important, he added,

> I think it is a disadvantage to the upper classes not to know the minds and the opinions of the rank below them, and I think that the battle of life will be better fought if as a boy you mingle with all classes, because as men you are obliged to mingle with all classes.[14]

Another ran a school in a rural area that involved all social classes, with different levels of fees being paid by the different classes. According to this witness, 'the tendency entirely is for the better class of boys to raise the character of the lower class boys', although he recognized some resistance to such mixing on the part of some parents:

> If you asked a farmer whether he would like his boy to be taught with boys of his own class or with the labourers' children, as a matter of course he would say he would rather have them taught with boys of his own class, but you cannot do it.[15]

On the other hand, a large number of witnesses to the commission emphasized the importance of separating the social classes. The Rt Hon. Earl Fortescue declared that it was 'rather desirable to mark a distinction in kind, as well as in amount, between the average education of the middle class and the lower class'. Although there should be a clear barrier, however, the emphasis here was placed upon the 'average':

> God forbid that any impassable line should be drawn between the lower class and the middle class, any more than between the middle class and the higher class: but in dealing with average human nature, and average lads, I think it would be desirable.[16]

The head of King Edward VI Grammar School in Southampton, C.W. Hankin, appeared to follow this general line as he supported the approach adopted at Cheltenham School that no tradesman's son should be admitted. He was endeavouring to make the fees for the modern department lower than for the classical department at his school, and by this means to provide for 'an exclusion of all mixture of classes'. There was in any case, according to Hankin, an observable 'difference between boys of different social positions in aptitude for study' in that 'boys from a lower stratum in society were not equally apt in intellectual pursuits generally'.[17] Such differences, combined with differences in manner and appearance, were repeatedly noted as ways of justifying a more or less rigid separation between the social classes.

In spite of this, some witnesses pointed out that scholarships, examinations and other devices could provide an important opportunity for allowing at least a few exceptionally able working-class pupils to progress into secondary education. One lamented that the new Revised Code, by restricting pupil-teachers, had lost a 'magnificent opportunity' of 'raising the clever fellows of the humbler class', who he described as 'perhaps extraordinary cases . . ., boys with considerable industry and talent'.[18] The issue that thus arose was how to cater for the 'extraordinary' or exceptional while excluding the 'average' or ordinary. This was achieved in a number of cases. At Liverpool College, for example, the three divisions of the school were 'absolutely separate' so that the upper school, the middle school and the lower school were effectively three separate schools with different curricula, each catering for a different social class. The buildings were arranged so that pupils from the different divisions could not mix in school hours, with separate playgrounds, dining rooms and entrances, and the teachers were also 'absolutely separate'. Within this rigid demarcation, the headmaster permitted one narrow 'link of connexion', which was that

> every half year one boy can be 'nominated' from the lower school to the middle school by election from merit, without any increase of payment; and one boy from the middle school to the upper in the same way; and of course that stream of promotion might reach the Universities.

According to this headmaster, there had been several boys who had risen in this way to 'very good positions at the Universities', but he insisted on restricting the flow to one nomination per half year, and a maximum of six promoted boys in any one school at one time.[19]

A similar arrangement was observed by one of the commissioners, T.H. Green, in his report on Aylesbury Free School in Buckinghamshire. In this case there were two departments, the higher and the lower, separated by curriculum and fees and taught in separate buildings:

> That appropriated to the lower department is old, and not in very good condition. The ventilation is bad; the floor is of brick, and uneven; the house of the English master, also, is in bad repair. The school of the upper department is new and good, though small.

Green noted that 'The boys of the lower department leave school half an hour before those of the upper, to avoid mixture in the streets.'[20] In these tightly controlled conditions, 'exhibitioners' could be promoted from the lower to the higher school on the basis of examinations, exempt from fees, and so 'the lower department serves as the avenue by which poor boys may rise to the higher education'.[21] Nevertheless, according to Green, the headmaster of the school 'did not look very favourably' on such transfers, for what he called the 'usual' reason, that 'the boys transferred, knowing plenty of arithmetic but no Latin, and only used to oral methods of teaching, did not fit satisfactorily into the system of the upper school'.[22]

Such 'lines of connexion' rarely seemed to include girls. One commissioner, James Bryce, noted that

> Although the world has now existed for several thousand years [*sic*], the notion that women have minds as cultivated and as well worth cultivating as men's minds is still regarded by the ordinary British parent as an offensive, not to say a revolutionary, paradox.[23]

The Treasurer of Christ's Hospital, W. Gilpin, concurred with this view, commenting that at this school there were pupils from all social classes but with few girls involved, because

> They are of that class that if you give them what is called a first-rate education, which several of the governors want them to have, such as music and French, you put them immediately above their parents, who, the greater part of them, are mere labourers, and there the governors felt they had great difficulties to contend with.[24]

Even for those who insisted on the importance of education for girls and the suitability of girls for an advanced education, there tended to be a greater aversion to mixing the social classes in relation to girls than for boys.

The final report of the Taunton commission faithfully adhered to the systematic separation of the social classes that was favoured by so many of its witnesses, and emphasized the distinct nature of the different grades of schools. However, it supported the development of 'some mode of selection by merit'[25] that would allow the schools to 'select the boys by their ability and attainments', preferably though 'open competitive examination' above the age of 13.[26] On this basis, it insisted, 'All who are admitted at all should be exactly on the same footing, and no distinction should be allowed, except that which depends on superior merit'.[27] It added that this 'open competition' should involve boys from different social classes, thus allowing at least the possibility that a small minority of working-class boys might be able to progress into secondary education, since, as the report stirringly concluded, 'If the son of a labourer can beat the sons of gentlemen that goes a long way to prove that he is capable of using with advantage the education usually given to gentlemen.'[28]

The ideas current in the 1860s therefore tended to encourage a sharp separation between instruction for the working classes and education for the middle classes, but allowed at least some scope for a few of the most able working-class children to benefit from secondary education. This kind of approach sanctioned a limited measure for secondary education for the working class, but did not allow for a distinct form of secondary education that might be more appropriate for working-class children.

## Working-class secondary education

The Elementary Education Act (1870) provided a means to 'fill the gaps' left by voluntary provision, and led to the establishment of popularly elected School Boards responsible for elementary education in their local area. This in itself tended to reinforce the existing divisions between 'elementary' and 'secondary' education, consolidating what Simon describes as 'a highly organised and strictly segregated system of schooling designed specifically for the working class'.[29] By the 1890s, there was a compulsory system of elementary education in force through which nearly all working-class children went to school. In this situation, educational debate increasingly revolved around two key issues: first, how far the ablest children in the elementary schools should be enabled to progress into secondary education, and second, whether the School Boards should be allowed to provide 'advanced' as well as strictly elementary instruction. This latter issue raised an important general principle as to whether there could be developed an alternative form of secondary education, a working-class secondary education, that would be more appropriate to the needs of the working class than was that provided in the grammar schools and the public schools.

The attitudes expressed in the 1860s remained strongly in evidence towards the end of the century. The Cross commission, investigating the effects and working of the Elementary Education Act in the 1880s, found a number of witnesses who strongly endorsed the maintenance of class based educational provision. Lord Lingen, a former secretary of the education department, was adamant that on principle 'it is not desirable, in my opinion, that the master should be educated in the same school with the man'.[30] Only a small number of working-class children would be capable of going into secondary schools, since, as he argued, 'if you take the natural capacity of the majority of children, and if you take the age at which they must go to labour, it is only a very few children that will emerge out of the elementary schools'.[31] Lingen also opposed 'bringing secondary education into the table of elementary schools', largely on the grounds that very few of the pupils would be suited to such education.[32] Another witness also emphasized what he called the *esprit de corps* that was present in some schools, by which 'Children of a certain social class will have none amongst them who do not belong to that class, and in some cases get rid of very poor children.'[33] This class consciousness existed in an uneasy tension with the idea of 'lifting' a 'clever boy' out of his own 'social station', although it was recognized that 'there are many men of considerable distinction who owe their distinction mainly to having been lifted out of their surroundings, and being given a fresh start in life'.[34]

Others argued the need for more advanced instruction for working-class children, although generally these still drew a distinction between this kind of development and the characteristics of secondary education. For example,

Sir Philip Magnus, a prominent advocate of technical education, supported the idea of 'higher elementary schools' into which 'the better children would be drafted' in order to allow them to gain 'systematic instruction during two or three years of their youth, which it is difficult, if not impossible, for them to obtain from any evening classes'.[35] Such schools would be limited to 'a better class of pupils, the more gifted pupils I would say',[36] but they would not be regarded as secondary schools not only because their curriculum would not be so advanced, but also because 'the secondary school would be adapted for a different class of children from those who, for the most part, would avail themselves of instruction in higher elementary schools'.[37] Magnus's proposals, far reaching though they were, therefore avoided making a direct challenge to the structures and assumptions that sustained the separation between elementary and secondary education.

Another supporter of higher elementary schools, the Revd Dr H.W. Crosskey of Birmingham, followed a similar line in emphasizing their distinctive nature in relation to secondary schools. Crosskey argued that higher elementary schools should give 'special provision' for children who had passed Standard VI, 'in the shape of adapting their education to their requirements and aptitudes'. Such schools would provide

> a continuation of their education [for] the children of working men who are going to work in manufactories on leaving school, and whose parents can keep them at school for two or three years after they have passed their Sixth Standard.

According to Crosskey, however, such schools would be 'entirely distinct from anything that can be properly called a secondary school, using the word secondary in its proper educational sense'. On this basis, elementary schools were 'schools for children who will be compelled to go to work at the age of 14 or 15', while secondary schools were 'for those who can remain longer'. It followed from this that there should be two separate systems of education, 'conducted upon different lines'.[38]

This view was supported by another witness to the Cross commission, James Scotson, the headmaster of the Higher Grade Board School in Deansgate, Manchester. Scotson argued that higher grade schools such as his own should 'form a connecting link between the ordinary elementary school and the really secondary school'.[39] A few 'extremely dull' pupils would be allowed to leave elementary school and enter employment without even having passed Standard II, on the grounds that they were simply unsuited to further education:

> The general condition of the human intellect is like the surface of the earth, there are mountains and valleys; and all that education will do will be to lift up the whole crust of it, still leaving the mountains and the valleys. We shall always have the hewers of wood and the drawers of water.[40]

Those who were more suited to advanced instruction would be allowed to proceed into schools such as his own, although these would still prepare pupils for industrial occupations.

Scotson's remarks reflected the emergence of a new kind of institution, the higher grade school, which provided more advanced education for the abler children in the elementary schools under the auspices of the local School Boards. These developed especially in the urban centres of the north of England in the 1880s and 1890s. By the end of the century, there were about 400 such institutions, either separate or part of a larger school.[41] They provided novel opportunities for advancement for able working-class children. In the 1880s, as witnesses such as Crosskey and Scotson made clear, they remained specifically 'elementary' rather than entertaining aspirations for a higher, 'secondary' status. By the 1890s, their ambitions were bolder and more assertive, and they cast themselves increasingly in the role of providing an alternative and more suitable form of secondary education intended for the children of the working classes. Such hopes were given voice in 1895 in the findings of the Bryce Report on secondary education.

Some witnesses who gave evidence to the Bryce commission retained convictions in favour of a more or less rigid separation between elementary education and secondary education that were reminiscent of the opinions expressed at the time of the Taunton commission, 30 years before. For example, Frederick Temple, the Bishop of London and a former Taunton commissioner, took a particularly hard line. He insisted that elementary schools should not provide anything that might be described as secondary education. He allowed that there were a few boys who might be suitable to be selected to progress from the elementary school to the secondary school, but drew a sharp distinction between the boy who has been 'carefully picked' and the needs of the 'average boy'.[42] The latter would be 'best educated in apprenticeship or in actual employment of various kinds', and would 'get on in that line but will not get on very much by having more book learning given to them'.[43] Also, he suggested, since a minimum fee should be attached to all secondary education and parents should be responsible for paying such fees, 'the impecunious class would have to be content with the elementary education unless they could get exhibitions to enable them to enter upon the Secondary Education'.[44] When questioned as to whether fixing an 'irreducible minimum' to the fees paid for secondary education would 'really be a kind of recognition or incorporation of social distinction in our educational system', the Bishop of London replied: 'I do not quite see the point of your question.'[45]

Other influential witnesses also adhered resolutely to the principle of a clear separation between secondary and elementary education on the grounds of social class differences. Sir John Donnelly, the secretary of the Science and Art Department, argued that

the education which is adapted to the boy who is going into work at
13 years of age is and ought to be a different kind of thing from the
education of the boy who is going to the secondary school – I mean
from the beginning; it is not a stepping from one to the other.

This being the case, he added, 'The education of the boy destined for the
secondary or higher school should be different, almost from the first, from
that of the boy whose scholastic life is to stop at 12 or 13 years of age.'[46]
The Hon. Lyulph Stanley, a leading member of the London School Board,
suggested that the line between elementary and secondary education was
'like the shading of a piece of paper from black to white'. On the one
hand, 'for practical purposes that education which is intended to lead to
industry and which will end at 14 and a half or 15 years of age comes
within the proper scope of elementary education'. On the other, secondary
education comprised 'that education which is intended to lead to higher
clerkships or business and professional training, say as a surveyor or engin-
eer or solicitor, a thing for which children who are not going out early in
life take scholarships chiefly and stop on to 16 and a half (and there are
plenty of them)'. In short, Stanley concluded, 'I think the thing that deter-
mines it is partly the age of leaving and partly what is likely to be the
employment of the child after leaving.'[47]

Similar views were expressed by the Revd M.G. Glazebrook of Clifton
College, who distinguished between elementary school teaching that 'trains
a boy to accept and retain knowledge which is put into his mouth', and
secondary school teaching that 'trains him to acquire knowledge for himself'. To Glazebrook, 'overlapping' was unnecessary and undesirable, and
he was pained to see 'promising "scholars" being spoiled at a higher grade
school' and 'future errand boys wasting their time on the classical side of
a grammar school'. In any case, he declared, advanced education should
not be given even to able working-class children since it made them dis-
contented and unfit for useful work, and 'merely swells the ranks of an
aimless, educated proletariate'.[48] On this view, the 'disposition and antecedents' of working-class children made them unsuitable for secondary and
higher education whatever their individual ambitions and talents might be.
Such arguments were especially common in relation to working-class girls
in particular. As another witness urged, since 'any system of education for
working girls should have for its object their training for the responsibilities
of married life', the education provided in the 'middle-class school' was

> therefore, wholly unsuited to the needs of working girls, and the attempt
> to draft them in large numbers to such schools by means of scholar-
> ships a mistaken policy, except (1) in cases where the girl shows ability
> remarkable even amongst girls who have had greater advantages, and
> (2) in the case of girls intending to become teachers in the elementary
> schools.[49]

Other witnesses, such as J.G. Fitch, formerly HM Inspector (HMI) of Training Colleges, were more willing to encourage scholarships for able working-class children to progress from elementary into secondary education, but showed little sympathy for the idea of secondary education of a suitable kind for the 'average' child from such a background.[50] Fitch suggested that secondary schools would still tend to be drawn 'from the middle and upper classes', but 'whatever is possible should be done to make the classification of schools depend on educational rather than social distinction; and to encourage the admission into them of all scholars, of whatever rank, who need the education they provide'.[51] Higher grade schools under such an arrangement should be regarded simply as the 'crown and completion of the Public Elementary School' rather than as a distinct form of secondary education for the working classes.[52] They were, however, 'a sort of *cul-de-sac*', and

> if you want to enable boys to go up higher than first grade school they must do it through the secondary schools pure and simple, those that have the proper secondary and liberal curriculum, not simply science schools, such as the higher grade schools.[53]

This was a clear formulation of the model of secondary education for the working class based on selective entry for the exceptionally able pupil through examinations.

However, several other witnesses differed from this kind of view by proposing a distinct form of secondary education that would be suited to the needs of all or at least 'average' working-class children. In some cases, the higher grade schools were regarded as providing an appropriate base for such provision, while others suggested that evening schools would be most suitable for this purpose. Such arguments were more limited and even more conservative than those that emphasized scholarships from elementary to secondary schools in the sense that they acquiesced in existing distinctions of social class, and sought to institutionalize a new form of class based provision. On the other hand, there was a profound sense in which they were more subversive. This was because they openly challenged the established notion of 'secondary education', first by claiming that working-class children in general might be suited to it, and second by asserting that different kinds of curricula and purposes might be entitled to such a label.

A good example of this notion of an alternative form of secondary education designed for working-class needs was provided by trades and labour councils in a joint submission to the Bryce commission. They argued that secondary education must be available for all 'as the education which follows and continues primary or elementary education'. The distinction between them should be 'strictly and solely *educational*, marking the successive stages of an educational curriculum; and not *social*, marking merely different grades of social rank'.[54] This could be achieved, they proposed, if children of the 'middle and upper classes' continued to go to secondary schools during the day, while 'the children of the wage-earning classes' went to 'secondary *evening* classes' after leaving elementary school at the age of 14 to go to work. On this scheme, there would be secondary evening schools of a higher grade that would give an opportunity to scholars who had passed the higher standards 'to continue their education so as to fit themselves to be scientifically-trained workmen, and to receive the fuller equipment and influence of such Secondary Education in preparation for the duties and enjoyment of life'. Ordinary secondary evening schools would also be available 'to give such lessons to our youth, who have not passed the higher standards, as they are able to receive, and in such a manner as to attract and profit them, so as to make them better workmen and better men than they would otherwise be'. The polytechnic institutes and social institutes already established in London might be suitable as bases for such an extension of secondary education, they suggested. Fundamentally, they were happy to acknowledge as a basic part of their argument their accommodation with established social class distinctions, since, as they stressed, 'The Secondary Education of the working classes must to a large extent be technical and manual. The first necessity for them and for the industries of the country is that they should be skilful and expert workmen and workwomen.'[55]

This kind of claim on behalf of evening continuation schools and classes was also advanced by several other witnesses to the Bryce commission. George Kekewich, secretary of the Committee of the Privy Council on Education, suggested that 'the evening continuation school, if it is a continuation school proper, is, and ought to be, a secondary school'. Secondary education in day schools would continue to be 'only for the few', but the evening continuation school would be 'the Secondary Education for the people, for the artisans, and for the masses'.[56] The Revd F.E. Anthony of the Association of School Boards similarly supported the role of evening continuation schools as providing 'Secondary Education for the working classes'.[57] Meanwhile, other witnesses emphasized what they saw as the 'legitimate sphere' of the higher grade schools in terms of 'an introduction to Secondary Education for the children who have been educated in the board schools',[58] that is, not simply as the culmination of elementary education but as the beginning of secondary education. Some recognition was also given to the needs of working-class girls so far as a distinct form of secondary education was concerned, and it was noted that 'some change must be made if Secondary Education worthy of the name is to be given to those belonging to the industrial class'.[59] Such an education, it was suggested, would need to differ widely from the secondary education of working-class boys, 'differentiated according to their future life'.[60]

Probably the most interesting and most fully developed contribution to the notion of working-class secondary education at this time was made by

John Brown Paton, founder of the National Home Reading Union. Paton refused to accept the idea that secondary education should be for the 'children of the middle classes', and insisted that an alternative form of secondary education should be developed that would be more suitable for working-class children after leaving elementary school.[61] There would be two different groups of working-class children involved in secondary education under Paton's scheme. The smaller group would be more intelligent and advanced, having already progressed through science and art classes, technical classes in connection with the City and Guilds, classes taught under the Evening School Code, trade schools, university extension lectures, or the polytechnics in London. The larger group would not have the same 'ambition' or 'faculty' to reach a high level as did the first, but Paton urged that

> for them, and they are the great majority, surely some further education is requisite which will give them training that they can appreciate and enjoy, that will elevate and purify their taste, that will prepare them for the duties of social and civic life which they will have to fulfil, and that will open to them some of those higher pleasures which, like the light and air of heaven, should be accessible to all men, whatever their mental faculty, or their social station.[62]

With these aims in view, he argued that a scheme of secondary education for the working classes should seek to combine social and recreative elements with the more practical and intellectual elements of education. The programme would have a physical character, involving exercises, the gymnasium, and organized clubs for sporting activities. It would include a social dimension such as training in music and drama. It would be aesthetic in its training of the senses to appreciate and produce forms of beauty. It would be practical in encouraging arithmetic applied to workshop practice, the making of common things, and home industries classes for boys and girls. It would be 'informational', with information related to personal hobbies and interests and leading on to an understanding of science, history and geography. Lastly, it would also be ethical, through its teaching of citizenship, hygiene, temperance, service and thrift. In Paton's grand design, social institutes would be

> planted in the very midst of the neighbourhoods where they are needed [and would] effectively provide the secondary education that has been spoken of, not only for the more able and ambitious of the youth of that district, but for all of them, whatever their ability or disposition may be.[63]

Similar principles would also be applied to 'the secondary Education of working girls and young women', although Paton largely confined himself to describing 'the special needs of working lads and young men'.[64]

This idea of a distinct form of working-class secondary education, with its own curriculum and ethos, therefore competed for the attention of the Bryce commissioners against the more familiar ideal of the selection of a chosen few to participate in the secondary education associated with the middle and higher classes. Very few witnesses suggested the idea of a free secondary education that would be appropriate for all pupils whatever their social background, although such an aspiration was occasionally expressed.[65] The Bryce Report itself, published in 1895, reflected this debate and incorporated its own proposals for a distinct form of working-class secondary education. This was all the more remarkable since the chairman of the commission, James Bryce, had himself been, like the Bishop of London, a member of the Taunton commission of 30 years before. Bryce now proceeded to recommend, against the vociferous protests of his former colleague, a crucial departure from the rigid, class based demarcation of secondary education that had been approved so strongly in the 1860s. Whereas the Taunton Report had specifically related secondary education to the middle classes, the Bryce Report allocated one grade of secondary education to a working-class clientele.

In the scheme put forward in the Bryce Report, 'higher grade elementary schools' were recognized as a form of secondary school of the third grade.[66] Indeed, the report pointed to a few higher grade schools that continued the education of some of their best pupils after the age of 15, preparing them for scholarships or for matriculation at a university, and described such schools as 'a secondary school of the second (and not merely of the third) grade'.[67] This inclusion of the secondary schools within the typology of the Taunton Report disrupted the straightforward correlation between secondary education and the middle classes, and also posed difficult questions about the nature of secondary education itself. It acknowledged the issue of differentiating between the secondary education of working-class boys and that provided for working-class girls, but emphasized what it regarded as the aims that were common to both groups.[68] These aims it portrayed as broad and general, and it went so far as to suggest that technical education could be included within secondary education alongside classical and liberal studies. In a general definition that challenged long held assumptions about the curriculum and class based character of secondary education, it insisted that technical education was a 'species' of the 'genus' of secondary education:

> Secondary Education, therefore, as inclusive of technical, may be described as education conducted in view of the special life that has to be lived with the express purpose of forming a person fit to live it.[69]

Bryce's delicate formulation was crucial in conceptualizing a particular form of secondary education that was designed to suit the specific needs of working-class people. It overturned the familiar tenets that secondary education was by definition middle class in nature and that it was based on a classical and liberal curriculum. It ruled instead that secondary education should be regarded as an advanced form of education that would prepare pupils to assume 'the special life that has to be lived' in a range of different ways that would be most suitable for them. Within this general approach, it could still emphasize the need for more scholarships as a 'means of transferring pupils from one grade of education to another'.[70] Nevertheless, the key strategic importance of the Bryce Report was not so much in supporting facilities for individual transfer between different types of schools, as in legitimizing the idea of a distinct working-class form of secondary education.

## Reverting to types

The alternative possibilities that were glimpsed in the 1890s and championed by the Bryce Report were rapidly closed off. At the turn of the century a new system of secondary education was introduced, under the auspices of the state, that was based on an academic and liberal curriculum and which selected limited numbers of working-class children from elementary schools on the basis of examinations and scholarships. Under the Education Act (1902), School Boards were abolished in favour of local education authorities that were responsible for both elementary and secondary education. Higher grade schools lost their special, if unofficial status, and either reverted to elementary schools or in some cases became secondary schools of the established type. The class divide between elementary and secondary education was reinforced, to render the hopes for a distinct form of working-class secondary education a derelict and abandoned ideal.

Higher elementary schools were to be retained in the new scheme, but these were to be kept strictly in their place and were not to aspire to become 'secondary' in nature. Sir John Gorst, education spokesman for the government in the House of Commons, was specific in his view that the curriculum of such schools should not include 'technological subjects' such as shorthand and typing because, as he put it, 'We are not to convert children at the expense of the State into more valuable wage-earners for the benefit of their parents.'[71] A report by the newly created consultative committee for the Board of Education, published in July 1906, strongly endorsed these sentiments and emphasized both the educational and the social differences between elementary schools and secondary schools.[72] The provision of more advanced instruction for working-class children, including for 'average' pupils from a working-class background, was thereby resisted, leaving many to question, as did one Rochdale higher grade school teacher, whether it was 'as easy now, as ten or twelve years ago, for the child of the self-sacrificing worker to obtain education higher than elementary in our large towns'.[73]

Rather than developing a distinct form of working-class secondary education, therefore, greater reliance was placed on providing scholarships for able children to transfer from elementary to secondary schools. In the interests of 'efficiency', as Searle has observed, secondary education was to be largely restricted to 'fee-paying children from the middle classes, plus a handful of exceptionally able pupils caught by the offer of free places or by a "scholarship" ladder'.[74] Such an approach could also enthuse Fabian socialists such as Sidney Webb, who also endorsed the key distinction between 'educating the *mass* of ordinary average children for the ordinary average life', and 'the other (educational) function, that of preparing the exceptionally clever boy or girl for exceptional work'.[75]

Thus the tradition of secondary education for the working class was entrenched in state secondary education. It was an approach that secured social and occupational mobility for a small minority of working-class children. By the same token, the ideal of a distinct form of working-class secondary education, widely endorsed in the 1890s, was undermined and marginalized in the early twentieth century. Any education specifically designed for the working class had perforce to be regarded as elementary education. Yet demands for more advanced instruction persisted and were not fully satisfied by the provision of free places and scholarships to secondary schools. The ideas expressed towards the end of the nineteenth century would again become broadly influential as a means towards defining an appropriate form of education for the working class in an era of secondary education for all.

# 3

## The education of the adolescent

The general idea of working-class secondary education returned to favour in the 1920s after its setbacks at the turn of the century. Debates focusing on the Hadow Report on the education of the adolescent, published in 1926, not only reaffirmed the radical implications of such a development for the received ideals and traditions of secondary education, but also produced clear strategies for containing the challenge that it represented. These debates also began to address the issue of how to develop a suitable curriculum and system of assessment for such a novel form of secondary education.

### Secondary education in the twentieth century

In the development of secondary education in different countries around the world in the early twentieth century, several related features are especially notable. First is the increasingly active intervention of the state in the provision of secondary education. If the nineteenth century had witnessed the widespread introduction of state systems of primary and elementary education, the twentieth century heralded the rise of organized state provision of secondary education. This led in turn to an expansion if not immediately to all sections of the population, then at least to a larger proportion than had hitherto been involved. The extent of this general growth of provision was more striking in some countries than in others. In Japan, secondary school enrolments rose from 100,000 in 1900 to 700,000 in 1910, and to 1,200,000 in 1920. An impressive expansion was also achieved in the United States of America, where high school enrolments rose from 200,000 in 1890 to some 500,000 in 1900, and by 1912 had reached

1,000,000. In France, expansion was more limited as enrolments rose only from about 100,000 in 1900 to about 150,000 in 1920.[1]

The nature of the secondary school curriculum also changed during this period, although again within particular bounds or constraints. The curriculum was often broadened in scope to cater for an enlarged and more diverse population, although it usually sought to retain an avowedly liberal rationale. At the same time, the secondary school curriculum increasingly became associated with examinations which were used to assess individual ability or 'merit', to such an extent that by the 1920s examination success was widely viewed as the central purpose of secondary education. This was also a consequence of the expansion of access to secondary education, as the schools strove both to provide for and to distinguish between a wider range of pupils.

In England and Wales, secondary education in the first three decades of the twentieth century broadly reflected these international developments. In this particular case, the growth of access remained limited to a relatively small sector of the population. The secondary school curriculum was only slightly broadened, but there took place a major growth in the role of examinations. The Education Act (1902), and the Secondary School Regulations that followed, introduced after long debate a system of state secondary education, responsible to the central Board of Education and administered by the local education authorities (LEAs). Many of the local secondary schools of the nineteenth century became state secondary schools under the Education Act (1902), although they generally continued to imitate the practices and traditions of the Victorian public schools, and indeed were largely encouraged by the Board of Education to do so. They remained select, largely fee paying institutions designed for a small proportion of the age range, although in the early decades of the new century this proportion did begin slowly to increase. The Grant List in 1904–5 consisted of 575 secondary schools with 94,698 pupils. By 1938, this list had grown to 1397 secondary schools with a total of 484,676 pupils. As the Spens Report on secondary education noted in 1938, this constituted in itself what it called a 'vast increase' in the provision of 'Secondary Schools of the academic type', as well as of the 'number and variety of pupils attending them'.[2] Even so, in the 1920s there were still only about 7 per cent of children of between 11 and 15 years of age attending grant-aided secondary schools,[3] and this proportion changed little during the 1930s. Many other secondary schools meanwhile remained privately organized and funded, with the aim of retaining their independence and established characteristics outside the direct influence of the state.

The curriculum and examinations of state secondary schools adapted to the 'number and variety' of the pupils involved in them, but also consolidated the select connotations of secondary education. The curriculum continued to avoid as far as possible any 'practical' or 'vocational' subjects such as engineering or domestic science that would be related directly either to industry for boys or to domestic work in the case of girls.[4] At the same time, examinations assumed an increasing influence as the basis for securing 'free places' or scholarships to the secondary school, and through the School Certificate and Higher School Certificate examinations that were established in 1917.[5] Pupils in the secondary schools were classified and graded on the basis of ability and achievement as measured in written tests and examinations.[6]

Secondary education in the early twentieth century therefore continued to be narrowly defined and constituted largely along lines of social class. It had been 'reconstructed' to ensure 'the resilience and extension of older cultural models suitably modified and disseminated through a set of reformed schools'.[7] Board of Education officials and Conservative politicians, themselves mainly familiar with the public schools, encouraged this process of cultivating elite traditions at the same time that they resisted further expansion of state secondary education to working-class pupils who would undermine its social and cultural characteristics.[8] The large majority of working-class children remained confined to elementary schools that were as Lord Eustace Percy, himself in the 1920s a Conservative president of the Board of Education, later recalled, 'as much "finishing schools" for manual workers as Miss Pinkerton's academy was a finishing school for young ladies'.[9]

### 'Mentals' and 'manuals'

By the 1920s, the issue of how to cater for working-class children beyond the elementary stage was again a matter for keen debate. This was partly due to a large growth in adult unemployment, which was related even before the First World War to a lack of advanced education for industrial workers.[10] The idea that this 'educational waste' was even partly responsible for national economic and industrial difficulties was a powerful incentive to review arrangements in this area.[11] Educational requirements for national competitiveness in times of war and peace were increasingly questioned as a result of the experience of the First World War, and then during the economic depression that followed. The social inequality inherent in the division between elementary education and secondary education also stimulated worries about how to encourage greater equality of opportunity for all children regardless of their social background. For many, the appropriate response to these issues was to ensure that all children should have a right to go on to secondary school. This view was increasingly taken up by the Labour Party and the trades union movement, and the idea of 'secondary education for all' became popularized during the 1920s.[12] At the same time, there was a renewal of interest in initiatives to provide a distinctive form of advanced instruction that would be particularly appropriate for working-class youth. These initiatives were centred on the development of 'central schools' and 'day continuation schools'.

Central schools were promoted, especially in London, as a means of giving an industrial or commercial training of an advanced nature to working-class children. The education committee of the London County Council (LCC) was conscious both of the anomalous position of higher elementary and higher grade schools since the Education Act (1902), and of a need to provide more education of a 'practical' kind. Elementary schools, it was suggested, should produce 'the boy who will have had an all-round training of his faculties, and will have acquired that readiness and adaptability which will enable him to turn his hand to the task that awaits him in the workshop or factory'.[13] Central schools, by comparison, should 'be schools which will give their pupils a definite bias towards some kind of industrial or commercial work while ensuring that their intelligence should be fully developed'. They should 'occupy a distinct position' from the secondary schools, although 'that position will not be in any sense inferior'. Their curriculum should be framed to suit a school leaving age of between 15 and 16. The courses of such schools would, it was declared,

> provide for the pupil the best possible equipment for entering upon the industrial or commercial world as soon as he leaves school, while at the same time qualifying them to enter upon a special course of training for some particular industry at a Polytechnical or similar institution if they desire to continue their education elsewhere.

Most importantly, according to the LCC's education committee, these schools would suit 'many boys and girls' much better than would a secondary school, and would prepare them better for 'the requirements of their future occupations'.[14]

These notions therefore again sought to accommodate existing differences in social class, as had many of the arguments in favour of more advanced instruction for working-class children in the late nineteenth century. Even this was too much for the Board of Education. The LCC represented the central school in terms of being 'the crown of Elementary Education', in which 'it was intended that when the scholar left at 15 and a half he should have finished his day school training and should be adequately equipped for the work of life'.[15] The Board responded by criticizing the cost of such schools and disputing the need for their special provisions.[16] Despite the constraints imposed by the Board of Education, central schools were developed further in the 1920s and 1930s and became, as has been observed, 'in practice secondary schools for the most able working-class children'.[17] As well as being class specific, these schools also catered separately for girls and for boys in preparing them for different kinds of employment. Some were 'selective' in that their children were selected for entry at the age of 11, usually through an examination, while others were non-selective.

The case of the 'continuation schools' was rather different. The Education Act (1918) made it compulsory for LEAs to provide day continuation schools for pupils between 14 and 16, giving part time advanced instruction, and it was hoped that this provision would be extended to include pupils beteen 16 and 18. By the early 1920s, however, far from being extended it had fallen into abeyance and was widely recognized as a failure.[18] On the one hand, they fell victim to postwar financial restrictions. On the other, although there was some sympathy for them within the Labour Party as being 'for the present, the secondary school and university of the vast majority of working-class children',[19] they were increasingly regarded as only a temporary expedient, inferior to the preferred solution of providing 'secondary schools for all'.[20] Very few were able to survive, with only the day continuation school in Rugby lasting until the Second World War. Their failure serves as a clear reminder of the marginal and insecure nature of initiatives to secure advanced instruction of a distinctive kind for the working class.

Even so, the question of how to provide such instruction, with all its inherent dilemmas, could be ignored no longer, and in the early 1920s it attracted the attention of the consultative committee of the Board of Education. This committee, established when the Board itself had been set up in 1899, was able to focus on difficult problems obstructing the growth of public education, and since 1920 had acquired new rights to propose urgent cases for inquiry.[21] Its members, especially J.A. White, who was the headmaster of a central school in London, argued that public awareness of this general issue had been raised by the Labour Party's support for the idea of secondary education for all and by strong criticisms expressed by the *Times Educational Supplement*. It seemed important to respond to these problems and in particular to suggest an alternative policy in case the Labour Party came to power.

Led by the chairman of the committee, Sir Henry Hadow (vice-chancellor of the University of Sheffield), a deputation strove to convince Board officials of the need to

> think out some alternative course of instruction for children up to 15 or 16 who would not be proceeding to the Secondary Schools and who would compose 'the multitude who labour with their hands' as opposed to those who entered Secondary Schools and proceeded to clerical occupations.[22]

This notion did not challenge the established class based structure of the separation between elementary and secondary education, but highlighted the need for 'the provision for the non-Secondary child of something better after 11'.[23] The importance of this was spelled out in crudely political terms as 'dispelling the Socialist and Labour war-cry of "Secondary Education for all" . . . , if possible before the Labour Party came into power; otherwise they would make the attempt and find too late that the philosophy of the project was wrongly based'. Also, as was noted,

> employers were coming more and more to demand in their shorthand-typists and clerical assistants a more advanced standard of general education, and the Committee would be able to explore the best means of providing this for children who did not go to Secondary Schools.[24]

Following protracted negotiations, it was left to the new president of the Board of Education of the incoming minority Labour government, C.P. Trevelyan, to approve the terms of reference for this inquiry. A broad remit had emerged, but it excluded consideration of secondary education, encompassing as it did 'the organisation, objective and curriculum of courses of study suitable for children who will remain in full-time attendance at schools, other than Secondary Schools, up to 15'. In doing so, it was to have regard on the one hand to 'the requirements of a good general education and the desirability of providing a reasonable variety of curriculum, so far as is practicable, for children of varying tastes and abilities', and on the other to 'the probable occupations of the pupils in commerce, industry and agriculture'. It was also to investigate suitable means of testing pupils at the end of their course, and ways of 'facilitating in suitable cases the transfer of individual pupils to Secondary Schools at an age above the normal age of admission'.[25] This formulation of the problem to be addressed was a resonant echo of late nineteenth century attempts to define an advanced form of instruction that would be suitable for the working class, but in line with the repeated edicts of the Board of Education it clearly acknowledged that such instruction could not be regarded as a form of 'secondary education'.

Several witnesses who were invited to give evidence to the consultative committee's inquiry adhered closely to this established principle of separating advanced working-class instruction from secondary education. H.M. Richards, chief inspector of elementary schools, acknowledged that strong demand existed for advanced elementary education, but emphasized the restrictions that had been imposed upon it since the beginning of the century. He admitted that he 'could not remember a time when Education Authorities and the Board were not constantly embarrassed by this pressure from below for something more than the ordinary Elementary School could give and yet a something which the Secondary School was not organised to supply'.[26] Richards accepted that an effort must be made to meet this need, and suggested that Senior Schools might be developed for children from 11 to 14 or 15. Such extended provision, he added, should not be based on the examination system that had been created for secondary schools, and it should maintain a clear separation of roles. Yet at the same time he reminded the committee that 'most of us in England were snobs', and so any 'alternative to Secondary Schools' that might be devised through extending the provision of senior schools and central schools must be made 'a good alternative'.[27] He left unresolved the difficult issue of how this might be achieved. Some, such as James Graham, the director of education in Leeds, argued that it would not be possible to create an acceptable alternative, and therefore recommended that the existing distinction between elementary schools and secondary schools should be rigidly enforced. Graham was emphatic in his conviction that 'there is no place in our system for a school intermediate in character between Secondary and Elementary'.[28] Others were more ambitious, and began to challenge the terms on which the inquiry had been set up.

One such witness was John Lewis Paton, high master of Manchester Grammar School and son of John Brown Paton, who had championed the cause of secondary education for the working classes to the Bryce committee in the 1890s. John Lewis Paton had long advocated the further development of continuation schools in order to foster a 'sense of social solidity' in citizenship based on a shared culture.[29] He took his opportunity now to point out that about 150,000 girls and boys between 14 and 18 years of age were currently in employment, with many others unemployed, and to argue that every effort should be made to educate such youngsters in these 'formative years'. This led him on to challenge the established idea of 'secondary education'. He favoured the idea of 'secondary education for all', but felt that it implied developing a new form of secondary education:

In the present accepted meaning of the term secondary education was meeting the need for which it was designed quite well. But he hoped that this was not the only type of secondary education to be provided. What was needed was to give a real humanity of culture to the boy who was not going into professional or business life. For him a new type of secondary education was required which was not bookish.[30]

This might mean developing some kind of differentiation between alternative types of education at the age of 11-plus, but allowing for late development after this age. Pupils, he suggested, could be divided at the age of 11 into what he called 'Mentals' and 'Manuals', although these should be given equal status. On the one hand, 'The Mentals would have in view the office or warehouse. Their education would be on commercial lines.' On the other, 'The Manuals would have in view the engineering shops. In the countryside the aim in view would be agriculture.'[31] This was highly significant testimony in that it revived the prospects that had been raised in the 1890s, albeit in a different and rapidly changing educational, social and political context. It was radical in its espousal of a broader notion of secondary education, but once again it identified the different kinds of curriculum that this would involve with differing positions in society.

Another prominent witness to the Hadow committee was Professor Percy Nunn of the University of London. Nunn was well known in policy circles and had recently produced what was to be his major work on *Education: Its Data and First Principles*.[32] Like Paton, he sought to encourage the committee to rethink the structures of secondary education, which would also entail revising its basic assumptions and purposes. He also proposed a 'clean cut' across the public education system at the age of 11-plus, leading on to three distinct grades of post-primary education. Grade (a) schools would be secondary schools of a grammar school or high school type which would aim to retain their pupils until the age of 18. Grade (b) schools, best represented by London central schools and junior technical schools, would end their courses at 16. Grade (c) schools, meanwhile, would 'deal with pupils who were not transferred to institutions of the former two grades'.[33] They could be modelled on senior elementary schools such as those in Carlisle, or on junior schools like those that were being developed in Bath. Nunn envisaged that about 25 per cent of pupils might ultimately go on to grade (a) schools, 45–50 per cent to grade (b) schools, and 25–30 per cent to schools of the grade (c) type. However, he acknowledged, the grade (c) schools raised the most difficult problems of all, since 'It would need to be openly recognized that the status of the third (c) grade school was not inferior to those of grades (a) and (b) but that it was a school designed to much better provision for certain classes of children.' In scattered rural areas with poor transport facilities, he suggested that grade (b) and grade (c) schools would need to be merged. Nunn also emphasized that the curriculum in grade (c) schools should be 'thoroughly practical in character', and that they should be equipped with 'simple work-rooms' for both boys and girls rather than separating manual training and domestic economy into separate centres as in the present system. At the same time, the teaching should also be 'cultural' in nature, with art, music, dancing, poetry and drama playing 'a very important part in the life of the schools'.[34]

It was the ideas suggested by witnesses such as Paton and Nunn, rather than the caution of Richards and Graham and of the officials of the Board, that were most evident in the final report of the Hadow committee published in December 1926. The report set out an ambitious programme for what it called the 'consummation' of trends towards a higher form of 'elementary education'.[35] It recognized the recurrent tendency over the past 50 years for elementary education to develop 'experiments' in more advanced provision, and also noted that although 'such experiments have again and again been curtailed or rendered difficult by legislative or administrative action', they had 'persistently reappeared in various forms'. This historical tendency in itself seemed to suggest what the report described in an exceptionally striking passage as the half-conscious striving of a highly industrialised society to evolve a type of school analogous to and yet distinct from the secondary school, and providing an education designed to fit boys and girls to enter the various branches of industry, commerce, and agriculture at the age of 15.[36]

This in turn would mean a need to 'take into account the probable future of the children and the nature of the industrial society into which, when their formal education has ceased, the majority of them will enter'.[37] It also implied the development of 'schools of varying types', which would take 'several different paths', each of these based on 'a due proportion in the outlay of thought and expenditure' so that 'the whole front may advance together'.[38]

Undeterred by the limitations imposed by its terms of reference, the report proposed to abolish the term 'elementary' altogether at the same time that it sought to 'extend the sense' of the word 'secondary'. Elementary education would be superseded by 'primary education' up to the age of 11 or 12. Moreover, it continued,

To the period of education which follows upon it we would give the name secondary; and we would make this name embrace all forms of post-primary education, whether it be given in the schools which are now called 'secondary', or in central schools, or in senior departments of the schools now termed 'elementary'.[39]

If this could be established, then the schools currently known as 'secondary' would be described as 'grammar schools', while those currently known as central schools would be given the term 'modern schools'. Thus, it concluded,

On such a scheme there will be two main kinds of education – primary and secondary; and the latter of these two kinds will fall into two main groups – that of the grammar school type, and that of the type of the modern school.[40]

The modern school would not provide secondary education 'in the present and narrow sense of the word', but it would be nonetheless 'in our view, a form of secondary education, in the truer and broader sense of the word'.[41]

The curriculum of the 'modern school' was envisaged in the Hadow Report as being both 'practical' and 'cultural' in its approach, 'under the stimulus of practical work and realistic studies', but still 'in the free and broad air of a general and humane education, which, if it remembers handwork, does not forget music, and, if it cherishes natural science, fosters also linguistic and literary studies'. More broadly, it would seek to cultivate the forming and strengthening of individual and national character, the training of boys and girls 'to delight in pursuits and rejoice in accomplishments', and the awakening and guiding of the 'practical intelligence' in order to ensure 'the better and more skilled service of the community in all its multiple business and complex affairs'.[42] The report asserted that the type of education that would be most suited to the needs of a large proportion of pupils between the ages of 11 and 15 would be less 'academic' and more 'practical' than in the present secondary schools, either because they were already looking towards the needs of their future occupations, or because they were 'ill at ease in an atmosphere of books and lessons, and are eager to turn to some form of practical and constructive work, in which they will not merely be learners, but doers, and in a small way creators'.[43] Such minds, 'and by no means minds of an inferior order', would respond best to 'practical or constructive activity' that would complement 'real life', with a significance that was 'made as plain to them as possible, by being obviously related to the work of the world, as they see it in the lives of their parents, their older brothers and sisters, and their friends'.[44] This approach was not the same as the technical and vocational education provided in junior technical schools, which the report argued should continue in their present specialized role of preparing pupils for particular industries and trades, but would imply using 'realistic' studies as 'an instrument of general education, as they are already used by a considerable number of secondary schools to-day, and as academic studies are used for the same object by existing "secondary" schools'.[45] A curriculum that provided 'large opportunities for practical work', the report insisted, could still give a 'good general education'.[46] A foreign language, usually French, should be learned in all such schools. At the same time, it was careful to add that easy transfer should be made possible from these schools to the existing 'secondary' schools, as well as, 'hardly less important, easy transfer in the opposite direction'.[47]

These proposals also had important implications for the assessment of courses. If the newer types of post-primary schools were to have an earlier leaving age and a shorter course of study than did the existing 'secondary' schools, the leaving examination would need to be different and less rigid. Although leading towards a 'definite objective', courses 'need not be influenced to the same extent by the requirements of an external examination', which would give the teachers in such schools greater freedom to frame courses in the different subjects. A special examination should therefore be introduced on an optional basis for pupils leaving these newer schools, but the report recommended that this should not be established for at least three years in order to allow more time for the 'free development' of the schools, and that 'the syllabus for it should be carefully adjusted to the needs of broad and varied curricula'.[48]

The proposals of the Hadow Report were in many respects highly radical and visionary. They effectively challenged and subverted existing preconceptions about the nature of secondary education, in the same way that the Bryce Report had done 30 years before. They also went further than the Bryce Report had done in outlining the nature and implications of the distinct form of working-class secondary education that it proposed. They suggested the possibility of a broad and humane curriculum unrestricted by the academic bias and examinations of the existing secondary schools. The report was acutely conscious that new arrangements would remain strongly influenced by past traditions,[49] but it set its store as an article of faith with the idea that 'public opinion' would accept 'other kinds of secondary education besides those given in schools which are "secondary" in the technical sense of the word', and that 'the larger significance which we wish to claim for the word will be accepted without any very great difficulty'.[50] Certainly the *Times Educational Supplement* was in no doubt as it acclaimed the triumph of its own campaign for reform. The Hadow Report, it averred, was 'a masterly document'. It meant that 'A change has come over the whole spirit of English education. The day of elementary education is over and the new Report of the Consultative Committee fully recognises that change.'[51]

Yet the Hadow Report also had overtones that were fundamentally conservative. Above all, its notion of secondary education remained, as that of Bryce had also been before it, solidly based on existing divisions of social class. It meant that 'ordinary' or 'average' working-class children should not aspire to the academic curriculum of the established secondary schools, nor to the professional careers to which they led, because they were more suited by their nature and background to a particular kind of curriculum and station in life. And it was this class based characteristic of 'education for the adolescent' that could most readily be exploited and sustained.

### The new prospect in education?

Following the publication of the Hadow Report, the officials at the Board of Education were concerned to resolve the legal and logistical issues that it raised. These had major implications both for the character of secondary education in general, and for the distinct kind of advanced education that it suggested for working-class children. The need to raise the status of this particular form of education was broadly accepted, but it soon became clear that established assumptions and ideals about the nature of secondary education remained well entrenched.

The first issue was to define which types of post-elementary schools, if any, should be included within the domain of secondary education. The strategic aspects of this decision came sharply into view, as it was perceived that it might be possible both to raise the status of particular types of schools while retaining important distinctions of function for the existing secondary schools. Much energy was expended attempting to draw an appropriate line. It was suggested that the most straightforward solution would be 'to define the highest type of Central School, calling it "Modern", and making room for it as part of Higher Education, while leaving the present "Elementary" law as it is'.[52] Special Regulations could be introduced in order to allow LEAs to choose whether or not to provide a 'modern' school in their area. For example, in the West Riding in Yorkshire it was often difficult 'to get a particular district to accept a Central School instead of a Secondary'. In such an area, rather than 'providing the more expensive school where it is not really needed', it might be helpful for them to be able to offer 'not an Elementary School at all, but a "Modern" school, under Higher Education Regulations, and to be distinguished from a Secondary School only in respect of its purpose and its age-range and what follows from that'.[53]

This strategy implied concentrating on the central schools rather than on the wide range of other kinds of institutions that had developed in this area such as the 'higher top' to the elementary school, and establishing them as an acceptable alternative to secondary or grammar schools. On the one hand, a secondary school would be

> a School which provides a progressive course of general education of a kind and amount suited to an age range at least from the age of twelve to seventeen attended by pupils who normally remain at the School for at least four years and up to the age of sixteen at least.[54]

On the other, a 'modern school' might be

> a School which provides a progressive course of general and practical education of a kind and amount suited to an age range from the ages of eleven to sixteen attended by pupils who normally remain at the school for at least four years and up to the age of fifteen years at least.[55]

Such suggestions reflected a continuing vagueness about the exact nature of the distinction to be drawn between secondary and modern schools in terms of their differing curricula and the length of their courses. There was no doubting, however, that they were to remain distinct, and it was observed that 'It is of the first importance, if these schools are to be included under "Higher Education", that they should continue to be subject to the existing conditions as regards fees, attendance, age limits, religious instruction and salaries.' The reasons for this view were explained as being 'partly social, partly educational, partly financial and partly political'.[56] That is, they would observe existing social distinctions, preserve educational traditions, save money, and avoid being drawn fully into accepting the idea of 'secondary education for all'.

The president of the Board of Education in the Conservative government of 1924–9, Lord Eustace Percy, was reconciled to the idea of elevating central schools in particular areas as a means of making an alternative form of secondary education acceptable. As he observed 'going about the country', in some districts 'parents would not accept a "Central School" because it was "Elementary" and the LEA would not provide a "Secondary School" because it was not really required'.[57] Modern schools might well be a suitable alternative: 'A "Modern School" i.e. the highest type of Central School, but regarded as part of the Higher Education system, seemed to be just what was wanted in such cases.'[58] Percy's strategic objective was readily interpreted by his officials as 'proposing some modification of the status quo' in order

(a) to remove the stigma of social inferiority which appeared to attach in some areas to the central as opposed to the secondary school [while at the same time] (b) retaining the central (or modern) school as an alternative to the secondary school in cases where it seemed to be a type of school best suited to the needs of the particular area.[59]

This could be achieved 'without recourse to what might prove to be extremely contentious legislation', but care would be needed to restrict the scope of the new 'modern' schools to children up to 16 years of age, and 'this age delimitation would have to be strictly enforced if the school was to maintain its existence as a definite and separate type'.[60]

The implications of maintaining 'definite and separate' types of school were, as had already been noted, both 'educational' and 'social'. Such a formula recognized the notion of a distinct form of working-class secondary education, an idea that had attracted supporters for the past 50 years as the best way to provide advanced instruction of a suitable type to working-class children. The restrictive nature of this class based solution was no less evident to those who now came to embrace the idea as a way to maintain social distinctions in education. One correspondent was especially anxious to spell out the social class basis of the 'modern' schools, asserting that 'craft and aesthetic work' should 'play a large part' in them, and especially for 'boys who are to be "hewers and drawers" and cannot therefore find much personal outlet in their occupations – people such as typists'. An example of this type was apparently to be found in Manchester at the Xaverian College in Victoria Park, a boys' Roman Catholic secondary school: 'Very remarkable things are done, at little expenditure and without elaborate training for the teachers. They get done because plenty of time is available and boys don't fritter that time away on half-a-dozen different things.'[61] Thus the potential 'financial' advantages of such an arrangement were no less explicit than the social and educational issues involved, as it was argued that by restricting the character of the modern schools in an appropriate way, the economic costs of the initiative would be contained at the same time.

Such was the logic that during the 1920s effectively transformed what had been at best a marginal tradition over the previous 30 years, apparently expunged as a realistic option at the turn of the century, into a widely approved basis for future policy. In spite of the consensus that was beginning to form, however, there remained several important unresolved dilemmas about how to put it into practice. The underlying tensions around the Hadow proposals were vividly reflected in doubts expressed by an influential educator, Cyril Norwood. As head of Harrow, a leading public school, and chairman of the Secondary School Examinations Council (SSEC) which reported to the Board of Education on examination matters, Norwood was well placed both to monitor and to influence contemporary trends. He was especially concerned to defend what he saw as the vital traditions of the public schools, and to apply these to the secondary schools that were now developing under the auspices of the state.[62] He regarded Hadow's proposals as potentially representing a threat to these traditions. For this reason, he vigorously challenged any concessions that might undermine the established notion of secondary education. Norwood was anxious about the effects of a growth in the number of pupils in secondary schools, which he felt was already taking place and which under the Hadow scheme would accelerate still further. He pointed out that the number of girls in state-aided secondary schools had risen from 33,519 in 1904–5 to 173,273 in 1925, while the number of boys had risen over the same period from 61,179 to 194,291. This expansion constituted, according to Norwood, 'a veritable flood of new material', which he claimed was 'not of the best intellectual material'. Moreover, he asserted, 'There is also in prospect an addition to these numbers, from the four year courses of the Central Schools, and from developments which may ensue from the Consultative Committee's Report on the Education of the Adolescent.' If the School Certificate examination which was currently the major award for secondary school pupils were to be amended to suit these new pupils, which there would be pressure to bring about, then, he warned, 'In accordance with the law that the worse drives out the better currency it is probable that in twenty years the conception of Secondary Education, as established by the Board, would disappear.'[63]

Norwood was also unhappy about other aspects of current changes in policy. He was especially worried about the increasing numbers of girls who were taking secondary school courses, and argued that there should be greater gender differentiation in curriculum and examinations in order to help direct them into an appropriate role in society. He was also very uncomfortable with attempts to elevate the status of 'practical' forms of education, especially where these threatened to undermine the established status of 'academic' types of curriculum. Again, in his view such arguments threatened to undermine the traditions of secondary education that had been cultivated over many years. His proposed solution to these perceived threats was to maintain the School Certificate examination in its current form, that is, 'demanding four subjects at least from Groups I, II and III, and thereby laying it down that a *full* Secondary Education does involve the mother tongue, a foreign language, and Mathematics and Science', but at the same time introducing a new 'General Secondary Certificate' which should be given for a Pass in Group I and any four subjects. This would achieve greater differentiation so that ' "School" and "General Secondary" would establish themselves in use, and the Professional Bodies, business and industry, would know what they were getting'. The alternative option of widening the School Certificate examination itself would, he warned, 'seriously throw back the great work of establishing a sound tradition of Secondary education that has been accomplished in the last twenty-five years'.[64]

The implications of Norwood's frank intervention in the debate were highly alarming to Board officials. It was noted that Norwood was 'in a difficult position', and that he should be dealt with 'in a friendly and unofficial way'.[65] Nonetheless, his proposal of a General Secondary Certificate which might be used for pupils in modern schools was 'lamentable' because it would undermine the status of these new schools. The creation of a suitable examination for modern schools was 'a matter at once delicate and important', as such an examination 'if it is to appeal to teachers, and above all employers, must have all the prestige of a fresh and living attempt to focus the work of the schools'. Norwood's proposals would not assist in this process:

> In the midst of our rather anxious deliberations on this point Dr Norwood presents us, rather contemptuously, with an Examination not good enough for the ordinary Secondary School pupil, but good enough for those who cannot take 'the full Secondary School course' and 'are not of the best intellectual material', 'not the right sort of material for the First School Examination'.

If the 'principal concern' of Lord Eustace Percy, the president of the Board of Education, was 'to defend the Modern School from the charge of being an inferior option to the Secondary School', such a strategy would be severely undermined by Norwood's intervention:

> Could any policy more effectively stultify the President's contention or more effectively stamp the Modern School as an inferior thing or more manifestly play into the hands of those who regard the Central School with suspicion than the course of action advocated by Dr Norwood?[66]

As a distinct form of secondary education for a clientele with its own particular requirements, the modern schools needed to be supported and developed with the utmost care.

These immediate responses had the desired effect. At the following meeting of the SSEC, Norwood withdrew the proposal to establish a General School Certificate that he had tabled earlier, 'as the result of communications he had received from the Board'.[67] Over the longer term, however, the episode was significant in defining the grounds of contention that would surround the idea of mass secondary education in general and the development of modern schools in particular. On the one side, Norwood and many others remained highly conscious of the established conception of secondary education that was based in the public schools and in the academic and liberal curriculum. Proponents of this general view were inclined, even where they accepted the development of modern schools, to emphasize the prior claims of the existing secondary schools – the grammar schools envisaged in the Hadow Report. On the other side, there was the unresolved issue of exactly how to promote the idea of mass secondary education that would involve cultivating a new form of education for a new group of pupils, with equal stature to the more traditional form. Some began to argue, as Norwood had predicted, that central and modern schools were able, 'often drawing on the less successful candidates for admission to secondary schools', to 'do work comparable with that of a secondary school'.[68] Such a view implied giving the pupils at the new schools the same opportunities and facilities as those enjoyed by pupils at the established secondary schools. At the same time, others feared that by moving in this direction, 'instead of finding its own aims, the central school may tend to duplicate the secondary school'.[69]

Such doubts and uncertainties were widely shared, and lay only just beneath the newly developing orthodoxy. They were obscured, at least in public debate, by the energetic avowals of the Board of Education that the Hadow Report represented a 'new prospect in education'. It emphasized the importance of maintaining a clear distinction between the new and old forms of secondary education, and noted in terms that Norwood would have approved that 'the ever present temptation to think that the use of existing examinations of an academic and pre-University nature will dignify the status of a Modern School' should be strongly resisted: 'It will indeed be nothing short of a calamity if the end of the Modern School is an anaemic reflection of the present Secondary School.'[70] The modern schools would need to 'think out their goal, feeling their way towards an appropriate curriculum and an appropriate examination'.[71] The prize that it offered was

> that of the adaptation of the existing Elementary School system so that all the older children, not a selected few, may receive an education suited to their age and special needs, practical in the broadest sense, and so organised as to allow for classification and differentiation between pupils of different types of capacity and of different aptitudes.[72]

This in itself would make it increasingly important, the Board averred, 'to maintain in their proper sphere the special standards' of the 'traditional type' of secondary education.[73]

Overall, therefore, demand for the further expansion of secondary education in the 1920s led in the case of England and Wales to an attempt to establish a distinctive type that would be suited to the needs of the working class, taking into account, in the words of the Hadow Report, 'the probable future of the children and the nature of the industrial society into which . . . the majority of them will enter'. During this period the outlines of 'modern schools' were identified, and their distinctive curriculum and forms of assessment were discussed in some detail. The conditions for such an experiment to be developed on a large scale were to become even more favourable as notions of a tripartite system of three types of secondary schools, each with different roles and functions, became increasingly prominent.

# 4

# Secondary education for all?

If there was to be a distinctive form of secondary education designed specifically for the needs of working-class children, with its own curriculum and assessment system, this would have major implications for the idea of 'secondary education for all'. It meant that there would be different kinds of provision for different social groups, although the relationship between these was not clear. A tripartite model of provision had major influence in helping to shape the notion of secondary education for all in the 1920s and 1930s. It was widely hoped, or assumed, that it would be possible to establish a broad equivalence, or 'parity of esteem', between these different types of provision. The major reconstruction of education that was carried out during the Second World War was strongly imbued with the ideals of tripartite provision, and also of parity, but concealed doubts that were already widespread as to whether the theory would correspond with the practical reality. Separate provision for different social groups thereby became the dominant educational tradition.

## International and comparative perspectives

Secondary education for all clearly suggested a major shift away from the exclusive provision for a select, elite group that had been characteristic of secondary education in the nineteenth century, in favour of an expansion of provision for the age range as a whole. And yet it left unresolved the key issue of how to cater for the needs and interests of such a broad group. In general terms, this problem could be tackled in one of two ways. First, it could be addressed through developing a 'comprehensive' model, designed to cater for all abilities and aptitudes, without regard for social differences and backgrounds. Second, it could be addressed by building on these social differences and establishing a 'tripartite' model that provided in different ways for different groups in society. Around the world, different nations found their own responses to this central issue acording to their own circumstances and traditions.

The structure of provision became a key issue in many different countries that was resolved in some cases by developing a comprehensive approach, and in others by emphasizing tripartite patterns. In very broad terms, the tripartite strategy was especially familiar in western European nations, although with important exceptions such as Sweden.[1] Comprehensive forms of secondary education came to be identified with North America, especially the United States. At the same time, the range of approaches was more complex than this general typology might imply. Those nations that developed tripartite forms of provision, for example, varied among themselves on the extent to which they allowed a common or core curriculum in the different kinds of secondary schools. Those that promoted comprehensive structures of provision also differed as to how far they encouraged other forms of selection or differentiation to develop within them.

The dominant European tradition of differentiation between educational institutions with distinctive curricular and social roles was especially strong in Germany and France. The German equivalent of the classical secondary school for the elite was the *Gymnasium*, but in the late nineteenth and early twentieth centuries other kinds of secondary schools for different groups of pupils emerged in the form of such institutions as the *Realgymnasium* and the *Oberrealschule*.[2] During the twentieth century, tripartite arrangements as opposed to a comprehensive pattern became the established pattern for secondary education, followed in the Federal Republic of Germany after the Second World War.[3] In France, the *lycée* was the most prestigious form of secondary education, again classical in nature, while the *collège* and other institutions also developed in the early part of the twentieth century.[4] In such cases, the advantage of encouraging new types of institutions for different groups of the population lay at least as much in protecting the elite prestige and traditions that had been cultivated in the established secondary schools as in extending opportunities more broadly.

The alternative pattern of provision was witnessed in particular in the United States, where the high school of the nineteenth century had also been an elite institution that catered for a small proportion of the population.[5] After the First World War, a comprehensive high school pattern was introduced for pupils between 12 and 18, to promote appropriate forms of curriculum for different pupils within the single institution.[6] This major development, building on the common school ideal that had already been established in the United States in the nineteenth century,[7] was perceived in terms of providing greater equality of opportunity and a common bond of citizenship. Nevertheless, different kinds of selection and differentiation between different groups of pupils remained potent devices even in this context, and the development of distinct 'social areas' in large North American cities encouraged differentiation based on the distinctive nature of particular neighbourhoods.[8]

Elsewhere, there were several cases of a trend towards comprehensive provision within a single type of secondary school. One especially notable example of this was Scotland, with a separate system that was in many respects more 'advanced' than that of England and Wales, building on a national tradition of social equality and encouraged partly by the need to cater for the full age range in a large number of smaller communities.[9] In other contexts, too, the familiar elite institutions of the nineteenth century were also challenged by the emergence of a pattern that favoured comprehensive provision.[10]

## Plato's children

The pattern of provision that developed in England and Wales in the early years of the twentieth century was strongly tripartite in that it catered in different ways, with distinct types of institutions and curriculum, for different social groups. It was encouraged in this partly through an emphasis on individual differences that was promoted by influential educational psychologists such as Cyril Burt, who argued that intelligence testing could serve as a scientific basis for differentiated schooling.[11] It was also an effective means of social stratification in consolidating distinctions between different social categories and creating a hierarchy among them. The respectable intellectual lineage of theories of tripartism also corresponded in a very convenient way with the realities of social class in contemporary England and Wales.

The Platonic theory of tripartism, based on the ideas of the ancient Greek philosopher Plato in *The Republic*, emphasizes the distinctions between three different groups in society that are discussed in terms of gold, silver and copper.[12] These distinctions provide a philosophical and cultural framework to rationalize different capacities and aptitudes, and the different roles in society to which they lead. The first class, associated with gold, was that of the philosophers, from whom the 'guardians' or philosopher-kings would be chosen. The second class was made up of the 'auxiliaries', or skilled merchants and tradesmen, and this was characterized as silver. Artisans and farmers, made up of iron and copper, constituted the third class. The first class would be given a liberal education, while the second class would be given a vocational training. Several commentators have noted the resemblance of twentieth century educational patterns in England and Wales to this general ideal. Some, like Richard Crossman in the late 1930s and John Dancy in the 1960s, have strongly criticized the enduring influence of Platonic educational ideas.[13] Others have cultivated it no less avidly.

Sir Richard Livingstone, a classical scholar based at the University of Oxford (educated at Winchester and New College, Oxford), was an active proselytizer on behalf of Plato's ideas, most strikingly perhaps in his Rede lecture delivered in 1944 under the title of 'Plato and modern education'. Livingstone argued that Plato's educational proposals were 'perfectly practical', and 'illustrate that uncanny power of divining what was yet unborn, which no other writer, ancient or modern, possesses so highly, and which makes him so often seem more modern than ourselves'.[14] Plato's age, he insisted, had confronted similar problems to those faced by twentieth-century society, so that Plato's philosophy remained vital in providing values and ideals for the future. He complained that this theoretical basis of education was often forgotten:

> Our eyes are blinded by a dust-storm of School Certificates, Higher Certificates, Scholarships, Degrees, Diplomas, Examinations beyond counting; the air is full of the loud demands of industry, commerce and the professions, and through the din and mist the figure of education is faintly descried.[15]

In particular, according to Livingstone, it was important for universities to teach what Plato had called the 'Idea of the Good' as an alternative philosophy to counteract the potential appeal of Nazism and Communism.

A wide range of influential social and political theorists in the 1920s and 1930s also exhibited a strong regard for the values articulated by Plato. Jose Harris has argued that a form of idealism strongly imbued with the social philosophy of Plato formed 'the overarching philosophy of the early days of the welfare state'.[16] According to Harris, 'early twentieth-century social scientists found in Plato not simply a system of logic and epistemology, but a series of clues, principles and practical nostrums with which to approach the problems of mass, urban, class-based, industrial and imperial civilisation'.[17] In addition, the 'vast majority' of these British Platonists were 'reformers, democrats and egalitarians, largely oblivious of Plato's apparent endorsement of absolute political obedience, a functional caste system, and the selective breeding of a master race'.[18] This tendency was especially noticeable in the field of education in the 1920s and 1930s.

The strength of the Platonic tradition in secondary education is perhaps best reflected not in those who resisted reform, but in those who advocated radical change. By the 1920s and 1930s, there were many critics who advocated a major expansion in the provision of secondary education that would entail its extension to the whole age range. It is important to note that these reformers did not challenge tripartism and in many cases actively sought ways to incorporate it into a system of 'secondary education for all'. This is apparent from the ideas put forward by three key prophets of reform in this period who were very different in many respects in their wider social and political affiliations but who all remained attached to a recognizably Platonic and tripartite approach to education: R.H. Tawney, Fred Clarke and Cyril Norwood.

## Secondary education for all

R.H. Tawney was a dominant influence in educational thought and politics during the interwar years, through his membership of key committees, his close involvement in the Labour Party, and his frequent contributions to the public debate through the newspaper the *Manchester Guardian*.[19] In spite of his strong commitment to socialism, he was also an admirer of Plato's philosophy. This was probably in large part due to his own education at Balliol College, Oxford when idealist thought based in Platonism had been at its height.[20] Early in his career, he suggested that 'real culture' should be offered to 'the mass of ordinary men who must pursue ordinary occupations in order to earn a living', on the grounds that 'changes in the structure of English Society are throwing more and more responsibility on the shoulders of men who had had no opportunity of obtaining the "synoptic mind", which, as Plato reminds successive generations of Oxford students, is desirable in "governors"'.[21] This helped to lead him to the conclusion that working people should gain access to higher levels of education. Tawney was also an acolyte of Albert Mansbridge, for many years the secretary of the Workers' Educational Association (WEA), who was a keen admirer of Plato's ideas. According to Mansbridge, for example, the university tutorial movement which he supported and in which Tawney was prominently involved in the early years of the century 'conforms in method to that of Plato in so far as question and answer developed in discussion are concerned', and helped to encourage 'the acquisition of knowledge as assisting the fulfilment of an educational ideal which is conceived not in the interests of the individual; but in the interests of citizenship'.[22]

Tawney argued strongly that social class was responsible for basic inequalities in educational provision, especially in the way that working-class children were largely denied access to higher levels of education. Social class assumptions were so prevalent, he noted, that 'in common speech elementary education has come to mean not preparatory education but that kind and quality of education which is thought sufficient for the majority of working-class children'. He regarded the imposition of financial restrictions as a thin pretext for the maintenance of this class-divided system, which obscured the powerful interests that motivated it. On the other hand, he proposed an alternative approach, a 'new direction in education', which would involve a 'new conception of the relations between primary and secondary education'.[23] It was this 'new conception' that he set out to convey in detail in a set of policy proposals published by the Labour Party in 1922 under the title *Secondary Education for All*.

The Labour Party's general objective, persuasively fashioned by Tawney himself, was that secondary education should be no longer regarded as the privilege of a small elite but as the prerogative of all. Primary education and secondary education, rather than being largely separate, should instead be 'organised as two stages in a single and continuous process; secondary education being the education of the adolescent and primary education being education preparatory thereto'.[24] The continued division of education into elementary and secondary was, it insisted, 'educationally unsound and socially obnoxious'.[25] The general organization of education on 'lines of class' was 'at once a symptom, an effect, and a cause of the control of the lives of the mass of men and women by a privileged minority'. Indeed,

> The very assumption on which it is based, that all that the child of the workers needs is 'elementary education' – as though the mass of the people, like anthropoid apes, had fewer convolutions in their brains than the rich – is itself a piece of insolence.[26]

Secondary education for all, by contrast, would help to 'lay the foundations of a democratic society' by creating a single system for all ('normal') children of the appropriate age-range.[27]

So there should be a single system for secondary education. Tawney's proposals were equally clear, however, that there should still be different types of secondary school. Indeed, *Secondary Education for All* emphasized the idea of 'various types of institution'. In particular, it explained,

> There must be local initiative and experiment. There is no probability that what suits Lancashire or the West Riding will appeal equally to London or Gloucestershire or Cornwall, and if education is to be an inspiration, not a machine, it must reflect the varying social traditions, and moral atmospheres, and economic conditions of different localities. And within the secondary system of each there must be more than one type of school.[28]

It proposed a broad notion of the scope of secondary education, defined as 'the stage of life for which it provides, . . . the education of the adolescent',[29] and argued that it should be fundamentally liberal in spirit. Even so, it concluded, 'Provided, however, that these general characteristics are present, the greater the variety among secondary schools the better for education.'[30] The overall aim was that 'primary and secondary education, instead of forming, as now, two separate systems with frail handrails thrown from one to the other, would form two parts of a harmonious whole'. In the new system,

> Secondary schools would be various in type, and not all children would pass to the same kind of school. But all children would pass to *some* kind of secondary school and would spend the critical years

from eleven to sixteen under the invigorating influence of a progressive course of full time education.[31]

In the years that followed, Tawney was insistent in denouncing attempts to offer what he called 'a cheap substitute for secondary education' to working-class children, but continued to suggest that secondary education for all should involve 'schools differing in type and curriculum, but all complying with secondary standards'.[32] By the beginning of the Second World War, he was confident that this view was widely shared: 'The policy of a universal system of secondary education, embracing schools varying in educational type and methods, but equal in quality, has made much progress outside official and political circles.'[33] This was his key concern during the war in the development of reforms that were to culminate in the Education Act (1944). He was anxious that fees should be abolished in all state-aided secondary schools,[34] but was consistent in his view that 'varying types of ability should move easily to the different schools best qualified to develop them'.[35]

## A middle way

These notions of cultivating diverse forms of provision suited for different kinds of children were also pursued by another leading educational reformer in this crucial formative period, Fred Clarke. Formerly a professor of education in South Africa, Clarke was director of the Institute of Education in London from 1936 to 1945.[36] In many ways, his ideas on educational reform were as radical and far-reaching as were those of Tawney, especially as they were represented in his short book *Education and Social Change*, published in 1940.[37] Clarke was acutely aware of the social class inequalities in which secondary education was based. He was also concerned to help to develop a new 'social philosophy' that would be 'in harmony with that which inspires a generous education'.[38] At the same time, his thinking, like Tawney's, was strongly influenced by Plato, and he was even more explicit than Tawney about retaining tripartite divisions in secondary education.

Clarke's general views about secondary education were well developed by the early 1930s. He perceived a strong parallel between the contemporary social and international situation and that which had faced Plato's Greece, and emphasized the need for the restoration of order in facing up to crisis. Education would be important as a part of this approach, and, in particular, 'Plato followed a profoundly true instinct when he found the answer to closely similar problems in what may fairly be called a scheme of secondary education.'[39] Just as in Plato's day, Clarke asserted, 'If free societies are not to fall to pieces under the strain, if a new age of Caesarism is to be averted, the alternative must be sought in the possibilities that are offered by a reformed secondary education.'[40] Such reform should not be based on what he called 'the prejudices of a mistaken equalitarianism', but should in fact help to encourage 'the deliberate creation of an *elite*', and should also retain an important role for 'selection'.[41] With these priorities in view, he sought a middle path between the egalitarianism of the American high school and the social class prejudices, 'that *damnosa haereditas* of class-feeling', of secondary education as it had developed in England.[42] On the classic Platonic model, he hoped to produce not only 'philosopher-kings' who would be able to provide wise leadership, but also the 'rank-and-file' who would be expected to follow their lead. It was in providing for 'the secondary training of the rank-and-file' that he saw the need for 'ever wider diversification of facilities', which would he felt 'include much more than the ordinary school as usually understood'.[43] Thus, he argued, could be fashioned 'some effective amalgam of the best elements in European and American ideas of secondary education', which could combine 'the generosity, the freedom from class-taint, and the experimental spirit of the American idea' with 'the exacting standards, the thoroughness of discipline, the subtler interpretation of equality, and the faithfulness to a great cultural tradition, which mark the European idea'.[44]

During the Second World War, Clarke also took part in discussions on the kind of educational reconstruction that should be attempted, and within this wider context of preparing for general educational reform pursued the social implications of secondary education for all.[45] Like Tawney, he insisted that secondary education 'must be defined quite shortly as *the education of the adolescent*, whatever its form might be, . . . and whoever the adolescents concerned may be', although he also argued that such education might be provided either in schools or elsewhere.[46] The 'stage of evolution that English society has now reached' meant that secondary education could no longer be confined to a select minority, and it was the 're-planning' of this area that was 'central' to 'any practical scheme of reconstruction in education'. He was also clear, however, that the creation of secondary education for all would mean providing 'a sufficient variety of forms of secondary education to meet the wide variety of needs and aptitudes', which in turn would entail 'variety of organized *curricula*, whether provided together in a multilateral large school, or distinctively in separate schools'. He suggested that this could be achieved not so much through the '*selection* of a few' as through 'the allocation of all alike, each to the appropriate form of education'. Towards this latter end he proposed that a period of special observation by teachers between the ages of 11 and 13 would be much more useful than an examination as a means of guiding the decision 'as to the form of secondary education to which the pupil should proceed'.[47] Although Clarke allowed for the possibility of a 'multilateral' form of secondary school, then, this was within the context of emphasizing the

importance of maintaining tripartite distinctions between different forms
of secondary education and curriculum.


## Parity of esteem?


A key debate also developed at this time over whether it was really possible
to foster parity of esteem between alternative forms of secondary school, and
on the kinds of reforms and conditions that might help to bring it about.
Such issues came sharply into focus during the 1930s around a further
inquiry into secondary education under the auspices of the consultative
committee of the Board of Education. This inquiry, chaired by Sir Will
Spens (himself educated at Rugby School and King's College, Cambridge),
sought ways of securing 'equality of conditions in post-primary schools of
different types', and a sub-committee was established towards this end.[48]
Tawney, who was fully appraised of the problems facing the committee,
feared that the Board of Education would resist the idea of 'equality of
conditions', partly for reasons of cost, such as the implications for teachers'
salaries, but also because of 'the real issue which won't be stated – principle'.[49] He insisted, in spite of this, that the introduction to the report
should reflect the weight of evidence from LEAs and others 'in favour of
equality for all kinds of post-primary education'.[50]

Such pressures resulted in the Spens Report, published at the end of 1938,
making a strong endorsement of the ideal of parity of esteem between different types of post-primary schools. The introduction to the report duly
emphasized that 'everything possible should be done to secure parity of
status for Grammar Schools, Technical High Schools, and Modern Schools'.[51]
Chapter 9, entitled 'Administrative problems', dealt at some length with the
implications of this view. It argued against the general adoption of multilateral schools, but suggested that what it called the 'multilateral idea' should
'permeate' the system of secondary education.[52] Existing barriers between
different types of secondary schools were, it insisted, 'the legacies of an age
which had a different educational and social outlook from our own'.[53] The
report conceded that it would be necessary to reduce the differences in the
regulations and conditions under which each of these kinds of schools operated. It made several specific recommendations designed to meet this objective. In particular, it proposed that teachers' salary scales should be reviewed
and revised, the provision of school buildings given equal treatment, payment
of fees abolished in all state secondary schools 'as soon as the national
finances render it possible',[54] the minimum school leaving age raised to the
same general level in all schools, and a new Code of Regulations developed
for secondary schools to embrace grammar schools, technical high schools
and modern schools.

Even before the publication of the Spens Report, strong doubts were raised as to whether such reforms would be effective in their declared aim of achieving parity of esteem. One leading official at the Board of Education, R.S. Wood (educated at the City of London School and Jesus College, Cambridge), was especially sceptical, and circulated a detailed rebuttal of such hopes. He could already visualize in outline the implications of including different forms of post-primary education within the domain of secondary education. He insisted that this should retain a strong element of differentiation in order to cater for all children in terms of their individual capacities:

> To attempt to put children through the same mental mill would be as stupid and dangerous a proceeding as to put all children through the same physical training without any consideration of their differing degrees of health or strength of physique.[55]

He suggested that a suitable degree of differentiation could be readily achieved:

> All would proceed alike to a 'Secondary' School, the majority to one of general type – the Modern School of the Hadow Report. A small proportion would go to the High School, the genuine Secondary School aiming at the professions and the University. There would be a place for the Technical High School corresponding to the Junior Technical School.

At the same time, Wood also pointed out that although the Spens proposals would 'eliminate to some extent the inferiority complex about an education confined to a so-called Elementary School, for all children alike would attend a Secondary School of one type or another', there might still develop 'a feeling that special advantage attached to the Grammar or High School and a consequent demand for an unreasonable expansion of this type of provision'. Indeed, he added, 'it may be urged that any scheme such as that outlined above is nothing more than an elaborate attempt to spoof the public mind, and by giving a new wrapper and a new name persuade them to accept the cheaper article as the higher class goods'.[56] Wood concluded that the proposals of the Spens committee would do little to remedy the 'disparity of prestige' between the existing secondary schools and new types of secondary schools.[57]

Wood's warning reflected an important tension between the ideals and practices of tripartism, and the doctrine of parity of esteem. Plato's theory of tripartism had not conceived of the different forms of educational provision being equivalent to each other in terms of their status, but was intended to rationalize and justify a clear social hierarchy. There was no obvious place for parity of esteem in such a theory. Nor did it sit at all comfortably with the realities of social class differences in the 1930s, when the distinct social origins of elementary and secondary education remained clearly evident. This tension, clear but unresolved, was integral to the idea of secondary education for all as it worked itself out during this period.

## Three types of mind

Another key figure in this period who also helped to shape conceptions of what secondary education for all should encompass was Sir Cyril Norwood. He represented a more conservative position on the nature of educational reform than either Tawney and Clarke. Norwood, who was educated at Merchant Taylors' School in London and St John's College, Oxford, was a devout admirer of Plato's ideals, and he adapted these to develop the most famous and elaborate typology of tripartite distinctions in English secondary education.

Whereas Tawney was fiercely critical of the social class basis of secondary education in England, and Clarke sought a compromise between English and American ideas, Norwood was unapologetic and fervent in his defence of what he called the 'English tradition of education'. He argued that this tradition had emanated in the Middle Ages from the ideals of knighthood, chivalry and the English gentleman, and had been maintained in the nineteenth century through Thomas Arnold of Rugby and the revival of the public schools. In the rapidly changing social and political situation of the twentieth century, he insisted, these same ideals should be enlisted to underpin any new reforms or expansion in secondary education.[58]

It was during the Second World War, through his chairmanship of a Board of Education committee on the curriculum and examinations in secondary schools, that Norwood was able to expound his views on the nature of secondary education for all. He began with the assumption that while 'freedom' was 'essential' as a principle for a reformed system, it was most important that 'the tradition of secondary education, the best in the world, must be preserved'.[59] As a starting point for discussion, he 'suggested that primary education might be regarded as a training in the three Rs and of the senses; from this there might be a path to various forms of secondary education'.[60] Norwood insisted on maintaining the grammar school as the repository of a distinct form of secondary education which he described as 'grammatical'. Such a treatment was 'concerned with knowledge for its own sake more than any other treatment is likely to be', and was most suited for 'the boy or girl who shows promise of ability to deal with abstract notions – who is quick at seizing the relatedness of related things'.[61] It was soon agreed that such grammar schools should continue to take their place in the 'field of post-primary education' alongside technical and modern schools. Moreover, following some discussion of alternative terms, finally it was decided that, as post primary education of whatever type would have one code of regulations and similar advantages in build-ings etc., it was best to indicate the stage by the word 'secondary' as an inclusive term, and to define the kind of 'secondary' school by the titles Grammar, Modern and Technical; thus there would be Second-ary Modern Schools, Secondary Grammar Schools, Secondary Technical Schools (which would cover also Commercial and Art and Agricultural Schools), and such nomenclature would bring Technical education and Modern schools into parallel with existing so-called Secondary schools.[62]

This was a clear endorsement of the principle of tripartite divisions within the general reform that would establish secondary education for all.

However, Norwood and his committee shared the doubts that had been expressed earlier by R.S. Wood as to the prospects of parity of esteem. In its deliberations the pointed question was raised: 'Can a school with a leaving age of 16 ever have parity of esteem with one with a leaving age of 18? Is it all a game of "Let's pretend"?'[63] The committee decided that use of the phrase 'parity of esteem' tended to create 'confusion of thought', and that therefore 'the Report should not give any encouragement to the use of the phrase but should rather expose it as meaningless'.[64]

The final report of Norwood's committee spelled out with startling candour the social and educational implications of tripartism. Part I of the report identified three 'rough groupings' of pupils which, 'whatever may be their ground, have in fact established themselves in general educational experience'.[65] On the basis of this, it argued that such distinctions should be both acknowledged and cultivated in the future provision of secondary education for all. According to the Norwood Report, the first type of pupil was 'the pupil who is interested in learning for its own sake, who can grasp an argument or follow a piece of connected reasoning'. Such pupils had previously been associated with the grammar schools, and went on to the 'learned professions' or into 'higher administrative or business posts'.[66] The most suitable curriculum for such pupils, it maintained, was one that 'treats the various fields of knowledge as suitable for coherent and system-atic study for their own sake apart from immediate considerations of occupation'.[67] The report concluded that grammar schools should continue to uphold an ideal of 'disciplined thought provided by an introduction to the main fields of systematic knowledge, which is valued first for its own sake and later invoked to meet the needs of life'.[68]

By contrast, the Norwood Report defined the second type of pupil as one who showed 'interests and abilities' that lay 'markedly in the field of applied science or applied art'. Such pupils would be better suited to a cur-riculum that was 'closely, though not wholly, directed to the special data and skills associated with a particular kind of occupation',[69] particularly in industry, trades and commerce, and this should be provided in secondary technical schools. At the same time, the third type of pupils identified in the report apparently dealt 'more easily with concrete things than with ideas', and demanded 'immediate return' from any endeavour: 'His horizon is near and within a limited area his movement is generally slow, though it may be surprisingly rapid in seizing a particular point or in taking up a special line.'[70] For these pupils, it suggested a curriculum with 'a balanced training of mind and body and a correlated approach to humanities, Natural Science and the arts', not with any specific job or occupation in view but in order to 'make a direct appeal to interests, which it would awaken by practical touch with affairs'.[71] The kind of institution that would best meet these needs, it considered, was a new kind of secondary school to be known as the modern school.

Overall, Tawney, Clarke and Norwood reflected differing stances on educational reform from the 1920s until the passing of the Education Act (1944), broadly socialist, liberal and conservative respectively. Together, they help to convey something of the strength of the tripartite tradition in secondary education that underlay the emergence of 'secondary education for all' during this period, as a central element in the ingrained culture of secondary education. This was the spirit with which the major White Paper *Educational Reconstruction*, published in 1943, was imbued. At the same time, the contradictions that were inherent within tripartism between separate provision and parity of esteem survived within this key basis for reform, as it promised that from the age of 11, 'secondary education, of diversified types but on equal standing, will be provided for all children'.[72] The White Paper declared that 'conditions in the different types of secondary schools must be broadly equivalent'.[73] On the assumption that this could be achieved, it was confident that the future of the modern schools 'is their own to make, and it is a future full of promise'.[74] It remained to be seen how these ideals would be realized in the new era of secondary education for all.

# PART 2

## The practice

I would santd a beter canst of get a good job in a work whit you like but all 4R are good for is the pit filling tubs and clevering roads why the B class get the top jobs.

(Secondary modern school pupil, *c*.1961)

# 5

## The secondary modern experiment

Following the Education Act (1944), there were many attempts on the part of the Ministry of Education and in different local contexts to articulate a distinctive ideal for the new secondary modern schools. Initially, the supporters of the SMSs sought to emphasize the unique and novel qualities of these schools, and to mark them off clearly in comparison with grammar schools and technical schools. In this regard, they drew heavily on the notion of working-class secondary education that had been developed over the preceding 50 years. Gradually, such appeals subsided in resonance, and by the 1950s and 1960s they were largely overtaken first by attempts to imitate the familiar practices of the grammar schools, and second by an increasing emphasis on undermining the alternative ideal represented in the comprehensive schools.

SMSs were intended to provide for the needs of about three-quarters of secondary school pupils up to the minimum leaving age, which was raised in 1947 from 14 to 15. They were to be non-selective in the admission of pupils, whereas both the grammar schools and the secondary technical schools were to select suitable pupils at the age of 11. It was also hoped that the SMSs would remain free of the constraints of examinations that were associated with the grammar schools, as the Hadow Report had envisaged in the 1920s, so that their curriculum could develop in an independent and distinctive manner to cater for the distinctive needs of their pupils. It was left to the local education authorities to determine the appropriate pattern of provision to suit local needs, but this was to be brought about on the basis of a development plan for each local area that had to be approved by the Ministry of Education.

By the 1950s, the introduction of SMSs had been successfully achieved at a national level. In 1955, there were over 3500 SMSs in England and Wales, of which one-quarter were boys' schools, one-quarter were girls' schools, and the remainder were mixed. There were over 1,200,000 pupils attending these schools, and almost 56,000 full-time teachers employed in them.[1] This general development obscured some important local variations. In many areas, such as in the urban centres of Leeds, Manchester and Sheffield, and in some rural counties like Berkshire and Montgomeryshire, SMSs were to form the major element in a 'tripartite' arrangement alongside grammar and technical schools.[2] In other localities, such as Brighton, Leicestershire and Merthyr Tydfil, a 'bipartite' arrangement was preferred in which grammar schools and modern schools were provided but technical provision was to be incorporated within each type as appropriate.[3] Some LEAs, like Darlington and Durham, proposed a tripartite system in highly industrialized areas but a bipartite structure elsewhere.[4] A few, most notably the London County Council, opposed both tripartite and bipartite approaches and sought to develop 'comprehensive high schools' that were designed to cater for all aptitudes and abilities.[5] By the 1950s, it was becoming clear that the secondary technical schools had failed to develop as widely as had been hoped, catering for less than 4 per cent of secondary school pupils rather than the 10–15 per cent that had been anticipated.[6] Meanwhile, an increasingly political debate served to focus growing attention upon the problems and failures experienced by the SMSs, and on the alternative offered by the comprehensive schools.[7]

### The great adventure?

A major priority of the Ministry of Education in the years immediately following the end of the Second World War, under Clement Attlee's Labour government, was to consolidate the tripartite arrangement of secondary education that had been foreshadowed in 1943 in the White Paper *Educational Reconstruction*, and in the Norwood Report. To this end, it was crucial to explain the new role that would be taken by the SMSs on behalf of the large majority of pupils from the age of 11. There was some good will on which this new type of school could build; the *Times Educational Supplement*, for example, referred to teachers in the SMSs setting out with 'renewed vigour' on a 'great adventure' to 'prove that these schools are as good as any'.[8] It would be necessary, however, to rationalize the distinctive ideals underlying the SMSs in terms that would support their existence as separate institutions.

The first attempt to do so was produced in April 1945 in the form of a Ministry of Education pamphlet entitled *The Nation's Schools: Their Plan and Purpose*. This set out to consider 'the objectives of different types of education and the conditions necessary to their attainment'.[9] So far as secondary education was concerned, it sought to balance a 'unity of purpose' with differences in 'general ability' and in the 'individual interests and aptitudes' of pupils.[10] SMSs would provide, it predicted, 'the secondary education of the majority of the nation's children',[11] and yet it conceded that the 'possibilities' that they offered were 'generally too little understood and too little appreciated'. It emphasized that they should remain free from the 'pressures' of external examinations, and that this 'invaluable freedom' should help them to 'advance along the lines they themselves feel to be right'.[12]

*The Nation's Schools* then went on to link the needs of SMS pupils with their future position in society and employment. They would cater, it pointed out, for 'a considerable number of children whose future employment will not demand any measure of technical skill or knowledge', but who would be needed for 'a growing field of repetitive and routine process work'. The education provided in these schools would therefore need to develop for many of their pupils the resources 'to find and pursue interests which will add to the meaning and enjoyment of life', as well as to fulfil their 'home-making' responsibilities which would also, it suggested, provide the 'basis of future happiness'.[13] Craft work and other practical activities, alongside more formal classroom studies, would help to ensure, it concluded hopefully, that the SMS would become

> one of the main pillars in the secondary structure, aiming at giving a full school life and a balanced education that is at once practical and general, which will equip a large number of the country's future citizens to enter the larger world trained in character, adaptable and awake to the possibilities that lie within themselves of finding and pursuing interests both of mind and hand that will aid their further development and add to their pleasure in life.[14]

For some commentators, *The Nation's Schools* was a mission statement that struck broadly the right note. Dr William Alexander, the highly influential secretary of the Association of Education Committees (AEC), declared that in his view it would be a 'major disaster' if the SMSs 'merely tried to ape the grammar schools or the technical schools', and claimed that some SMSs had already developed 'a very fine form of general education'.[15] The *Journal of Education*, while also supportive, argued that the pamphlet had not in fact done enough to 'adequately convey' what it called the 'immense and adventurous task' that awaited the SMS, in the form of 'the discovery (for it is no less) of a curriculum suited to the needs and interests of boys and girls of no more than average intellectual gifts'.[16] In its forthright description of the role of the SMS, however, the pamphlet helped to consolidate the terms of debate between supporters and opponents of the policy.

Officials at the Ministry of Education were acutely aware that the ministry would need to take the lead in articulating the ideals that underlay the tripartite structure of secondary education, 'to speak in bolder tones and more definite terms', although, as was also noted, 'if we are wise, as we become positive rather than neutral, we shall continue conscious that we must carry our partners and the public with us'.[17] It was a key part of this approach that the new minister of education, Ellen Wilkinson, was as enthusiastic about tripartism and the SMSs as were her senior officials. The contradictions apparent between Wilkinson's deeply held socialist convictions and her support for different types of secondary schools have often been noted.[18] She was convinced, however, not by the idea of the 'cream' going to one type of school while the 'rest' went to another, but by the notion of helping to improve the status and standards of the SMSs to the level of other types of secondary schools.[19]

Wilkinson, herself the product of a higher elementary school as well as a graduate of the University of Manchester, emphasized the need to persuade the parents of potential pupils that modern schools would provide 'secondary' education rather than being a second-best alternative:

> The idea of the school must be presented to them so clearly and convincingly, that they will help us in putting pressure on difficult authorities to get them. Equally important they must be convinced that a grammar school is now a specialised type of secondary school, and not the *real* thing any others being substitutes.[20]

This was her consistent message during her period as minister of education. The 'true Modern schools', she argued, were those in 'fine new buildings', and these where they existed 'had won a considerable measure of public confidence in the type and standard of the education which they were giving'.[21] Others, meanwhile, were developing 'a good "Modern" type of education in cramped out-of date premises', while 'many, inevitably' were 'nothing more than the top halves of former elementary schools'. The lesson that she derived from this situation was that 'We must work as quickly as possible to make all schools of this type "Modern" in education as well as in name.'[22] This view led Wilkinson increasingly into conflict with many members of her own party, which at its conference in June 1946 called on her to repudiate the Ministry of Education pamphlet *The Nation's Schools*.[23] Despite such opposition, she remained unrepentant, insisting that she was not 'promulgating a wrong social philosophy', and openly taking issue with 'those people who say that by setting up distinctions of brains between people you are only producing another kind of distinction'. Indeed, she commented, 'I am sorry if people feel that, but I am glad to think we are not all born the same. We are people, not postage stamps.' Moreover, she added, not everyone wanted an 'academic education', and

> coal has to be mined and fields ploughed, and it is a fantastic idea that we have allowed, so to speak, to be cemented into our body politic that you are in a higher social class if you add up figures in a book than if you plough the fields and scatter the good seed on the land.

According to Wilkinson, it was essential to 'reorientate our whole attitude on this subject'.[24] At the same time, she continued to insist that the 'premises and staff' of SMSs 'have to be made not only adequate, but equal to anything given to the other forms of secondary schools, and the curriculum has to be planned as a secondary course.'[25]

Wilkinson's approach was strongly supported by her parliamentary secretary at the Ministry of Education, David Hardman. Educated at Coleraine Academical Institution in Ulster and Christ's College, Cambridge, and now the Labour MP for Darlington, Hardman argued that the SMSs could be regarded as novel institutions that, far from being inferior to the older established schools such as grammar schools, were actually in many respects superior. He challenged the idea that had been promoted, in his view, by 'Plato and the liberal educationists' that 'there is education for a livelihood (practical things) – but a superior education in the liberal arts which we call non-vocational'.[26] On the contrary, according to Hardman the SMSs could demonstrate the importance of an alternative approach to education:

> What is wanted in the Modern secondary school is NOT a tame copy of a so-called superior education taken up to 16 at a Grammar school; nor is it to be a hotch-potch of manual jobs with a bit of Art thrown in. We want definite scholarly things for the child to do and a recognition that hand done things of the highest creative type (architectural draftsmanship, painting, modelling, handicrafts, etc) are of equal status because they provide a sense of concrete achievement in the growing child.[27]

He took a strongly idealistic view of what he saw as 'our new conception of secondary education for the majority of our children',[28] relating the SMSs to the experiment of the village colleges led by Henry Morris in Cambridgeshire,[29] to insist that 'there is something new being born in our educational system'. Indeed, he told his minister,

> Forgive me if I tend to labour the point too much, but I do feel our job is to educate many in our party to a new and better conception of education for the adolescent, rather than an apish imitation of what in many respects in secondary education has been a failure in the past.[30]

Hardman's missionary zeal on behalf of the SMSs was also reflected in his public pronouncements. At a conference of modern school heads in May 1946, for example, he praised their commitment to 'activity' which was destined to supersede what he derided as the 'dismal reign of mere chalk and talk, the mechanical use of the text-books and the piling up of parrot facts'.[31] Like Wilkinson, he was unapologetic about the idea of 'three kinds of mind', and he argued forcefully that 'There are differences in intelligence among children as well as among adults. There are distinctions of mind, and these distinctions are imposed by nature. I am afraid that is a fact which we cannot get over.'[32] In a more positive vein, he insisted that there was an opportunity to 'create in the secondary modern school a curriculum and a training the like of which our educational system has never before known'. This would carry with it the need to give greater credit for 'activity' and 'that sense of achievement which comes from manual skill'. If this could be achieved, he proclaimed, 'The ideal of the secondary modern school as indic-ated in the best of our secondary modern schools between the wars and in the Cambridgeshire Village colleges, presents us with boundless opportun-ities.'[33] At another public meeting in Leicester later in the year, speaking on behalf of the minister, he emphasized the need for 'variety' in the provision of secondary education so as to cater for differences in 'capacity and interests'. Many pupils, he claimed, 'will do best in a school that provides a good all-round education which enables them to develop freely on their own lines'. This would require 'a flexible curriculum, reasonably small classes, skilled teachers, up-to-date buildings, modern equipment, including radio and a cinema projector', and it would also mean 'looking on the traditional sub-jects in the curriculum not as a body of knowledge to be imparted, but as an instrument to stimulate the children's interests'. The SMS, he insisted, 'suits the majority of the children', and would evolve a 'true secondary course' that would 'be as great a milestone on the road of English educa-tion as was the large-scale development of grammar schools after the Act of 1902'.[34]

The aspirations voiced by Wilkinson and Hardman are testimony to the ideals that underlay the SMSs, in particular the conviction that a distinct form of education could be developed in them that would be most appro-priate and rewarding for the mass of secondary school pupils. This deter-mination was vividly reflected in the Ministry of Education pamphlet *The New Secondary Education*, published in 1947. Chapter 7 of this publication attempted to explain the defining principles of a 'modern school education'. It pointed out that the SMS was still 'a growing tree with strong roots, but so far rather a limited number of branches',[35] since there were 'very few schools of this type in this country that represent, in conditions, buildings and general curriculum, the standard which all must reach as soon as pos-sible'.[36] With this important proviso, it defined the aim of the SMS as being 'to provide a good all-round secondary education, not focused primarily on the traditional subjects of the school curriculum, but developing out of the interests of the child'. It would cater for a wide range of 'ability, aptitude and social background', and so it 'must be free to work out its own sylla-buses and methods',[37] in order to achieve as much 'freedom' and 'flexibility' as possible. The best existing SMSs, it argued, 'already offer convincing examples of the lines on which this general objective can be attained', by providing 'a broad and balanced general curriculum' and 'by means of many kinds of practical activity'.[38] Such schools would be given 'parity of condi-tions with other types of secondary school', but they must be prepared to achieve 'parity of esteem' only through their 'own efforts'.[39] Above all, it concluded, the SMS must not be 'dominated by traditions that derive from an education that was planned for quite different conditions and with quite different aims'.[40] The pamphlet radiated an unruffled optimism in the conviction, as it proposed, that

> As the modern schools develop, parents will see that they are good; it will become increasingly common for them to keep their children at school beyond the compulsory age, and to select a modern school as the one best suited to their children's requirements on grounds unhampered by considerations of 'prestige'.[41]

It was on this hope that the fate of the 'great adventure' would depend.

### Secondary schools in name only?

Even as Wilkinson and Hardman were preparing their strategy to bolster the SMSs, there were many critics of the 'great adventure' who argued that it would serve in practice simply to maintain the social differences and inequalities of the past. Sir Robert Wood at the ministry stressed the potential advantage of developing a variety of schools as abolishing 'class distinctions' in favour of 'intelligence distinctions or differences – distinctions imposed by Nature and outwith the control of man'.[42] Even so, Wood could clearly anticipate the objection that

> by having different types of secondary school we should only be re-placing social class distinctions by equally objectionable intellectual distinctions – creating an aristocracy of talent in the Grammar Schools and putting the 'runners-up' in the Secondary (Technical) Schools, and 'the field' in the Modern Schools.[43]

The chief inspector for secondary schools, R.H. Charles, also reflected on what he saw as 'undoubtedly a widespread view that the division in the Norwood Report of children into three categories is really theoretical and artificial, and that if it is pressed and translated into bricks, mortar and regulations, it will have anything but a happy social effect'. At the same time, Charles hoped that the new SMSs, alongside the secondary technical schools, would be able to 'develop and liberate powers in pupils which at present are ignored and perhaps not dreamed of'.[44] A wide range of educational agencies articulated similar anxieties, often relating current problems to the social origins of the SMSs in the elementary schools of the nineteenth century, and concluding that they would struggle to achieve any form of parity of esteem especially in relation to the grammar schools.

Such criticisms were evident, for example, in many submissions that were made during 1945 and 1946 to the first major inquiry undertaken by the new Central Advisory Council (CAC) for Education (England). The successor of the consultative committee to the Board of Education which had produced the Hadow and Spens Reports in the interwar years, this new body was commissioned by the Ministry of Education under the Education Act (1944) to advise the minister on issues related to educational theory and practice. The first substantive inquiry to be set up, by agreement between the minister and the first chairman of the CAC, Sir Fred Clarke, was on 'the transition from school to independent life'. Through this inquiry, Clarke no doubt hoped to develop and promote his earlier ideas about the relationship between education and the community. It soon became clear that, at least for many observers, the realities of a tripartite system would contradict any such lofty ideals.

The key issue that was repeatedly stressed in submissions to the Central Advisory Council was the pervasive legacy of earlier forms of provision which continued to be reflected, both in theory and in practice, in the schools of the 1940s. The AEC pointed out that education had been viewed for many years in terms of 'a provision on the one hand of a limited elementary schooling for the great majority of children and, on the other, of provision of a system of higher education for a selected few'. This situation, it suggested, had created a 'doubt in the public mind' over 'the value of expensive provision save in respect to higher education'. A 'fundamental modification in the educational philosophy underlying both statutory requirements and existing practice' was necessary in order to redress this imbalance. According to the AEC, such a shift in thinking was embodied in the Education Act (1944) with its 'conception of education for all children in appropriate stages and related to their individual requirements'. If accepted by the public, it argued, this could provide the necessary support for 'making effective standards of accommodation and of staffing which have hitherto been unacceptable, even where provided by regulation'.[45] Other witnesses were less optimistic, and argued that the new reforms, far from alleviating earlier inequalities, would prove superficial in their effects.

The Association of Municipal Authorities also pointed out the financial obstacles that lay in the path of ventures such as the SMSs. After the First World War, it recalled, there had been pressure to provide new schools to serve housing estates, but this had been resisted on grounds of cost. Older buildings had been regarded as 'out of date' by educationists, but 'from the point of view of the advocates of economy were regarded as weather proof'.[46] It was widely feared that the legacy of these previous restrictions would hamper the chance of success unless the opportunity was now taken to reconstruct and rebuild the facilities themselves. The National Federation of Class Teachers also expressed this concern when it suggested that the 'prevailing standard of accommodation' was rooted in 'the low estimate of the value of education among the majority of the population'. The 'commercial outlook' of the nation, it suggested, 'always requires a concrete return for expenditure and is not ready to expend money for a return that cannot be measured'. It concluded that such attitudes led directly to major differences in the standard of provision. For example,

> In a township in one Urban area all the junior children attend the same school. 500 boys and girls are congregated in a pre-1870 building with a railway goods yard on one side, a gas works on another, with a colliery 200 yards away. In the same area the Secondary Grammar School adjoins the park and is a fine modern building. ALL the children of this area have to be educated in the pre-1870 building while 40% at the most enter the Secondary School. The best possible facilities should be available for children of all ages.[47]

The County Councils Association (CCA) in its evidence attributed such striking inequalities to the dominance of an 'academic tradition' that implied 'that those who could not or would not benefit from that type of education were less worth educating'. It urged that the ministry should learn from this to ensure that there would not now develop what it called 'a stereotyped school system in which are repeated previous mistakes'.[48]

Similarly, the Association of Teachers in Colleges and Departments of Education also emphasized the importance of raising the standard of accommodation. It again linked this issue with broader attitudes to mass educational provision. Like the CCA, this body could point out examples of inadequate and neglected facilities:

> One school accommodating 300 girls has only two wash-basins, only cold water, no soap, two roller-towels changed once a week. Lavatories are across the yard. Toilet paper has to be asked for. This school is in a highly-populated area. In the same area many schools are typified by one which was built in 1871, is unaltered, and has one classroom which has to be used as a passage way to other rooms. There are at least six schools of this type in a city of 270,000 population. Several others consist wholly or in part of army huts put up as a temporary expedient after the 1918 war. In a boys' central school in another area in 1937 there were no toilet fixtures and no toilet paper in the lavatories, and this was remedied only after a prolonged campaign on the part of the teachers.

The causes of this neglect, it proposed, were a general unwillingness to spend money, together with a tendency to spend money on a few new schools rather than on older buildings, but it also identified 'the slow-dying conviction that "anything will do" for the schools provided for the children of the poor'.[49]

Perhaps the most striking evidence submitted to the Advisory Council at this time was the submission prepared by the Workers' Educational Association. This comprised a detailed analysis of the deficiencies of school

accommodation, combined with a stong critique of the principles that underlay the provision of the SMS. It insisted that 'the present state of provision
for a majority of the children, as a preparation for life is lamentable', and
argued that the financial as well as the social and educational implications
of this must be 'faced' rather than 'evaded'. In Manchester, it pointed out,
out of a total of 248 buildings now in use for primary and secondary
schools, 14 were over 90 years old, 10 others were over 80 years old, 32
more were over 70, a further 52 were from 50 to 60 years old, 66 dated
from between 1896 and 1914, and only 69 had been built since 1918.
Over 700 schools in the country as a whole had been 'blacklisted' in 1924
but were still in use, and there were many schools

> without proper lighting, with inadequate heating; with primitive sanita-
> tion, and with no inside water, with a single washbasin and towel for
> scores of children; with defective ventilation; schools where children
> who have come some distance have no place to dry their clothes . . . ,
> old fashioned furniture, unsuitable for children; cramped and incon-
> venient classrooms; small rough playgrounds and no playing fields; as
> well as a deficiency of equipment, and especially of books, so serious
> that teachers are to be found in desperation supplying the lack as best
> they can out of their own pockets.

The 'school to which the majority of children will probably go', it continued,
was 'the one about which not nearly enough has been done'. It also suggested
that too little thinking had been devoted to how the SMSs should cater for
the majority of school pupils, for example in terms of its curriculum and
methods of teaching. Lastly, it expressed open scepticism in the ideas put
forward in the ministry's pamphlet *The Nation's Schools*, 'under which at
the age of 11 separate and segregated training of three classes of future
workers is implied'. The WEA strongly opposed the development of

> three parallel schools, one of which is rather self-consciously 'cultural'
> in its aims, while another is 'vocational' with cultural 'subjects' rather
> obviously 'tacked on', without any real integration with the main work
> of the school; while the third, the Modern school, has no very clearly
> developed purpose at all

in favour of a more 'democratic' conception of education that might
be encouraged more fully in 'multilateral' or 'comprehensive' forms of
organization.[50]

These trenchant criticisms of the historical legacy of the SMSs, as well
as of their underlying principles and their general facilities, had an important influence on the findings of the Advisory Council. As it developed its
inquiry, it began to raise several unresolved issues about the nature of the
SMSs and how they would seek to cater for their pupils. The distinctive
values of the SMSs, and the extent to which their teaching would be

frustrated by 'the present conditions in the schools', were identified as key problems.[51] It was queried how examinations and tests should determine what type of secondary school each pupil should go to at the age of 11, and which schools each should go to.[52] The CAC also considered the implications of secondary school education for British industry, and it was suggested that health and industry should form the basis of the educational system, 'with much greater emphasis than at present on the education of the great majority who must always remain "the working class"'.[53] The nature of the curriculum to be prescribed 'for the dull and backward, the non-academic child of average ability, the child who wants to be a technician, the academic child respectively' was also discussed.[54] More tellingly, the CAC began to criticize the nostrums that had been put forward in previous reports such as the Norwood Report and *The Nation's Schools*. A draft statement on educational objectives contributed by Clarke himself noted that in *The Nation's Schools*, for 'the modern schools to be attended presumably by the rank and file, the criterion of social need is applied in what might almost be called an inverted form',[55] since the main destiny of the pupils involved would be for work that 'may offer little, if anything, to keep minds alert and interests alive'.[56]

Such doubts were also vividly reflected in a detailed survey of criticisms of a tripartite arrangement in secondary education that was prepared for the Advisory Council's inquiry. This noted the insecure basis of the 'experiment' that was being conducted:

> While it is generally agreed that a new order must incorporate in some way the schools we already have providing education beyond 11+ (grammar school, junior technical school, and senior school), it is contended that to assume that these three types afford the right basis upon which to erect the whole structure is to assume the result of a long-term experiment before even setting the experiment on foot. It would be hazardous to contend that the deposits which have resulted from the improvisations of the past, influenced as they were by considerations that were not always purely educational, are precisely the same as the result we should have achieved by a longer term experiment in secondary education for all, conducted from the first on purely educational principles, and uninfluenced by adventitious considerations of social prestige or administrative expediency.

The Norwood Report of 1943, it continued, had attempted to 'rationalise, in terms of curriculum, the three kinds of post-primary school that have emerged from the improvisations of the past'. The ultimate effect of this might be, 'in view of the past history of the three types, the relative advantages they have offered hitherto and prevailing social attitudes towards them', that 'what are represented as three co-ordinate types will in fact be *three social grades*, arranged in this order of prestige and preference:

grammar, technical, modern'. Such a situation would hinder easy transfer of pupils between different types of schools, and might also bring about 'a concentration of the abler pupils in the grammar school, while at the other end, the modern school, will tend to become a receptacle for the rejects from the other two types'.

The different social origins of the three types of schools were also clearly observed by the Advisory Council as an obstacle to the goal of 'parity of esteem'. The grammar school was 'continuous with the great cultural tradition of Europe originating in Greece and passing by way of the Roman Empire, the Christian Church, and the Renaissance, to our own time'. The technical school was 'a development of the very recent junior technical school, which was never truly organic to the English system, but rather a sort of floating kidney in the educational anatomy'. Meanwhile the modern school was 'a direct derivative of the elementary school and its traditions it is suggested, is that of the 19th century Poor Law'. In such a situation,

> How then it is asked, can entities so different in their social and cultural origins come to be regarded as having 'parity of esteem'? Administrative action of itself could hardly achieve the result. Can it ever be achieved in English society apart from profound changes in prevailing social attitudes and habits?

The prospect that such a system might serve instead to 'classify and stratify our population and to predetermine destinies at the tender age' seemed more likely and at the same unacceptable, and so it was concluded that 'before the proposed tripartite system of secondary schooling is finally adopted, the more remote and possibly less obvious social effects of such policy ought to be looked into'.[57]

In view of these issues, expressed in such a manner, it was not surprising that the draft of the final report prepared by the Advisory Council raised fundamental criticisms of what it described as 'the contrast between theory and practice' in secondary education. This went so far as to suggest that hopes advanced on behalf of 'secondary education for all' through the Education Act (1944) had been disappointed and betrayed.

> What has happened [it complained] is that a number of schools have changed their name and are now designated Secondary Grammar, Secondary Technical and Secondary Modern to satisfy new official requirements. But, as parents well know, they are the same schools and many of them fall far short in personnel, premises and equipment of the old secondary school standard. [Indeed, it ventured,] There is a great danger of an onrush of cynicism as a result, and the growth of a feeling that the Education Act is just a scrap of paper like the Day Continuation School classes in the Fisher Act [of 1918].[58]

The final report that was published at the start of 1947 under the title *School and Life* was much more moderate in its language, probably in order to avoid undermining the position of local schools.[59] Nonetheless, the report as published did still point out that 'Many secondary schools under the new Act are secondary schools in name only', and it also emphasized that unless a high priority was given to school building, 'the majority of our children will for a long time to come be denied secondary education, in spite of the great expectations awakened when the Education Act was passed'.[60]

These debates therefore reflected widespread anxieties about the wisdom of the 'great adventure' or 'experiment' on which the Ministry of Education had embarked through its support for the SMSs. The principles on which these schools were based, which embodied more than half a century of agitation on behalf of a distinctive form of mass secondary education especially suited to the needs of the working class, were about to be exposed to empirical scrutiny of the most severe kind.

## 'A good orthodox blueprint for the future'

The Education Act (1944) had indicated that LEAs would all produce local development plans suitable for the needs of their area. The implications of this for the organisation of secondary education were spelled out in Circular 73, issued by the ministry at the end of 1945. This provided 'guidance' to the LEAs along the lines that had been proposed in the White Paper *Educational Reconstruction*, the Norwood Report of 1943, and the ministry pamphlet on *The Nation's Schools*. As a general rule, the proportion of accommodation to be allocated to the different types of secondary education would be about 70 to 75 per cent for modern schools and 25 to 30 per cent for the grammar and technical schools combined. Where such types of schools were developed together as bilateral or multilateral schools, the Circular advised, they should not in general cater for more than about 500 to 600 pupils, and the interests of the SMSs should be placed foremost.[61]

In the often protracted negotiations that followed with the LEAs of England and Wales, the Ministry of Education was especially concerned to ensure that the different forms of secondary education were clearly observed in their proper proportions. Although the SMS was itself a novel experiment, it enjoyed official approval and LEAs were expected to follow suit and provide it, while other kinds of 'experiment' had to be explained and justified in detail. Thus for example, in relation to Manchester's development plan, it was pointed out that the LEA should be asked to 'define and to describe any experiments it proposed for the future organisation of secondary education'. In particular, 'If the Ministry's tripartism is being challenged then a statement of justification for any novel or unorthodox treatment should be given.'[62] In spite of this, many LEAs voiced doubts about the separate provision of SMSs, and proposed a range of 'novel or unorthodox' alternatives. Others were more comfortable with the framework proposed by the ministry and with the principles that underlay it.

Strong opposition to the tripartite approach sanctioned by the ministry emerged in some local development plans, and also often in debates that took place at the local level. The Darlington County Borough Education Committee was among those that took an open stand against the principle of tripartism, arguing that 'this method of organisation will merely perpetuate the existing hierarchical structure and with it, those differences in status, prestige, staffing and amenities which spring from a complex of causes as largely social as educational in their origin'. In such a situation, it predicted, 'the position of the modern school will be an invidious one and prejudiced from the start'.[63] In Swansea, a protracted conflict developed over the multilateral plans of the local authority.[64]

In Durham, a compromise was sought in order to avoid the problems that were anticipated both in tripartism and in the multilateral alternative. So far as multilateral schools were concerned, Durham's director of education, Thomas Tilley, commented that although he had 'much sympathy' with their 'theoretical aspect', practical difficulties of finance and transport, added to the fact that 'in my view the educational advantages are problematic and are more apparent than real', led him 'to hesitate to recommend such a violent experimental change especially having regard to the safeguards with which the Minister evidently intends to hedge around such an experiment'. On the other hand, he felt unable to recommend a plan based on three separate types of schools:

> It must be admitted that the Norwood Report is backed by the opinion of a large body of educationalists of nationally recognised standing and prestige; to disagree with that Committee's recommendations cannot be done lightly. I hope that it is not due to any lack of modesty on my part – and in this hope I am fortified by the fact that I am supported by all my educational colleagues on the staff – that I am unable to accept the recommendations of the Norwood Committee.[65]

Tilley proposed instead that grammar and technical schools should be combined to form selective schools with a technical component for 25 per cent of pupils, but that 'the grammar-cum-technical school together with the modern school of the same contributory area be regarded as a multilateral unit with the head teachers of the schools in the unit working as a joint committee of head teachers'.[66] Tilley himself retired soon afterwards, leaving his proposed compromise to be debated further while a 'major battle' continued within the County on the possibility of a fully multilateral alternative.[67] A revised development plan for the area specified general provision in grammar-technical and modern schools, with highly industrialized areas providing three types of schools (grammar, technical and modern) grouped in multilateral units. The ministry accepted this plan despite the protests of the Central Division of Durham Education Committee, which insisted that a multilateral alternative should be developed.[68]

Not all local debates were as fierce as those that took place in Durham, but there were many other cases in which a bilateral structure involving selective grammar schools and non-selective modern schools came to be preferred to a tripartite approach. The separate provision of secondary technical schools came under severe pressure in such instances. In Brighton, for example, the tripartite pattern of the initial development plan was reviewed and then replaced by the provision of two 'broad types' based on 'the varying intellectual ability of the pupils', each type giving 'a wide range of courses to meet the special interests and aptitudes of the pupils'.[69] The work hitherto done in the secondary technical schools would be followed either in the grammar schools or in the modern schools, so that grammar schools might 'expand their science sides to include more of the applied sciences and to prepare pupils for advanced work in colleges of further education', while modern schools could develop 'adequate provision for craftsmen and technicians who will later become apprentices and/or receive training at the branch technical colleges'.[70] This proposal was accepted by the ministry.[71] In Hertfordshire, meanwhile, it was agreed that types of secondary education other than grammar would not be differentiated, and that the necessary facilities for technical education would be incorporated into the modern schools, if necessary by increasing the proportion of practical rooms to classrooms in the SMSs.[72]

A further implication of a bilateral approach was an evident hardening of the barriers between 'selective' and 'non-selective' education based on differences in pupils' intellectual abilities, or more specifically their 'intelligence'. It was assumed that although 'technical ability' might be difficult to assess at the age of 11, 'intelligence was not so hard and it would undoubtedly be the fact that the duller threequarters of the population would go to Modern Schools and the more intelligent quarter to Grammar and Technical'.[73] Such a differentiation, if it became widely established, would be unlikely to further the cause of 'parity of esteem' between the different kinds of secondary school. However, there were many avid supporters of SMSs in a range of local contexts who were determined to explain their distinctive rationale in more flattering terms.

In Lancashire, the largest LEA outside London, catering for a quarter of a million pupils over a large and diverse geographical area,[74] the tripartite policy was generally maintained intact in spite of some vagueness over the purposes of secondary technical schools and the proportion of pupils that should be allocated to them.[75] As the chief education officer, A.L. Binns, made clear, this was not merely a pragmatic approach intended to follow the lead set by the ministry. Binns acknowledged the need for further 'experiment', and that 'we should do well to keep an open mind on many points until we have further information based on experiment'.[76] Nevertheless, he was already 'quite sure' that the grammar school curriculum was suited only to a minority of children, while the modern school would provide a range of education for about 75 per cent of pupils. The latter would include a 'very wide range of ability and aptitude', from 'very able children who are not academically minded but are destined nevertheless for leadership in the community', to 'children so backward that they only just escape classification as sub-normal'. For this wide range of pupils, the 'limited purpose' associated with the elementary schools of the nineteenth century should have no place, and the SMSs should be established as real secondary schools. Binns was clear, even so, that they should be as distinctive as possible in relation to the grammar schools. The teachers and headteachers of the SMSs, he insisted, should assume major responsibilities in their development, and they should be allowed 'a very wide measure of freedom' to experiment, especially with regard to the curriculum. In particular, he argued, the SMS curriculum should not be allowed to become 'a reflection of the Grammar School' which 'could only be a pale one', whereas 'the Modern School can, I am sure, achieve remarkable success by striking out on entirely different lines in its curriculum, while adopting all that is best in the Grammar School and Public School conception of a complete education'. Also, he counselled the SMSs against the 'temptation' of using external examinations, which would shape and restrict the curriculum of the schools. If they could develop on this general basis, according to Binns, there might soon be 'great Modern Schools that will be famous throughout their county, and maybe throughout the country', and they could indeed become 'a great bond of union between different classes in society'.[77]

Binns's lavish aspirations were characteristic of local support for the SMSs in the late 1940s. The aim was to generate a new form of secondary education that would be appropriate for a particular section of the population, in fact for the mass of the population, in a way that grammar schools were not. The insistence on freedom for staff to be able to develop the curriculum of these schools in their own way, unrestricted by external examinations, was an important aspect of this approach. Like Wilkinson and Hardman at this time, these local supporters of the SMSs were drawing on the ideals of working-class secondary education that had been developed earlier in the nineteenth and twentieth centuries.

In Wakefield, too, the assistant director of education, G.F. Maw, identified the main constituency of the SMSs as being pupils who would form the 'majority' of the population, who 'may never become the nation's leaders in thought and action', but who 'need not therefore become a race of automata or sub-men merely serving the material needs of an increasingly mechanised civilisation'.[78] In the same vein, Stewart Mason, director of education in Leicestershire, hoped that external examinations would not be allowed to 'creep into' the SMS: 'As such they have only just started and we certainly don't want an exam to cabin them before we even know in what direction they will find themselves going.'[79] In this regard, Mason noted, they would need to resist the demands of many parents, 'who will want a piece of paper of more than local currency for their children to show employers', and of many teachers and head teachers 'who welcome an external exam as giving their pupils "something to work for", and also as providing a readymade standard of efficiency'. Succumbing to these pressures, according to Mason, would undermine 'the basic conception of "what the Modern School is about"', which was fundamentally different from the idea of the grammar school.[80]

Similarly, in Sheffield, the aim was to produce a distinctive form of secondary education through the provision of SMSs that would be different in its function from that of the grammar schools. Here, the basis for policy had been developed during the war years under the then director of education, Dr William Alexander, who went on to become the secretary of the AEC from 1945. Alexander, a product of Paisley Grammar School and the University of Glasgow, was strongly in favour of cultivating what he regarded as the inherent differences between children, especially with regard to their individual 'intelligence'. The provision of secondary education, he insisted, should reflect these basic distinctions, 'not merely in *degree* of ability but in *type* of ability'.[81] In 1942, Alexander drafted a final report for a special sub-committee established in Sheffield on postwar reconstruction in education. This envisaged the introduction of different types of secondary schools with the aim of catering for 'different types of ability'.[82] It acknowledged that such a development might well have the effect of dividing 'those who will later lead the community from those whom they will lead',[83] although it suggested that junior colleges from the age of 16 might help to bridge the 'gap' that this would create. Between the ages of 11 and 16, it supported the introduction of a tripartite system of grammar schools, technical schools and modern schools. Pupils would proceed into the different types of secondary schools on the basis of their record in the primary school 'together with suitable tests', although it was confident that 'The problem will be no longer one of selection, but rather of allocation of different children to different types of school.'[84] The report was accepted, and established a strong basis for the LEA's development plan.

In September 1944, following the introduction of the Education Act, Alexander made a further report to this special sub-committee. He insisted that separate types of secondary schools, 'on a parity so far as buildings, staff and other requirements were concerned', would be able to 'emerge equal in public esteem as the Technical Schools and the Modern Schools had opportunity to develop themselves fully – an opportunity which, up to this time, has never been allowed'. Just as the technical school in the city had already achieved 'full parity' with the grammar schools, and in some cases was regarded as 'an alternative to be preferred to admission to a Grammar School', so the modern schools would provide what he called 'appropriate education for those pupils seeking a sound general education without marked bias either of an academic or of a technical nature, an education which will develop skill of hand, clearness of thought and understanding of social events'. There would be a need to review existing buildings to establish which would be suitable for the purpose of modern school provision, and he acknowledged that 'substantial numbers of new Modern Schools' would be necessary. Overall, he concluded, 15 per cent of 11-year-olds should be allocated to grammar schools, 10 per cent to technical schools, and 75 per cent to modern schools. Alexander was authorized to prepare Sheffield's development plan on this basis.[85]

The development plan itself predictably endorsed tripartite provision for secondary education, and argued strongly that the SMS curriculum, 'still in the experimental stage', should be left for a number of years 'free from the influence of the Grammar School atmosphere to develop on individual lines and to determine how best they can make their proper contribution'.[86] Unsurprisingly, too, the plan was rapidly approved by officials at the Ministry of Education. It was, as one noted, 'carefully prepared', and the LEA had worked 'hard and conscientiously on a very difficult job', especially within the limits imposed by the topography of the city with its 'long high hills and valleys, all converging on the City centre'.[87] The 'final impression' was that Sheffield's plan represented 'a good orthodox blue-print for the future'.[88] It was, in fact, another official enthused, 'a terrific bit of work', which he should be 'delighted to approve forthwith'.[89]

Thus, in spite of many local differences and debates over the SMSs, there was at least some agreement at the local level that the 'experiment' should be pursued to its logical conclusion. The clear wishes expressed by the Ministry of Education had a strong influence on such thinking, but it was based also and more fundamentally on a desire to establish a new form of secondary education, suitable for the large majority of pupils, that would be different in kind from that provided in the grammar schools. Like Ellen Wilkinson and David Hardman at the Ministry of Education, these were the heirs of the idealized tradition of 'working class secondary education' that had flickered fitfully for over half a century. Its historic opportunity had now finally come, in the form of a 'great adventure' and 'experiment', on whose outcome the lives of a generation of pupils would ultimately depend.

# 6

# The world of Stonehill Street

The secondary modern schools that developed in the immediate postwar period generally reflected the working-class associations that had been anticipated for this form of secondary education. A closer study of the experiences of these schools also highlights the limitations and contradictions that were involved in working-class secondary education. The reality very often had little in common with the idealized notion of a distinctive and even superior type of education that would be suitable for the needs of the mass of the population. Many struggled with inadequate resources and failed to establish themselves alongside more prestigious institutions.

### Social class and the secondary moderns

The largely working-class composition of the SMSs was clearly apparent by the 1950s. A strong correlation soon emerged between SMSs and a relatively high proportion of working-class pupils. However, not all working-class children attended SMSs, as some were enabled to attend selective grammar schools by passing the so-called '11-plus' examination. Then again, not all children who attended SMSs were working class, principally because many middle-class children failed their 11-plus examination and were allocated to SMSs.

Research published in the early 1950s demonstrated major differences in the social composition of SMSs as compared to grammar schools. In London, it was soon observed, SMSs catered mainly for the children of manual workers, especially the semi-skilled and unskilled, both in the suburban areas and in the largely working-class districts of the East End and the centre of the city. At the same time, relatively few children from what was described as the 'lower working class' were educated in grammar schools, which tended to be largely middle class in their social composition.[1] Working-class children who did attend grammar schools tended to be from small families rather than large families, and were generally the eldest children in their family rather than of later birth order.[2] As Himmelweit noted, attendance at a grammar school represented in this context 'the main avenue for upward social mobility for the children of the "working class"'.[3] Conversely, the SMSs were readily associated with social inequality that was likely to undermine the prospects of parity of esteem between the different types of secondary schools.[4]

More recent research has confirmed the social class characteristics of SMSs that were observed at the time. One detailed study, by Halsey, Heath and Ridge, concludes that 'To arrange the types of school, whether public or private, in a widely acknowledged hierarchy of academic prestige is also to arrange them in the same order of probability of access for boys of different class origins.'[5] Three-quarters of working-class boys in this period went to elementary, secondary modern or comprehensive schools, while nearly three-quarters of boys from what they call the 'service class' attended a selective secondary school. Moreover, they add, 'Looking from inside the schools back towards the social origins of their pupils, it appears that two-thirds of the secondary-modern boys were working class, while two-thirds of the "public school" boys were from the service class.'[6]

The term 'working class' itself embraced a wide range of social and occupational groups, and the SMSs vividly reflected this heterogeneity. In the early 1960s, M.P. Carter's study based in Sheffield found a general tendency for SMSs to be regarded as the 'depository of the unsuccessful – the rag bag into which children who have not made the grade are put'.[7] Carter also noted that a disproportionate number of working-class children were allocated to SMSs.[8] At the same time, he discerned a great deal of variety among the SMSs themselves that could also be traced to the particular social circumstances of each school. Some SMSs, he saw, remained 'still anchored to the old conception of "elementary" education'. These were, in his view, ' "secondary" only in name', and they had departed 'only slightly or not at all from the idea of the basic "3 Rs"'.[9] According to Carter, such schools generally lacked accommodation and equipment, suffered from a shortage of teachers, and were in a 'poor' local environment.[10] By contrast, others veered towards an 'academic' approach, becoming in some cases a 'pale shadow' of the grammar schools: 'The academic orientation has been particularly apparent in modern schools built in the post-war period – many of which, with panelled libraries, impressive assembly halls and well-equipped laboratories, compare favourably in their facilities with grammar schools.'[11] These schools, Carter observed, might well be situated on 'the right side of town', with relatively larger numbers of pupils from middle-class and aspiring middle-class homes, and with higher social and occupational aspirations.[12]

It was within these parameters that the SMSs worked out the realities of working-class secondary education. According to Harold Dent, an assiduous observer and sympathetic critic, the schools fell into five general categories that were closely associated with the kinds of clientele that they served. These differences, in his view, also tended to influence the kind of curriculum that they provided. The first group of schools remained what they had been previously in all but name, and continued to fulfil the function of public elementary schools.[13] The second group of schools, which provided 'highly effective senior elementary work', either served 'culturally poor neighbourhoods', or were in areas where they received the 'rejects' who were left behind while the grammar schools attracted the most able pupils.[14] Third, according to Dent, came a large group of schools that were attempting to work out official policies and ideals in practice. These taught academic subjects in much the same way, although to a less advanced level, as in grammar schools, although they usually omitted some of these subjects, such as foreign languages and the specialized physical sciences, and gave more time to art, handicrafts, and social and cultural activities. Some, alternatively, departed from traditional academic subject divisions and methods, and attempted to build their curriculum around 'projects' and 'centres of interest'.[15] Fourth, a small group of schools made one particular activity, such as music, dancing or art, the key dynamic of school life. Lastly, there were some that offered vocationally biased courses to some or all of their pupils, as the secondary technical schools also attempted to do.

Such differences among the SMSs themselves served to highlight the importance of the school environment and neighbourhood. A study of the 'Crown Street' schools in Merseyside by John Barron Mays in the early 1960s, for example, emphasized the local variations in provision. In working-class districts of the city, it was observed, 'Horizons are apt to be narrow, the sights aimed low, ambition and curiosity limited to the local and the concrete.'[16] This led in turn to an especially limited purchase for the ideals generated by the Education Act (1944), which 'filters with difficulty down through the obscuring smoke and gloom of the older and less privileged neighbourhoods'.[17] Schools in such areas, it was suggested, 'do not and cannot yet provide a true secondary education within the full meaning of that term',[18] and reflected indeed the continued influence of the 'two nations' in education.[19] A 'gaping and almost unbridgeable chasm' separated such schools from the grammar schools.[20] In addition, the distance between the pupils in these SMSs and the teachers who taught them was held to be no less immense, especially since, as Mays observed, nearly all members of staff lived outside the Crown Street area.[21] The physical conditions of the schools were also a major influence on their curriculum, being 'for the most part physically outmoded and inadequate for modern needs, with a serious shortage of space both inside for work and outside for play'.[22] Such was the physical and outward legacy of the schools' prehistory, 'the heritage for the most part of an age which took a crudely functional view of elementary instruction and was not prepared to lavish space, money or equipment upon children of the labouring class'.[23]

It was especially these SMSs, in the most difficult physical and social environments, that were left to work out the realities of working-class secondary education. The image that attached itself to these schools above all led many observers to the conclusion that the experiment of the SMSs had demonstrably failed, even though these were only a minority of such schools. At the same time, they constituted both the most conspicuous, and the most unflattering, examples of what working-class secondary education really meant.

### Slum schools

In many cases, the buildings in which the schools were housed and the neighbourhoods that they served gave them the reputation of 'slum schools'. The accommodation of the schools in the form of their buildings and facilities often reflected their prehistory as elementary, senior and central schools that had catered principally for working-class children, to such an extent indeed that they struggled to justify their new status as secondary schools. The nature and shortcomings of the facilities were recorded in detail in the school inspection reports that were produced by visiting teams of HMIs.

In Manchester, for example, where 51 SMSs were established before the end of the 1950s, many remained housed in buildings that had seen long service as elementary and central schools. One such, Higher Openshaw County Secondary School, was housed in a building that had been opened by the Manchester School Board in 1897, and shared its premises with a junior mixed school and some classes from a nearby Roman Catholic school.[24] Another, New Moston County Secondary School, resided in premises that had been built in 1902, with practical rooms for cookery and woodwork and extra classrooms added in the 1930s.[25] The building of Birley County Secondary School (Girls' and Boys') had been originally opened in 1884 as a school for girls, and had gone through different phases of existence as a higher grade school and then a selective central school. It was also shared with Birley Primary School, and so catered for about 1200 pupils on a site of just over one acre. The accommodation for the boys' school consisted of a hall (containing rolled up judo mats for evening classes and used as a passage way), ten classrooms, a double room for handicrafts, a large laboratory, a large space in Ardwick Lads' Club that was used for a remedial class, and two small rooms for the headmaster and fourteen teachers.[26] Such buildings were generally inadequate, insanitary and overcrowded.

Many SMSs in other local areas were also housed in out of date and unsuitable buildings that dated from the Victorian era or earlier in the century. The main building of Harper Green County Secondary Girls' School in Farnworth had been opened in 1928 as two selective central schools, with another section housed in another school, a mile away.[27] Another, built in 1906 and shared with junior and infant departments, was regarded as 'solidly built and old-fashioned, and, in many ways, substandard for the work of a secondary school', and was handicapped especially by what was described as 'lack of space both inside and outside its building'.[28] The only boys' SMS in Penge, Kent, was housed in a building that had originally served from its foundation in 1900 as an elementary school four storeys tall, with two classes in a church hall 300 yards from the school.[29]

The problems raised by such outdated and inadequate conditions for the development of SMSs were vividly reflected in a number of inspection reports. In Cardiff, for example, Stacey County Secondary School occupied the first floor of a building on a restricted site. According to its inspection report, in May 1956,

Many of the essential requirements and amenities of a secondary school are lacking, and some facilities, such as those for Housecraft, Wood and Metalwork are so situated, and are shared by so many other schools, that considerable problems of organisation exist for this school.[30]

The lavatory facilities were shared with a junior school, and there was no staffroom or cloakroom and only one lavatory for the staff. The inspection report concluded that 'The school is severely handicapped by the inadequacy of the general accommodation and by the lack of special teaching facilities necessary to the normal curriculum of a secondary school.' Indeed, it continued, the school had failed to move 'far from the concept of Elementary School Education', and this was largely because of the 'restriction of accommodation and the impracticability of introducing and using necessary equipment'.[31]

Also in Cardiff, Splotlands County Secondary Boys' School occupied the upper floor of what had originally in 1882 served as the Splotlands Board School. After the Second World War it had been known as Splotlands All-Age School until the district was reorganized in 1951 and it became an SMS.[32] It was acknowledged that the accommodation fell 'very far short of what is required for the proper secondary education of 352 boys', and that this factor also prevented the development of a curriculum that might 'fully meet their needs'.[33] In this particular case, although the 1959 building regulations specified a minimum teaching area of 18,290 square feet for the number of pupils on the school roll, the actual teaching area that was available was only 8313 square feet. The school had no gymnasium, hall, or library, and its lack of showers and washing facilities was judged to be 'particularly unfortunate in this area where many houses have no baths'. There was no provision for handicrafts, and no usable storage space in the school.[34]

Similar examples could be found in most other large cities. Harehills County Secondary School for Boys in Leeds was housed in a building that dated from 1897, 'trying to provide secondary education in obsolete premises and with much obsolete equipment', conditions that were in themselves 'a serious handicap to its development'.[35] Only two classrooms in this school had furniture that was judged suitable for boys of secondary school age, with many of the desks being too small for the purpose and with an insufficient number of chairs and tables.[36] Similarly, Roseville County Secondary School for Girls, also in Leeds, was housed in a building that had opened as an elementary school in 1898, and lacked adequate sanitation, facilities and equipment.[37] In Birmingham, meanwhile, Summer Lane County Modern School, a mixed school with 672 pupils, was based in a building erected in 1877, on a site of 1.52 acres. In this particular instance, it was observed, 'The buildings as a whole impose difficulties upon the school, since stairs are narrow and the accommodation is often dark and sometimes cold.' There were separate staffrooms for men and women, both of which needed improving, and the halls, which were used as passages, required reconditioning, but 'the over-riding necessity in this school is for more modern wash-basins, the provision of hot water and of showers for both girls and boys'.[38] Slade Boys' County Modern School, also in Birmingham, was in buildings put up in 1910 that, as the inspectors again made clear, 'can only be regarded as improvisation for a secondary school; the obvious deficiencies are a hall, a gymnasium, a metalwork room, meals accommodation and storage space'.[39]

The continued existence of such buildings and facilities as accommodation for the SMSs was a standing reminder of the social origins of these schools in elementary education for the working class. There was a patent contradiction between the limitations imposed on such schools by the premises within which they worked, and the aspirations that were associated with secondary education. This was often true even for schools with relatively adequate facilities but housed in elderly premises, such as Chillingham Road County Secondary School for Boys in Newcastle, which despite recent improvements to its buildings still had 'the look of an elementary school'.[40] Some schools in buildings of a more recent vintage also presented a similar picture. Sharston Secondary School in Manchester, for example, was opened originally in 1938 as a senior elementary school with 'comparatively up-to-date buildings', but these were already in an 'unsatisfactory state' because of their use in the evenings by the Youth Centre and Evening Institute, combined with vandalism and graffiti. It was readily acknowledged, especially after six years of war, 'much remains to be done before it attains the standard as well as the name of a Secondary Modern School'.[41] Hatfield House Lane County Secondary School in Sheffield, opened in 1942, still suffered a decade later from 'some of the disadvantages associated with the war-time opening'. Its grounds were in particularly poor condition and as its inspectors commented, these provided 'an extremely poor environment for what is the most recently opened Secondary Modern school in this major city'. Moreover, it was added,

> This atmosphere of external shabbiness, regrettably, has crept into the school. The internal walls are dirty and need redecorating; the staff rooms are bare places without reasonable comfort. The school furniture, generally, is poor and there is a shortage of pictures which would add interest to the corridors and classrooms. Dignity can only be restored to this good modern building when these disadvantages are removed.[42]

Meanwhile, Tretherras County Secondary School in Newquay, opened in January 1954, as the first school of its type to be built in Cornwall, was intended to accommodate 510 pupils but in fact soon catered for 647, which meant that its hall and library were often used for teaching and some craft rooms were partitioned. It also suffered from a serious shortage of textbooks and equipment, and from a general misuse of the facilities. According to its inspection report,

> An attempt has been made to clean up the premises, which got into a deplorable condition soon after the school was opened, and evidence of this misuse is to be seen on desks and tables. The pupils still need training to help them to have a sense of personal responsibility and to respect public property.[43]

Such deficiencies were especially glaring when preference was given to improving the facilities of grammar schools rather than those of the SMSs. Bitterne Park County Secondary School in Southampton, for example, had two grammar streams and four 'general' streams. Its accommodation was recognized to be 'wholly inadequate' for its needs, as its 'outstanding deficiencies' included no library, no gymnasium, no showers or changing room, no adequate hall, no dining room, insufficient classrooms, few preparation rooms, little storage space, very limited accommodation for practical subjects, and inadequate lavatories. In this situation, the inspectors observed that priority had been given to providing equipment and apparatus for the newly formed grammar course, and that 'Now that this is reasonably satisfactory, more attention should be given to the needs of the majority of the pupils in the school.'[44] This order of priorities, in which the needs of grammar schools and their pupils were attended to before those of SMSs could be considered, seemed only too symbolic of a wider condition. In Lancashire, too, Hyndburn Park County Secondary School, built in 1906 and shared with junior and infant departments, was recognized to be 'solidly built and old-fashioned and, in many ways, sub-standard for the work of a secondary school'.[45] It suffered from a lack of space both internally and

externally. At a meeting with the school governors, however, it was made
clear that the needs of the school were of low priority. The HMI explained
that 'the Grammar Schools had been given priority because they supplied
the brains of the country', although she added considerately that she per-
sonally 'was as much concerned as the governors about the plight of the
Secondary Modern Schools'.[46]

## The local environment

This plight was made even more evident through the nature of the local
environments and clienteles that these schools often served. The poverty
and social problems characteristic of many districts, especially in the large
cities, were especially familiar to the SMSs. In Birmingham, for example,
Lea Village County Modern School for Girls had been originally opened in
1939 as a senior mixed school on the recently developed Lea Hall Estate,
to which many families had been moved from the poorer and more central
districts of the city. After the war, with further housing developments and
houses allocated to families from a city housing list, the character of the
school was clearly affected by the nature of its local community. According
to the school inspection report, moreover, the local district was 'singularly
lacking in social and cultural amenities'.[47] Severe social problems were also
witnessed in the case of Manor Park County Modern School for Girls, also
in Birmingham:

> There is much poor housing in the area of Aston served by this
> school, and the majority of the pupils live in small terraced dwellings.
> In many cases both parents are working and, in consequence, the girls
> are often required to carry heavy domestic responsibilities, and not
> infrequently to cook the mid-day meal.'[48]

Domestic instability and 'parental neglect' were not uncommon. It was
also observed that the 'native speech' of many of the girls at the school
was 'indistinct and ungrammatical', and that 'a significant number appear
to be of low innate ability', while 'ailments often associated with poor
housing conditions are relatively common'.[49]

Similarly, in Splotlands County Secondary Boys' School in Cardiff, the
difficulties of the accommodation were compounded by the circumstances
of its pupils, 'many of whom come from homes that provide a poor cultural and social background'. It was described as a 'slum school', sited 'very
close to the notorious Tiger Bay area of Cardiff'.[50] The docks, railways,
steelworks and ship repairing yards provided most of the employment in
the area, and it was noted that new housing estates on the outskirts of the
city and slum clearance in areas not far from the school had caused 'better
families' to move away and 'less ambitious families with lower standards'

to move in.[51] At the time of the school inspection in 1960, 28 pupils were serving varying periods of probation imposed by the Court.[52] At the same time, many of the parents were acknowledged to be 'keenly interested in the school and in the educational progress of their children'. Indeed, the inspection report concluded,

> The School achieves a remarkable measure of success in conditions which could be thoroughly discouraging. . . . In spite of the background of the pupils and the Court record of many of them, good tone and discipline are maintained in the School as a result of the sympathetic vigilance and understanding of the Head and his staff.[53]

Many schools were unable to overcome the difficulties imposed by such conditions and environments. Central County Secondary Boys' School in Southampton, for example, housed in buildings that were 70 years old on a very restricted site, and located 'in what is now a less well-to-do area than formerly', was afflicted with a 'considerable social problem' that was 'affecting adversely the educational attainments of a number of boys'.[54] In this case, although the 'grimness of the premises' was 'somewhat relieved by the redecoration that was done in 1952', facilities and equipment were inadequate and there was a general shortage of books and equipment. The standard of teaching was apparently not high and discipline was difficult to maintain. The school's inspectors acknowledged the basic difficulties involved, but held out some hope for improvement:

> The solution of the many problems, often of a social nature, mentioned throughout this Report, is not made easier by the old premises in which the School is housed or by the ungenerous staffing. Even so, something might be done by more deliberate planning and consolidation of the courses and, in particular, by exploiting the cheerful, if rough, enthusiasm of the boys.[55]

In other cases, it was found to be possible to overcome the problems caused by poor accommodation, facilities and local conditions, even if only to a limited extent or in a restricted manner. Belle Vue County Secondary School for Girls, in Leeds, was housed in a substantial building erected in 1883, 'situated in one of the oldest and once prosperous parts of the city'. The local area was now much less prosperous: 'It [the school] is surrounded by large blocks of houses now used as tenements and by small back-to-back dwellings, many of which are due for demolition under the slum clearance scheme. These are the homes of the girls who attend this school.'[56] The site was restricted and inadequate, but it was noted that the LEA had done much to improve the premises since it had become a secondary school. The importance of the headmistress was also acknowledged in that she 'fully understands the problems of this particular neighbourhood and recognises that it is highly necessary to provide the girls with security, friendship and good living standards'. In such a school, it was judged to be 'impossible to measure success by its academic achievements', since its success lay more simply 'in its ability to give the girls a secure and acceptable way of life'.[57]

Meanwhile, Woodhouse County Secondary School, also in Leeds, resided in an old building in 'one of the poorer parts of the city, a district where there is much old, condemned property'. In these circumstances, it was observed, the headmaster and his staff attached 'considerable importance' to the 'social side' of their work. Indeed, the inspectors' report on this school noted in 1956,

> There is every sign that in recent times much has been done to promote the social welfare of pupils, to foster good standards of behaviour and to offer a variety of communal activities tending to develop self-respect and consideration for others.[58]

Much emphasis was given in such cases to the potential role of the school in 'elevating' its pupils above squalid conditions and surroundings, both socially and morally. The 'social welfare' provisions of the school therefore often became at least as important as the formal education or curriculum that the pupils underwent.

This was again true in the case of Cambridge Street County Secondary School, in Newcastle. Many of the pupils at this school lived in what were viewed as 'appalling conditions', and the buildings of the school itself were 'grim and forbidding'. In these circumstances, it was judged that 'The first duty of their teachers, therefore, is to provide a school life which gives these boys and girls a sense of security and consequent confidence in themselves.'[59] This was largely achieved, according to the inspection report on the school, as the pupils were treated 'kindly and courteously', and 'in return they show themselves eager to give of their best'. The midday canteen meal, for which nearly three-quarters of the pupils made no payment, was viewed as a 'pleasing social occasion', and it was noted that there were very few juvenile delinquents at the school. Further confidential remarks by the inspectors, not included in the report itself, highlighted the extent of the achievement of this particular school in overcoming adversity:

> The school is situated in the worst area of Newcastle and it might reasonably be expected that it would have a large number of juvenile delinquents but this is not so. The H.M. has outstanding qualities in his human relations with his pupils and has his own methods of dealing with the potential bad boys and girls.[60]

In spite of such successes, the prevailing impression was one of a struggle against the odds that often failed to meet the expectations of secondary education.

Bow County Secondary School for Boys, in the East End of London, was an instructive example of this. The school, built in 1914 on the site of an earlier school, became a secondary modern school for boys in 1946, with the main school and an annexe about a quarter of a mile apart, and a decade later had 500 boys on its roll. Most of these lived in the 'busy area' around the school.[61] According to its headmaster, the school served a 'working-class neighbourhood', and the parents of the pupils were 'stall-holders, factory workers, dock labourers, furniture makers, general labourers, in surrounding factories, breweries etc'.[62] Its work was therefore assessed against what was described as 'a background of drabness and materialism, so depressing that only dedicated or well-rewarded teachers would go to the school and stay there'.[63]

The inspection report for Bow School, in 1956, emphasized its 'considerable achievements', which were held to be 'all the more laudable' in that 'only firm and kindly discipline, with work suited to the boys' capacities and interests, can enlist their efforts'.[64] The inspectors were particularly impressed with the weekly assignments of work, which apparently encouraged a 'sense of responsibility and avoiding waste of time', with the pupils' written work, which had 'quantity, quality and natural sincerity', and with the boys themselves, who 'impress visitors as clean and tidy (despite the shoddy clothes that many of them wear), friendly to their teachers and to strangers, and commendably industrious'. The teachers at the school, it was observed, endeavoured 'above all things to train boys in orderly and considerate behaviour, to foster habits of persevering effort, and to stimulate pride in work well done', and they appeared to have achieved 'heartening success' in their 'difficult task'.[65] In private, the school was described as adopting a 'friendly but authoritarian masculine approach' which ensured that the pupils were generally 'cheerfully content to behave themselves, to exert themselves, to be interested in their work and to be loyal to their school'.[66] This faint praise did not disguise the 'essential feature' of the school which was recognized to be its 'difficult environment', and for all the encouraging aspects of the school in terms of discipline and behaviour the 'main impression' remained 'that of a school functioning very much on the lines of the old elementary schools'.[67]

### Secondary modern discipline

The role of the teachers in such circumstances often reflected the social class differences between them and the pupils. In some cases, rigid class barriers could be erected between the teachers on the one hand and the pupils on the other. This relationship of mutual antagonism was portrayed in striking fashion in the novels of Edward Blishen, an English teacher in Archway County Secondary School for Boys in north London in the 1950s. Blishen's

fictional accounts of his teaching experiences in 'Stonehill Street' evoked
much of the reality of life in the SMSs. In his best known novel, *Roaring
Boys: A Schoolmaster's Agony*, published in 1955, Blishen introduced his
readers to many of the problems that confronted the schools. The building
itself is depicted as being 'as unkind as a prison'.[68] Although not of the 'worst
period of State school architecture', it remained reminiscent of prisons: 'Its
gates were so obviously meant to be locked; its high walls were so plainly
meant to imprison; its hard playgrounds were so suggestive, not of play,
but of penal exercise.' It was also a standing reminder of what the school
had been before it had become an SMS: 'And over the doors were announce-
ments in stone: "Senior Boys", "Senior Girls". These words were no longer
relevant, but their terse statements of categories made it easy to imagine the
mute pinafored ranks of fifty years before.'[69] The headmaster of the school,
Mr Perry, had taught for most of his career in elementary schools, and the
replacement of such schools by SMSs had done little or nothing to change
his working assumptions and practices:

> Why, at the end of his life as a teacher, should he try to face the
> enormous pretence (as it seemed to him) that Stonehill Street had been
> changed by a piece of legislative conjuring into something new and
> superior! He had gone on being the head of an elementary school.[70]

Blishen's work emphasized the contradictions between the outward appearance of secondary education in the SMSs and their inner reality which
remained rooted in the elementary schools of 50 years before. In spite of
the introduction of a school uniform and a change in the name of the school,
Stonehill Street is persistently a cheap and inferior imitation of the familiar
forms of education that had hitherto been reserved for the middle classes,
as Blishen notes: 'I thought often of the well-dressed, cosy crocodiles of
prep school boys I had led, not so long before, on their chattering way to
the playing-fields. By comparison, a crocodile of Stonehill Street boys was
a procession of scarecrows.'[71] This general verdict was exemplified in the
relationship between the pupils and their teachers. According to Blishen,

> The staff in their neat suiting, even in their old sports jackets and
> flannels, looked like visitors from another world. And, in fact, in
> Stonehill Street two worlds clashed. You couldn't help seeing it that
> way. The masters and the boys had very different backgrounds.[72]

These differences were clearly social and cultural in nature, as the teachers
represented middle-class authority while the pupils were visibly and un-
repentantly working class. Most of the boys, in Blishen's view, 'hated school
with a coarse sullen hatred', and 'endured their education; at no point did
they come happily and healthily to meet it'.[73] In many cases, the teachers
were obliged to assert strict discipline, but this simply reinforced the barriers
between themselves and their pupils, since 'even though a teacher managed

in the end to master the manners of his charges, it was always an act of mastery and never an act of intimacy'.[74] Indeed, Blishen observes, 'Even the most experienced members of the staff would discuss the boys as barbarous Celts might have been discussed by a Roman garrison.'[75]

Although Blishen's account of Stonehill Street was fictional, it was intended to evoke the actual experiences of teaching and learning in an SMS. Blishen himself noted that while the story was not 'literally true', he had 'tried to make it true in a wider sense'.[76] Moreover, as he later confessed, his work was in fact 'much more close to the literal truth than perhaps I should have allowed it to be'.[77] It also helped to confirm the growing suspicions of many who themselves had no direct experience of the SMSs that these were outdated and restrictive institutions, inherently inferior to the grammar schools, and bastions of class warfare. Blishen, unlike many other authors of novels about the SMSs,[78] resisted such simplistic conclusions especially in the way that he affirmed the complexity and variety of the relationships that could be formed in the schools. He argued strongly that the SMSs were tending to become increasingly informal in their management of pupils as a means of lowering class barriers. In disarming the pupils' distrust of school authority, he suggested, 'one is bound to become less the conventional pedagogue, more and more the relaxed informant, guide, and provider',[79] developing in the process fresh and innovative approaches to pedagogy and the curriculum.

This notion in itself reflected a central tension within the SMSs, between on the one hand a 'pedagogic shift' towards encouraging 'licence' and 'insolence' in the classroom,[80] and on the other hand a tendency towards a severe disciplinary approach. It was the latter that was emphasized by Richard Farley in his practical advice to teachers in SMSs on what he called 'secondary modern discipline'. Whether housed in 'poorly equipped old schools' or in 'municipal nirvanas of glass and concrete', according to Farley, secondary moderns were 'the focal point of the duller, less responsible, maladjusted and potentially criminal young people'.[81] This conviction formed the basis of his ideas on planning and organization in the classroom:

> Ninety per cent of the work in a Secondary Modern School is control and discipline; the lesson content is, or should be, fairly simple, but if you don't carry out certain checks, then your lessons will be a fiasco. It is wise to keep a check on your cupboards – if you have any – for cupboards get very untidy unless constantly watched and are fair game for any curious malcontent, so keep them locked.[82]

At the same time, Farley also acknowledged the wider influences of a changing society, and accepted albeit grudgingly that 'You cannot beat them down all the time within our present social framework and expect things to run smoothly, because they won't.'[83] A measure of 'tolerance' was therefore necessary, as 'the classroom is the prototype of a changing world and it is changing very fast'.[84]

This evocation of 'secondary modern discipline', together with outdated and inadequate accommodation and squalid local environments, became established as the dominant public image of the SMSs. It was certainly inaccurate and unfair to portray all SMSs in such unflattering and even pathological terms. One survey conducted in the early 1960s found that only about 18 per cent of SMSs and 15 per cent of their pupils were in urban 'slum or seedy' areas.[85] About 29 per cent of the schools had 'clearly inadequate' indoor provision, 30 per cent had clearly inadequate outdoor provision, and 19 per cent were clearly inadequate in both respects.[86] It was these schools, however, that gave the deepest impression of the outcome of the SMS experiment, and which fatally damaged whatever prospects the SMSs might have had of achieving parity of esteem with the grammar schools. They were an enduring testimony to the power of a class based tradition in education, but they did not evoke a novel ideal of working-class secondary education, as had been hoped. Instead, they radiated uncomfortable reminders of working-class elementary education, and even of the Victorian workhouse and prison. The great adventure of the SMSs had introduced a new generation of children to the world of Stonehill Street.

# 7

# The quest for virtue

In spite of the persistent problems that afflicted many of the SMSs, the Conservative government of the 1950s remained doggedly optimistic about their future, and continued to support both their existence and their further development. However, by the later 1950s there was a palpable shift away from the notion that the SMSs were providing a distinct and alternative form of secondary education that would be especially appropriate for working-class children, towards an emphasis on the academic and social opportunities that should be made available in such schools.

### Counter measures against the comprehensives

The Conservative government that was elected into office in 1951, and which was sustained through two further general election victories in 1955 and 1959, proved to be a staunch and vigorous champion of the SMS. It was motivated in this not so much through an admiration for the distinctive qualities of these institutions in their own right, but increasingly by its opposition to the widespread introduction of multilateral or comprehensive schools. Conservative ministers were especially concerned to safeguard the grammar schools and public schools against the threat that comprehensive schools were seen to represent, but the SMSs were of fundamental strategic importance for their role in maintaining the status quo and holding the line against a radical change in policy. In its defence of the SMSs, however, the Conservative government abandoned the claim that they were distinctive and even superior in relation to the grammar schools, which had been an integral part of their appeal at the outset of the 'experiment' in the 1940s. Instead, an attempt was made for the SMSs to develop many of the familiar curricular forms usually associated with the grammar schools.

It was hoped that imitation or emulation of the grammar schools might help to counter the gathering public impression that the SMSs were inferior schools for failures.

In the early 1950s, the Conservative government was quick to emphasize the importance of the SMSs, although it was noticed that the Conservative general election manifesto of 1951 said 'nothing whatever' about these new secondary schools, while committing itself to improved conditions in the primary and grammar schools.[1] Florence Horsbrugh, who was appointed as minister of education, publicly declared that the SMS represented one of the few attempts anywhere in the world to provide an education suitable for the 'bulk of secondary school pupils'. She continued: 'If it succeeds, as I believe it will, it may yet prove to be this country's most characteristic contribution to education in the second half of this century.'[2] Of particular value in these schools, according to Horsbrugh, was that

> They gave their pupils a thorough mastery of the skills that life in a complex civilisation demanded – manual and domestic skills as well as those that made for literacy – and they were not afraid or ashamed of having their courses dubbed 'vocational' by those who gave that word too narrow a connotation. [In addition, she affirmed] They kept a balance between clever and stupid children, and did not pin their faith to a particular method or approach.[3]

This kind of overt support for SMSs that were clearly differentiated from other kinds of secondary schools underwent subtle revision especially through the efforts of Sir David Eccles, minister of education from 1954 until 1957. Eccles, himself a product of Winchester and New College, Oxford, was acutely conscious of the growing appeal of comprehensive schools, and in particular the adoption of comprehensive schools as the official policy of the opposition Labour Party. Preparing for a general election in April 1955, he advised the new prime minister, Anthony Eden, of the dangerous implications that were involved in this trend: 'The most political problem in education is the 11+ examination and the Socialist proposal to abolish it by rolling up all secondary schools into comprehensive schools.'[4] This advice acknowledged the unpopularity of selection at 11 for different types of secondary schools, and the method that had increasingly been adopted to achieve it. The so-called '11-plus' was already a symbol of the tripartite system, and was held responsible for unfairness and inequality by critics of the system.[5] If it were to be undermined, the tripartite system would itself be endangered, and with it the grammar schools that Eccles cherished. Against this alarming prospect, Eccles proposed a series of what he called 'counter measures'.[6] The SMSs formed a major element in these plans.

The general purposes or objectives of the SMSs were not readily apparent to Eccles as he began to review their position. He noted the aims of the SMSs that had been propounded in *The New Secondary Education*, produced by the Ministry of Education in 1947,[7] but he was dissatisfied with its vision of 'a good all-round secondary education', since, as he explained to his officials, 'I do not know what this has come to mean, i.e. what HMIs have told teachers it should mean. Unsystematic education? the children doing what they like best? or find easiest?' He inquired pointedly: 'How has this doctrine stood the test of experience?'[8] A new HMI survey of the SMSs quickly served to reassure him as to their value, and the continuing validity of the experiment that they comprised. Indeed, he enthused, 'The moment in time seems comparable to that in industry when a big investment and expansion of staff is just getting through its teething troubles. The flow of results should soon increase fast.'[9] The political issue therefore was how to forestall public criticisms of the SMSs that might overwhelm them before they were ready to achieve their goals.

The minister of education was restricted in this endeavour. Most notably, perhaps, as Eccles soon discovered, he was limited to issuing 'guidance' so far as the curriculum of the schools was concerned. He had strong opinions on curriculum matters which he wished to see pursued, for example noting in relation to the SMSs that

> I do not like the idea that social studies should completely replace history and geography in any school. Children should be patriotic before they are committee men or any-questioners. And how you can be patriotic without a little history it is hard to see.[10]

He pointed out at the same time that

> If I am to say useful things about the desirable number of grammar school places I must know what is being taught in the modern second-aries. What alternative in academic education has the child who just fails to get into a grammar school? and this is relevant to the practical possibilities of transfer, which if few academic studies have been taken in secondary moderns from 11 to 13, must be restricted thereby.[11]

His officials hastily advised the minister that the Education Act (1944) prescribed only religious instruction and left the LEAs responsible for the secular curriculum. Hence,

> It follows that the Minister could not 'insist' on greater emphasis on English. But he can give guidance about the curriculum. Leaving aside the ordinary process of inspecting, and reporting on, individual schools, such guidance is given through the medium of Handbooks of Suggestions – the very title is significant – and pamphlets on particular subjects written by Her Majesty's Inspectors – again the title is significant.[12]

This statutory and practical limitation created major difficulties for a minister of education who was concerned to consolidate and develop the SMSs, although it also allowed the schools an opportunity to improve themselves in their own way.

The minister was in a stronger position to influence issues relating to entrance to secondary schools at the age of 11, transfer between schools at 13, and exit from secondary education into a range of different fields. Eccles hoped to minimize the inequities of the 11-plus, or at least to divert attention away from them, by emphasizing the opportunities that were available for suitable pupils to transfer between schools at 13. He was aware that the 'problem' of transfer at 13 was 'crucial'.[13] By discouraging transfer, it might be possible to develop 'self-confident secondary moderns'. However, by 'skimming the able children off into Grammar Schools',[14] public concern about the unjust effects of the 11-plus might be alleviated. He acknowledged himself that, as he put it, '11+ is early to show your paces if you come from a bad or dumb home.'[15] More extensive use of transfers at 13, he anticipated, might reduce the pressures involved at the earlier age.

Eccles was clearly attracted to this option despite its manifest implications for reducing the prospect of developing 'self-confident' SMSs, and he looked for ways of emphasizing the possibility of such transfer in appropriate cases.[16] He retained some ambivalence about the idea, even noting that he did not 'much like' such transfers in principle, but he argued more forcefully that small SMSs made such transfers more appropriate, and he left it for his officials to advise him how these would affect the nature of the SMSs as he inquired of them: 'How important to a Secondary Modern is it to keep a few bright children?'[17] There was little apparent response to this important question.

More fundamental than the issue of transfers at 13, to Eccles, was the problem of ensuring that pupils emerged from whatever kind of secondary school with an adequate preparation for adult life and work. 'In the long run', he ventured hopefully, 'our maintained schools will not be judged by how fairly a child enters at 11 but by how successfully he leaves at 15+, i.e. how he makes his way into the big world.' If this was true, he suggested, 'Parents will be satisfied when every secondary school offers a number of bridges to jobs which are worth having.' Indeed, he added, warming to the theme, 'The Englishman will not ask that the bridges should all be equal in wealth, or should all lead to the same suburb, but he will expect to see them in clear outline and to hear them well-spoken of.'[18] He was encouraged by the rise of full employment in the 1950s, which meant that nearly all secondary school pupils would be virtually assured of securing a job, and he was especially heartened to think that there would be a large increase in the number of 'good jobs' in industrial and other non-professional occupations over the next 25 years (that is, to the end of the 1970s).[19]

In the context of these social and economic changes, the minister saw fresh opportunities for improving the status of SMSs and achieving parity of esteem. For example, he noted, 'The dislike of vocational education may be a hangover from unemployment.' If this was the case, he asked, 'If we have full employment does it matter so much what is taught, provided it is well taught and arouses the interest of the children?; always assuming that what is taught is used as a vehicle for reading and expression?'[20] Such an argument encouraged Eccles in his view that what was needed were 'balanced groups of secondary schools',[21] each school with a different emphasis and catering in the main for different types of pupils, but each equally valued, and all leading to a range of rewarding and highly esteemed occupations in the changing and more prosperous society of the future. He was especially attracted, as he noted, to the notion that 'The most effective challenge to the idea of the comprehensive school is closer unity between a group of schools, all working together unselfishly for the good of each individual child.'[22] The only threat to this pleasing prospect was, he warned, for 'the public to think more about the entry to secondary education than about the exit from it to the great world'.[23] This was the 'last thing we want', he insisted, because 'Such jealousy would lead to absorption of the Grammar Schools in monster comprehensive schools.'[24] In the last resort, as usual, the perceived threat was not to the integrity of the SMSs, nor even to the delicate balance between groups of schools, but to the grammar schools.

Another device that was available to the minister was to reform the organization as opposed to the curriculum of secondary education. Eccles was increasingly drawn to such a solution, although this was also danger-ous territory. By the summer of 1956, he was more convinced than ever of the threat posed by comprehensive schools, and of the need to prevent their spread. He was conscious also that an impending 'bulge' in the numbers of secondary school pupils over the next decade would be likely to heighten criticisms of existing provision.[25] In addition, he had come to the conclusion that not only the grammar schools but also the public schools were at risk if the Labour Party was able to 'push education to the front as a political issue', a strategy that he felt it was avidly pursuing.[26] He pointed out that 'All sections of the Labour Movement are pledged to replace the tri-partite system with Comprehensive Schools', and that the 'first shots' were being fired 'against the Public Schools'. This was all the more dangerous, as he explained in detail in a seven page memorandum whose declared purpose was to 'save the Public Schools', when education 'must be the most urgent of all social problems' in the next decade and, at the same time, education remained divided into two separate systems.

According to Eccles's memorandum, 'Thanks to the 1944 Act the gap between the two systems of education is being narrowed, but not fast enough. The pressure to take some short cut is steadily mounting.' He continued to defend the status quo:

> We claim that when the Secondary Modern Schools, to which 3 out of 4 children must go, have found their feet, parents will accept the 11+ examination realising that the authorities do an honest job in direct-ing children to go to the schools that suit them best.

Even so, he was acutely conscious that as the bulge in secondary school places developed the inadequacies of the tripartite system, and especially the 'obnoxious' aspects of the 11-plus examination, would be increasingly evident. He acknowledged that there was not enough money available to build new schools and replace older ones, and that the priority continued to be to channel any additional funds into grammar schools rather than other areas: 'the only request which I shall put to the Chancellor for additional investment is in respect of science blocks in maintained Grammar Schools'. In this situation, he proposed, the most effective solution might be to postpone the 11-plus examination to the age of 15. This would turn all maintained secondary schools into comprehensives from 11 to 15, at which age pupils would go on either into a sixth form college or else 'out into the world to earn his living'. Such a scheme, he observed, had already been proposed in Croydon, 'but unfortunately was abandoned before I had a chance to approve it'.[27] This was a drastic, virtually last ditch proposal that visualized effectively abandoning the SMSs to their fate.

Not surprisingly, Eccles's proposal was met with a chorus of disapproval from his officials. One acknowledged both the 'apparent finality' of the results of the 11-plus examination, 'occupationally as well as educationally', and also 'the fact that few modern schools are as yet regarded as an acceptable alternative to the grammar schools', but argued that such criticisms would not be allayed by the pretext of 'abolishing the examination and pretending that a congeries of non-selective "senior schools" would somehow be equal to another in a way in which the present secondary schools are not'.[28] This was a revealing argument in that it also suggested a basic weakness in the alternative claims on behalf of the comprehensive schools. Another observed acidly that there had been little support for the Croydon scheme when it had been mooted locally.[29] Apparently undaunted, the minister continued to inquire into such a possibility, going so far as to invite for discussions a leading proponent of new experiments in comprehensive education, Dr Robin Pedley, who took the opportunity to suggest the postponing of selection to 14-plus.[30] Eccles remained convinced of the need to select and classify pupils in terms of their individual abilities, which he continued to insist was a 'natural and necessary consequence of real differences between children'.[31] However, he was prepared to compromise in a dramatic and arguably a far sighted manner, to avoid what he saw as the worst excesses of the alternative policies represented in the comprehensive schools.

## A new drive

In spite of Eccles's drastic proposals, there continued to be strong support from within the Conservative government for maintaining and developing the SMSs as separate institutions. Indeed, in the late 1950s, following Eccles's departure from the Ministry of Education, a renewed attempt was made to improve the standing of the schools. This set of initiatives accentuated the departure from the ideals of working-class secondary education that had already become apparent, and emphasized the claims of the SMSs for respectability and rigour in emulation of the grammar schools.

The incoming minister of education in the early months of 1958, Geoffrey Lloyd (educated at Harrow School and Trinity College, Cambridge), was especially concerned both to emphasize his strong support for the SMSs, and to promote their further development. Lloyd, like R.A. Butler and Eccles before him, was conscious that education was now a pivotal aspect of social policy, with an 'amazingly keen popular interest in Education' that had grown since the Education Act (1944).[32] He regarded further progress in the field as essential not only 'in the national interest' as a whole, but also since education was in his view 'the type of social reform which fits most perfectly into a general Conservative theme'.[33] This notion reflected the priority of Lloyd's longer term educational programme which was to provide 'varied opportunities for the able and the keen'.[34] Such a policy, it was hoped, would 'carry out the intentions of the 1944 Act' and also, no less important, 'take the sting out of the complaints arising from selection at 11'. The intention was to develop in a pragmatic fashion on the basis of the foundations that had already been put into place, rather than to make a radical shift through more 'sweeping measures'. More cautious reform should be promoted, it was argued, with the aim of securing 'worthwhile gains in a measurable time', and such gains should include 'a better basic secondary education for all in the vital 11–15 ages – no more all-age schools, better teachers, better buildings, but not just yet, unfortunately, smaller classes'. Such an approach would offer 'greatly improved opportunities for the able or the keen to go on after 15 to full-time or part-time schooling'.[35] The SMSs retained a key role in this strategy in helping to provide 'varied opportunities' for the 'keen', if not for the 'able'.

Lloyd had an early opportunity to display his enthusiasm for the SMSs through a major debate on education in the House of Commons on 20 March 1958. In this debate, prompted by opposition criticisms of educational policy, Lloyd made a robust defence of the 'educational record' of the government, and went on to emphasise the major contribution that was being made by the SMSs:

I must tell the House that getting to know more about these schools as I have visited them while going around the country has been the most stimulating single experience I have had since coming to the Ministry of Education. They are tremendously important, and three-quarters of all our children go to them. They are the one almost entirely new element in British education as it develops under the 1944 Act.[36]

Although, as Lloyd acknowledged, the public did not 'on the whole, take too easily to new institutions', he admitted that he had been 'a little surprised, but immensely encouraged' to find that the SMSs were already 'beginning to take root in the local communities'.[37] For example, in North-ampton 'I noticed the evident pride they have in the secondary modern schools there and the way each was developing special links with particular local industries'.[38] Furthermore, he noted, a particularly encouraging fea-ture of the schools was a trend that he discerned in them towards staying on at school beyond the compulsory leaving age, reflected for instance in SMSs in Birmingham. He conceded, however, that it was important for such schools to have a new school building, especially as in his view it 'contributes enormously to the prestige of the school for both the parents and the children'.[39]

These aspirations on behalf of the SMS were embodied in a further White Paper produced by the Ministry of Education in December 1958, entitled *Secondary Education for All: A New Drive*. The title itself was testimony to how far Tawney's ideal of 'secondary education for all', so radical in the 1920s, had now become common currency, but the White Paper as a whole again demonstrated how it was possible to interpret this ideal by envisaging a range of different types of courses and institutions. It acknowledged what it called existing 'defects' in the system, especially large classes, old school buildings, the continued existence of 'all-age' schools, and also 'a more general defect in our system of secondary educa-tion – a defect which is the root cause of the concern that is currently felt over what has come to be known as the "11-plus" examination'.[40] This latter defect was essentially one of inequalities of resourcing, quality, and the range of courses between different secondary schools.

SMSs in particular, it acknowledged, suffered from a lack of resources, which was why 'many parents still believe that, if their children go to a sec-ondary modern school, they will not have a fair start in life'.[41] The White Paper proposed, therefore, a five year programme of school building to the value of £300 million that would give priority to improving the provision of secondary schools, together with an increase in the volume of 'minor' works that would allow 'a steady flow of much-needed improvements, for example to sanitation, staff rooms, and playgrounds'.[42] It insisted, finally, that 'a substantial element of selection, in the broadest sense of the word' must be retained in secondary education 'if we are to do justice to the dif-ferent needs of individual children'.[43] Children, it urged, differed considerably in their 'mental powers', in their special gifts, in their vigour and industry, and in their ability to concentrate. Different courses and institutions to meet the needs of different types of children were therefore the best way of organizing the provision of secondary education, with the aim of ensuring 'the widest possible range of opportunities for boys and girls of different capacities and interests'.[44]

The message conveyed in this White Paper was clearly consistent with Lloyd's hopes of consolidating and developing the SMSs, and with the long term strategy of promoting both 'varied opportunities for the able and keen' and 'a better basic secondary education for all'. Brian Simon has argued that the White Paper 'seems now like a last-gasp defence against comprehensive education',[45] and it was certainly in the line of counter measures against the idea of comprehensive schools that the Conservative government favoured throughout the 1950s. Even so, there remained a strong element of optimism in the prevailing policy that the line could be held, and also a willingness to revise the existing system in order to minimize its most manifest inequities. These continuing aspirations, combined with the subtle changes in tone and presentation that had characterized Conservative policies on the SMSs during the 1950s, were well recapitulated by the chief inspector of secondary schools, W.R. Elliott, looking back at the end of the decade on the development of secondary school organization. The key development in the SMSs since the early 1950s, according to Elliott, was that they had become more aware of the needs and aspirations of their more able pupils, and it was this trend that the White Paper of 1958 had been attempting to encourage, 'to preserve and develop the existing system, removing any premature limitation of opportunities and the anxiety and sense of grievance which such limitation might create in some parents and pupils'.[46] While it allowed the grammar schools 'to continue their good work and to develop naturally and at their own pace', it also enabled the SMSs 'to continue playing their traditional role, while at the same time extending their scope in order to do justice to their full range of pupils'. Overall, Elliott suggested, the system envisaged in the White Paper would allow schools of all kinds to develop 'naturally and without undue restrictions', and he concluded with some satisfaction that

> It provides schools where those schools' pupils who are sound but not brilliant, and who thrive best under encouragement, can be the top people. It preserves a variety of settings and a width of choice for pupils. It enables schools to keep within bounds as regards size, and it permits the use of existing buildings, given reasonable room for improvements and extensions. It does not interfere arbitrarily with existing and flourishing institutions. It accords well with the British tradition and temperament in being evolutionary rather than revolutionary.

Although in Elliott's view there still remained significant difficulties such as the continuing 'feelings of disappointment' on the part of parents when their children failed to secure a place in a grammar school, and a lack of 'able teachers' who were prepared to teach in the SMSs, he recommended that the policy instituted in the White Paper should be maintained, developing the SMSs further along the proposed lines and consolidating 'our present resistance to schemes involving the transformation of grammar schools into comprehensive schools'.[47]

The unresolved issue in this line of thinking was over how far the SMSs should be encouraged to blur the lines between themselves and the grammar schools in the process of 'extending their scope in order to do justice to their full range of pupils'. It was increasingly argued that they should be encouraged to enter their pupils into external examinations, especially the General Certificate of Education (GCE) examinations that were associated with the grammar schools, in order to demonstrate that their more able pupils also had the opportunity to succeed in the academic sphere. This remained a matter of some contention. HMIs responsible for the SMSs pondered whether the GCE might be a legitimate goal for the school, and agreed that 'both staff and pupils might benefit from such a stimulus', but still suggested that such a stimulus 'might well be provided by other types of examination, apprenticeship schemes and industrial courses appropriate to local needs'.[48] On the one hand, there was strong pressure to show greater support for the 'reserve of able children' in the SMSs, both in the national interest and in the interest of the individual child, to enable them to stay on for further education. On the other hand, there continued to be an emphasis on flexibility, based on considerations of the nature of local communities, parental demands, local industrial demands, and the qualities of the teachers and headteacher.[49] These reservations about whether the SMSs should be encouraged to develop examination courses reflected at least in part a residual notion of the distinctive character of the SMS in relation to the grammar schools. Examinations, it was argued, would come to dominate the curriculum of the SMSs and would make them little more than pale shadows of the grammar schools. Others no doubt feared that involvement of the SMSs in the GCE examination would undermine and devalue the examination itself, a spectre that had been raised with regard to the School Certificate examination in the 1920s, 30 years before.

Similar issues were at stake so far as the idea of homework was concerned. HMIs expressed strong opposition to the notion of homework being expected in SMSs, and the senior inspector, Withrington, was clear in his view that he 'hoped that secondary modern schools would not copy grammar schools in the pattern and scope of homework'.[50] There was some support for what was described as 'semi-voluntary homework', or 'the gathering of information for some project', but HMIs tended to be sceptical of its value and emphasized its possible drawbacks, as it was observed that 'There was undoubtedly a case for an extension of homework in secondary modern schools, and certainly development could already be seen, but any suggestion for compulsory homework was full of dangers.'[51] Such arguments suggested lukewarm support at best within the inspectorate for practical measures designed to improve the capacity of the SMSs to provide for their more able pupils, in spite of the implications of this for limiting the appeal of these schools. In spite of this, throughout the 1950s there was a strong tendency for many SMSs to resort to such devices in order to broaden their appeal and to improve their local standing.

### 'Worth a second glance'

In the effort to consolidate the SMSs as separate institutions, it was recognized that examples of successful SMSs would help to alleviate public scepticism as to their future prospects. Such examplars were not always easy to find. A meeting of the secondary modern inspectorate in April 1956 noted that there might be a list of more than 140 SMSs that were 'worth a second glance'.[52] This was hopefully not an exhaustive list, since there were over 3500 such schools in existence at this time. It was suggested that the most successful schools should be publicized more widely in order to promote a 'quest for virtue' on behalf of the SMSs.[53] The fruits of this campaign were not apparent four years later, when a similar meeting again looked for likely role models. In particular, as was forlornly remarked, 'Evidence would be welcome of good secondary modern schools in poor areas.'[54] The problems that faced SMSs in substandard accommodation and in difficult local areas seemed virtually to rule out their chances of success or quality in the terms that were here being sought. The schools that were identified as 'good' or successful tended to be located in suburban areas with a broader clientele, and tended to try to emulate the provision offered by grammar schools in an attempt to blur the differences between them. The developments in such SMSs are readily apparent through exploring the experiences of two of them in greater depth: first, Greaves SMS in Lancaster, and second, Campions School in Hertfordshire.

Greaves SMS in Lancaster was originally opened in April 1907 as Greaves Council School. As a mixed elementary school with both junior and senior departments, its accommodation had been regarded as suitable for its initial purpose.[55] In 1921, the school was described in an HMI report as being 'housed in large and convenient premises', and 'conducted on modern lines and with considerable success'.[56] It became a central school from 1926, catering for children from 11 to 14 years of age.[57] In the 1930s, the school continued to be seen as a success. Its accommodation was still considered appropriate for its purpose, constituting 'bright and roomy premises containing the necessary "activity" rooms in addition to sufficient classrooms and two halls', and it was noted that the LEA had been 'generous, though not extravagant' so far as equipment was concerned.[58] By this time, the school was attracting wider attention, and headteachers from other schools, LEA officers, and also senior politicians visited to inspect its facilities.[59]

In 1938, J.H. Sutton, educated at a grammar school and a Master of Arts Honours graduate in English from the University of Manchester, was appointed as the new headmaster of Greaves. He was to remain in this post with the school until his retirement in 1965. It was Sutton who was primarily responsible for the successful transition of the school to become a leading SMS in the 1940s and 1950s. As an SMS, the school remained in the same accommodation that had housed the earlier elementary and central schools, in spite of plans to move to a new building that were included in the development plan for the area.[60] It catered for a broad range of pupils, boys and girls from both urban and rural communities, with a wide catchment area that at first included outlying districts such as Galgate, Glasson Dock and Garstang until the growth of new schools began to reduce its rural intake and the number of farmers' children at the school,[61] and it began to be identified more clearly as a suburban school within Lancaster. Pupils went to Greaves if they were unsuccessful in their 11-plus examination, and its most able pupils were often 'creamed off' to go either to the Lancaster Royal Grammar School or to the technical school, but it maintained a strong local reputation in relation to other SMSs in Lancaster during the 1950s.[62]

Sutton himself was an articulate and persuasive advocate on behalf of the Greaves school in particular, but also for SMSs in general. At the school's first annual Speech Day in November 1948, during which prizes were presented by the headmistress of Lancaster Girls' Grammar School, he took the opportunity to explain his notion of the scope and purpose of such schools. In general, he noted, the purpose of the SMS was 'to cater for boys and girls of a wide range of ability, from eleven years to the leaving age, and in that period to prepare them both to live and to get a living'.[63] He emphasized that this involved four types of educational activity: classroom, practical, sport, and conduct. The SMS was 'fortunate in that it is not in any way hampered in its choice of subjects by outside considerations', and it was therefore free to 'experiment',[64] but still he stressed the importance of first training in the use of the English language, and second of the elements of arithmetic. History, geography, physical training and games, dancing, literature, science, music, art and crafts, handicrafts, and domestic science were also included in the school curriculum, while French was taught to the most able forms, and religious instruction was a pervasive influence. Practical subjects involved close contact with woodland, farms, and local industries. He suggested that the SMS was distinctive, but still he argued that the school should do all that was possible 'to build up the fine tradition of devoted and disinterested service as revealed by our Grammar Schools'.[65]

As Greaves developed its role as an SMS, Sutton maintained its distinctive character while continuing to maintain its affinity to the ideals of the grammar schools, and increasingly also to many of their most familiar practices. On the one hand, he noted the uniqueness of the challenge that confronted such schools, as they had 'to cater for 75 per cent of our age groups and are therefore responsible for the largest and most difficult unit, e.g. I.Q.s of 70–115, of our school population', and he was convinced that 'as time goes on', they would become 'widely recognised as one of the most important units in our education system'.[66] On the other hand, as the product of a grammar school himself, he reflected that

> the more thought I gave to the matter led me to the vital conclusion that the aims of the school did not differ fundamentally from those of any other type of secondary school, except in so far as the range of curriculum and teaching approach had to be related to the abilities of our boys and girls, limited as these were known to be in certain ways.[67]

He therefore rejected what he saw as the over-rigid and artificial divisions envisaged in the Norwood Report of 1943, but he also resisted the development of external examinations in the SMS, and emphasized the need to take advantage of the freedom to experiment. The forms at Greaves were based on streaming, classified as Express, Practical and Remedial which corresponded to A, B and C streams, with an intelligence test used to classify pupils as well as record cards from their primary schools. During the 1950s, there was an increasing role for external examinations in the school, but Sutton sought always to temper their influence.[68] Such concerns were maintained despite the effects of a continual process by which the school was 'heavily creamed by transfer to the Technical and Commercial Schools'.[69] The building in which the school was housed had also 'changed little in spite of the Education Act of 1944', and seemed 'grimly determined to withstand any Education Act which may come its way'.[70] In these circumstances, the achievements and wider reputation enjoyed by the school were all the more impressive.

One pupil who took maximum advantage of the opportunities that Greaves SMS offered was Michael Worth, who became a prefect and head boy at the school and was captain of the school cricket team. He had failed the 11-plus examination, but recalled in later years that this failure was 'the making of me', and he did not regret going to Greaves.[71] He attended the school for five years, and was in the Express stream. While he was at the school, during the 1950s, it began to develop GCE work for its ablest pupils rather than sending these to the grammar school, although those who achieved good Ordinary level (O level) results were obliged to transfer to the grammar school at that stage if they wished to go on to take Advanced level examinations (A levels). The English and drama teacher, Arthur Nicholson, was an especially strong influence on Worth, who also admired the work of Sutton as headmaster. In his position as prefect and head boy, Worth was involved in keeping order in the school, echoing the roles developed much earlier in the public and grammar schools. Worth left Greaves in 1957 after passing the Local Government Entrance Examination and also gaining GCE O level passes in English language, mathematics, general science and geography,[72] and went on to join the Post Office.[73]

Greaves SMS was already well known and repected in the local community of Lancaster.[74] Sutton himself became president of the Association of Headmasters and Headmistresses of Lancashire Secondary Modern Schools, and later also president of the Lancaster and District Teachers' Association.[75] An HMI inspection in November 1957 served to confirm the progress being made by the school, with the chief education officer (CEO) offering Sutton his 'very warm personal congratulations', and emphasizing that 'You at Greaves have by no means the kind of conditions we would like to see our schools enjoying but in spite of this you have shown how a Secondary Modern school can afford a real secondary education.'[76] By the early 1960s, the school also began to achieve some national recognition for its work. Miss Hopwood, the deputy head, was awarded an MBE in 1960 for her innovative teaching methods in French.[77] The school was also visited in 1961 by members of the Central Advisory Council for Education. These distinguished visitors observed the deteriorating conditions of the school, and commented in their report that

> The School is hampered mainly in making provision for the most able groups by unsatisfactory and over-crowded premises. A considerable amount of work has been done in adapting suitable rooms for science and for craft but the school is old and over-crowded and the rooms used in the neighbouring Methodist Church are very unsatisfactory, dull and dirty.[78]

In spite of these shortcomings, they acknowledged,

> The special feature of this school which is more outstanding than any other is the close care and attention taken by the Headmaster and staff of the individual pupil and the determination to plan for the future of secondary modern education with imagination and foresight.[79]

Another SMS that was 'worth a second glance' was Campions School in Boreham Wood, Hertfordshire, opened in September 1955 in a new building. This school also catered for a broad range of pupils, both boys and girls, most of them drawn from council estate housing in the northern area of Boreham Wood, the rest from the longer established village of Shenley. By 1959, the school had reached a full pupil roll of over 600 pupils.[80] The head of the school, Janet Holman, was the first woman head to be appointed at a coeducational SMS in Hertfordshire. She had begun her teaching career at a senior elementary girls' school, and had already been the deputy head of two different SMSs before taking up her appointment at Campions.[81] She was to remain as head of Campions until she retired in 1979.

The official opening of Campions School in March 1956 was an occasion of some celebration for the school itself, and more generally also for Hertfordshire's impressive school building programme.[82] In her speech to mark the opening, Miss Dickinson, Principal of Wall Hall Training College, near Watford, emphasized the qualities of what she called its 'dignified, workmanlike and radiant building'.[83] This included classrooms, laboratories, domestic science rooms, craft rooms, wood and metalwork rooms, a gymnasium, and a hall with a stage. 'We can be certain', Miss Dickinson ventured,

> that good use of all the equipment will be made and that boys and girls will learn to draw and paint, to cook and sew and to construct in metal and wood, to use balances and test tubes and to grow physically strong and play games, to act plays and to make music, to write and to read and to calculate.[84]

There were still several limitations even with this accommodation. The HMI inspection report on the school in June 1962 noted that the buildings were 'modern and pleasant' and 'well situated on an open space', but added that it had been originally built for fewer pupils and was short of teaching spaces. In practice, also, the library was used as a classroom, mainly for the teaching of English, and also as a form base and prefects' room. The school suffered from a shortage of storerooms, toilet facilities for the staff were inadequate, and the playing fields were found to be insufficient.[85]

Holman's work at the school was actively supported by the chief education officer for Hertfordshire, John Newsom (educated at Imperial Service College and Queen's College, Oxford), who was anxious to encourage SMSs to achieve their full potential. Newsom had already publicly expressed his support for the SMS experiment and a conviction in its ultimate success. He noted that the population of the modern schools consisted of three-quarters of the children of England, of whom two-thirds were '"average" sort of people who will grow up into "average" men and women', while the remaining one-third were 'at the age of eleven somewhat below average attainment, but not necessarily below average capacity'.[86] Newsom conceded that the SMSs had a difficult task, especially in view of the superior prestige that was still associated with the grammar schools, but he was confident about the future:

> The Modern School is still at an experimental stage, but already its future is assured; not only because it provides the secondary education of 75 per cent of the population, but because some of the best minds in English education are being attracted to its service.[87]

He was resistant to the notion that the SMSs should try to emulate the grammar schools by providing what he called a 'watered-down version of the traditional curriculum', and sought to encourage them to cultivate their 'unique advantage', which in his view was their 'freedom from the restrictive effects of external examinations'. If they could be given the 'tools for the job', Newsom argued, 'the Modern School can design an education to meet the varying needs of its pupils, and it will be judged by their quality rather than by certificates and diplomas'.[88]

In June 1955, just before Campions School opened its doors for the first time, Newsom invited Holman to attend a one-day conference at Hatfield Technical College with a group of secondary modern heads.[89] His background notes prepared for this conference reflected many of the issues that confronted schools such as Campions. He argued that it was 'really very early to assess the quality of the work that has been accomplished' in the SMSs, and that the 'relatively limited experience' of the schools left some major problems still unresolved.[90] For example, he noted, so far as 'basic principles' were concerned, it was unclear whether the curriculum of the SMSs should be 'general' or specifically for vocational training, and what each of these approaches would involve. There were particular issues in this regard in the 'increasingly chancey business' of the borderline between SMSs and grammar schools. For those children who were in the A stream of SMSs, and who were 'difficult to distinguish from those at the bottom end of the grammar school', the question was how to ensure equality of opportunity:

> When a middle class child fails the grammar school the parents, not infrequently, send them to an independent school where, if they stay until they are seventeen, they often pass GCE in four or more subjects at 'O' Level and thus have a wide variety of careers open to them. If the parents are not able to do this then, in many ways, the children are assumed to have no 'academic' ability, not to find books the natural idiom of instruction, and are assumed to acquire knowledge more effectively by hammering metal or learning basic laundry work.

Newsom concluded: 'This forcing of children into categories is administratively tidy, but offensive to the wide variety of ability and need which exists.' With this in mind, Newsom proposed that there remained an important future for the SMS if it was envisaged as 'really comprehensive with the exception of those children who are *quite obviously* in the top 15 per cent or so of *intellectual* ability'. This would entail a 'much wider variety of treatment' in the SMS, which would contain 'everything from the "near miss" for the grammar school to children who are verging on the dim and backward'. Such variety of treatment might be 'virtually impossible' in many SMSs because of the inadequacy of their buildings, but in new schools such as Campions there might be new possibilities for innovation and experiment.[91]

Many of the innovations that were developed at Campions bore a strong similarity to the practices and customs that were already familiar in grammar and public schools. School prefects were appointed, and then Houses were introduced to encourage 'loyalty'.[92] Also, for pupils who were 'capable' and showed 'determination' the opportunity was provided to enter for public examinations in the form of the GCE or Part I of the Preliminary Nursing Examination.[93] The school established a fifth form from 1958 which began to develop O level examination work, and a sixth form the following year for an O level and a small Pre-Nursing group. The pattern of provision that developed in the first few years was, as Holman noted, one of 'general education'.[94] In the third year, pupils, parents and staff considered which course of study each pupil would study in their fourth year. The headteacher explained to parents at the school's Speech Day in 1958 that

> While in some cases the choice may be influenced by a child's future choice of employment, these courses are not given a marked vocational bias. They are planned to develop the children's interests, to encourage them to assess themselves and their abilities, to give them the opportunity of making decisions.

At the same time, she added, 'The approach changes from the rather formal teaching of the earlier years to the development of projects involving groups of children.' Holman was also conscious of the 'increasing competition' for what she called 'worthwhile jobs', and stressed the importance that employers would place on 'honesty, integrity, a willingness to work, a willingness to learn, a pride in doing a job well'. The kinds of employment taken up by former pupils would be the real 'test of our success', she asserted: 'Some have drifted from one job to another as we feared they would; others have unexpectedly stayed with the determination to become a success.'[95] Youth employment officers were used to advise the pupils, and also arranged for talks on different occupations such as nursing, catering, the retail trades, the Post Office, and the armed forces.

As well as being able to lead on to 'worthwhile jobs', Holman was anxious to persuade local parents that the school could offer the opportunity to gain examination success and to stay on beyond the compulsory leaving age of 15. In 1960, she was

> proud to announce [that] this year twice as many children sat for the General Certificate of Education, and they came from all the original five forms in the 1st year, they took three times as many subjects as last year – and the result as you'll see – 21 children with G.C.E.

She continued pointedly:

> And this is something I'd like you to talk about. Do tell the neighbours. Down by the Brook they haven't heard yet that at Campions we not only take G.C.E. we also get successes in G.C.E. 9 of the candidates passed in three subjects or more. 6 of them are staying at Campions for more 'O' level work, 2 of them have gone on to the 6th form at Grammar School, and 1 has gone to Hatfield Technical College. Got to have good teaching to get results like this in a modern school, and I know the children sitting here in front of me will readily endorse that, won't you?[96]

For pupils who left at 15, the school also introduced its own 'Campions Leaving Certificate', devised by the staff, which could be taken on three levels (A, B and C) in any subject: 'The vital point is to give to every girl and boy a sense of personal achievement – and I wish you could have seen the transformation of some apparently slack, happy-go-lucky individuals when the end of term presentation of certificates took place.'[97]

Holman urged parents to encourage their children to stay on at school as long as possible, partly to take examinations, but also to gain in 'personal qualities, in maturity, in sense of responsibility, in an understanding of other people both old and young, which will help them immeasurably when they go into employment'.[98] By 1962, 70 pupils were staying on after they were 15, about 40 per cent of the original age group, and were able to take A levels at Campions rather than having to transfer to the grammar school.[99] For such reasons, Holman was able to argue, 'No longer is the Secondary Modern School the end. It is now a stage between Primary and Further Education, and the children with the will and the encouragement from home will go on.' For example, she enthused,

> I had quite a surprise last Saturday to meet a girl who left a year ago, now sixteen, who is studying at the College part-time for 'O' level in English, Mathematics, Physics and Chemistry. She wasn't at school at the top of her age group, but she's got determination and a sense of purpose, and I wish her every success in her course.[100]

These kinds of developments were designed to convince local parents that Campions could offer a secondary education just as well as the grammar school, and they did so by imitating the forms and practices that were generally associated with grammar school education. The aim was to establish the school by achieving respectability, much more than by emphasizing distinctive, novel or experimental ideals that might have hardened the suspicions of the parents. There were several major problems in pursuing this approach, especially in relation to the misbehaviour of many of the pupils and a high rate of teacher turnover. In 1960, Holman explained to the Speech Day guest, Sir Ronald Gould of the National Union of Teachers (NUT), that most of the pupils at the school had been rehoused by the London County Council in Hertfordshire, 'and come therefore from very varied and in some cases very unstable backgrounds'. Although individually many of these did well, she continued, 'they find it difficult to retain their own standards within the group'. While many of the parents were 'co-operative and eager for their children to do well at school', she added, 'recently we have met antagonism amongst some parents'.[101] Teaching staff tended to move on to other schools very quickly, to such an extent that by 1962, Miss Holman found herself bidding farewell to the last of the original team of teachers who had founded the school only seven years before.[102] These problems were noted in the HMI report on the school in

June 1962. This observed that only five of the twenty-six full-time staff had five or more years of service at the school. Twelve had been at the school for one year or less, and ten were in their first teaching posts, which meant that a high proportion of the staff were young and inexperienced, although many of these appeared to be 'already useful teachers, and they form a source of potential strength'. So far as the pupils were concerned, the HMI report went on,

> The great majority are prepared to work readily with the Headmistress and Staff, but there is a rougher element which, while not behaving badly, could benefit from a stronger demand for discipline and sustained effort. Despite the influence of the teachers, the manners of a few pupils leave something to be desired. The prevailing atmosphere, however, is one of willing and friendly co-operation, and many of the pupils seem to derive benefit from being allowed to proceed at a natural pace.[103]

The 'quest for virtue' at both Greaves and Campions was a search for upward mobility, with the overriding aim of retaining abler pupils and winning the confidence of the local community and parents. This was done through a cultivation of the ethos of the grammar schools, and in spite of a residual reluctance also through the device of external examinations for the abler pupils. In order to be accepted as successful or improving schools, they had to leave behind the idea of constituting a distinctive form of working-class secondary education, which had been so important in the origins and rationale of the SMS, in favour of promoting a suburban middle-class respectability.

The process that took place at these schools, and others like them around Britain, was an integral part of the attempts to consolidate the SMSs in the 1950s in the face of the challenge of the comprehensive schools. They sought to override the unacceptable image of the Stonehill Street schools, and to obscure the inequities of the 11-plus examination, by demonstrating the opportunities for success that could be found in the SMSs. In so doing, they supplanted the notion of working-class secondary education in favour of the idea of secondary education for the working class, emphasizing individual social mobility at the expense of a distinctive social and cultural form of education that would be especially appropriate for a particular group. By subverting the rationale of the SMSs in this way, however, they raised the question of what the social mission of the SMSs really was, and why they should be retained as separate institutions in their own right. It was this issue that returned to haunt the schools in the early 1960s.

# 8

# The ordinary child

The 'experiment' of the SMSs, begun in the 1940s, was thoroughly tested and examined over the following 20 years, and in the early 1960s the results were widely discussed. There remained some support for continuing to invest in the schools and for developing them further, but strong doubts were expressed as to their general rationale and also their educational and social effects on the pupils who went through them. Increasingly, the debate turned towards trying to find alternative means of catering for such pupils, not only through changes in the organization of secondary education, but also by promoting distinctive forms of curriculum and examinations that were assumed to be especially suited for 'less able' pupils.

The Crowther Report, *15 to 18*, produced by the Central Advisory Council for Education in 1959, was a major influence on this debate. Its principal focus was on a phase of educational provision, after the compulsory school leaving age, in which most SMS pupils were not involved. However, it was also concerned to promote the development of extended courses and external examinations for suitable pupils in the SMSs which would allow more pupils to stay on at school beyond the leaving age. In this regard, it distinguished between different kinds of SMS pupils. A small group 'whose knowledge, comparable to that of many grammar school pupils, makes it worth while to do this'[1] was judged to be capable of taking a written examination at the age of 16 or 17. These were 'the modern school's potential G.C.E. candidates, and must not be robbed of their chance'. A second group, 'larger than the first', might be suited to an external test with a 'well defined objective'.[2] On the other hand, a third group, 'which is certainly larger than either of the others and probably as big as both together', consisted of pupils 'for whom an external examination at the age of 16 is an absurdity, and whose education ought to be developed on quite different lines'.[3] These latter pupils it defined as average and below average in ability. Some of these were 'physically and emotionally, as well as mentally' below average, but a larger number were 'physically quite as developed as any boys and girls of their age, and who are straining at the leash to get out into the world'.[4] It was this 'middle group', who were 'neither the brightest nor the dullest', that the report tagged 'the ordinary child'.[5]

Albert Rowe, formerly headteacher at an SMS, expressed similar concerns in a book published the same year entitled *The Education of the Average Child*. Rowe argued that the abler children in grammar schools and in SMSs should be encouraged to attempt GCE examinations, but that the courses that led to these did not meet the needs of the 'average child'. He continued:

> These average children comprise more than half the children under fifteen in all the nation's schools, and four-fifths or more of all those in secondary modern schools. They will therefore in due season form more than half our total adult population. Surely there can be no question that their education is just as important as that of the other half?[6]

In order to create an 'educated democracy', Rowe maintained, it would be necessary to give full attention to 'the 50 per cent or more who are average'. Moreover, he added,

> The most important (though not the only) task of the modern school is still to evolve a true secondary education for them, and its ultimate triumph will be to show that, given the right educational approach, the average child can learn more and, even more important, *be* more than has hitherto been thought possible.[7]

With this end in view, Rowe insisted that 'a re-examination and a rethinking of the way in which the average child can best be educated has never been of more vital urgency than it has to-day, for the future well-being of our nation may well hang upon it'.[8]

Much of the debate over the future of secondary education that developed in the 1960s revolved around seeking a suitable form of provision for this middle group of 'ordinary' or 'average' children. In particular, the CAC for Education itself developed a major inquiry on the 'education of pupils aged 13 to 16 of average and less than average ability'. This new inquiry was undertaken under a new chairman, John Newsom, formerly the chief education officer for Hertfordshire. It provided an opportunity first to review the experience of the SMSs, and to discern their successes and failures. It also permitted a more detailed investigation of the characteristics and future needs of the 'ordinary child'.

## 'The puzzled search for an aim'

Following the setting up of Newsom's committee under its new terms of reference, it was agreed to approach a wide range of interest groups, leading educators and others to discover their views and recommendations on provision designed for average and below average children of 13 to 16 years of age. In the course of this investigation, the committee was given a large amount of advice on how well the SMSs had provided for such pupils. Most of this advice was negative and often strongly hostile to the outcome of the SMS experiment.

A spirited case for the defence on behalf of the SMSs was submitted to the committee by the HMI sub-panel for SMSs. It argued that the SMSs had 'on the whole not only held together but also made progress in many ways', and that this was 'something that the public as a whole is only beginning to understand and appreciate'.[9] By and large, it claimed, 'the Modern Schools are better than they are thought to be, and the teachers work harder than they have ever done'. The key problem for the future, according to the sub-panel, was to resolve the uncertainties that continued to surround the SMSs. It identified strong doubts 'both about what to teach and how to teach it' in such schools, and suggested that these doubts were due to a lack of understanding as to how to apply the idea of 'secondary education for all' to average and below average pupils. This idea had become widely accepted, it noted, but it was 'a far more searching matter to interpret the phrase in terms of what should be offered in actual classrooms to pupils of particular ages and particular abilities'. Indeed, it asserted, the 'major problem' that faced teachers was 'to hammer out of the whole body of their experience some conception of the word secondary which is applicable to less able as well as to able pupils'. Such a task, it added, was hampered further by what it called the 'misconceptions of the general public', who 'still take secondary education to mean something approximating to what is done in Grammar Schools'. The tendency to 'react to the opposite pole' was also unhelpful when it led to 'false oppositions' in which it was often assumed

> that those who find abstract ideas difficult should abandon them for reality; that those who find the use of words difficult should reduce their contact with them and do something practical; that those who learn slowly from the printed word should see less print and be taught through the use of pictures and the like.[10]

The real way forward for the SMSs, the sub-panel argued, lay somewhere between these polar opposites, between imitating the grammar schools and reacting against them, but the SMSs had so far failed to define this alternative route with any clarity or precision. Even in Wales, where a much higher proportion of children went to selective secondary schools than was the case in England, there was little evidence of 'any special development of curricula, methods of teaching etc., appropriate to our children', and although more practical work was commonly proposed for 'the improvement of the education of the less able child', there were 'no particular detailed comments on this forthcoming, nor was anything seen which indicated that the idea was the subject of experiment along new lines'.[11]

The Newsom committee became acutely conscious of this failure on the part of the SMSs. One of the sub-committees set up for the purposes of its new inquiry, focusing on the needs of the school curriculum, observed pungently that the key issue was to ask 'What do we mean by Secondary Education for all?' It demanded to know

> how is it that we and the teaching profession are not at all clear what are the more obvious characteristics of secondary education for all? How is it that the glorious freedom of the Senior Schools has turned into the puzzled search for an aim of the Secondary Modern Schools? Should not more of us have exclaimed Eureka by now?

It reflected dissatisfaction with past attempts to define the nature and purposes of education in the SMSs:

> The phrase 'a good general education' contains three very imprecise and difficult words. The words are 'good', 'general' and 'education'. They provide a nice soft warm cocoon for our thoughts about education, and they send the mind to sleep for the duration.[12]

These attitudes and those of the HMI sub-panel on the SMSs amounted to a severe indictment of the SMS experiment, which had been intended to resolve such issues. In 1947, the ministry's widely circulated pamphlet *The New Secondary Education*, echoing the aspirations of the Hadow Report of 1926, had stated that the aim of the SMS was to provide a 'good all-round education'.[13] In the light of experience, such an objective appeared much too vague to be of use in defining secondary education for the majority of children, or for the 'ordinary child'. Thus the SMSs had clearly failed to achieve what was probably their most important objective. This was also a failure that could be contrasted with the experiences of other countries such as the Netherlands, where D.B. Bartlett, chief education officer for Southend-on-Sea, noted that schools were divided into units of limited aim: 'The fact that the modern school is so multipurpose that any clear aim is sometimes difficult to see, and whether this constitutes an advantage or disadvantage, is something which can profitably be investigated.'[14] Such issues raised basic questions not only over the curriculum of the SMSs, but also and even more profoundly over their rationale, and whether they should be allowed to continue in their existing form.

The generally low levels of attainment achieved in the SMSs were also a matter of concern. This problem was emphasized in several submissions, especially from employers, that came before the Newsom committee. Another of its sub-committees, on school and work, observed that employers 'fairly commonly' expressed their 'dissatisfaction' over 'the attainments of not all, but a substantial number, of modern school leavers', and that they tended to assume that the schools were 'at fault in not giving sufficient attention to "basic education" in the 3 Rs'.[15] The British Employers' Confederation (BEC), for example, insisted that 'while the quality of many secondary modern pupils, particularly those in the extended courses, is a tribute to the work of the schools, many other pupils of ordinary ability have apparently not been educated to the fullest extent of their abilities and aptitudes'.[16] The urgent need, according to the BEC, was to ensure that a much larger proportion of SMS pupils reached the standards that were currently being achieved by relatively few, at least in the 'key subjects' of reading, writing and arithmetic, and that financial and material resources and 'good teachers' should be deployed towards this end.[17] This message was endorsed by the National Coal Board (NCB) in its submission to the inquiry. The NCB pointed out that it took about 11,000 juvenile recruits into the coal industry every year. About 5 per cent of these had 'such a low standard of attainment in the three Rs as to be scarcely literate', but a much larger percentage had a poor standard of proficiency. It noted that an inquiry carried out in its Preliminary Training Centres in 1952 had shown that 25 per cent of entrants at that time 'would not be able to read properly an elementary text book or understand a description of a piece of mining equipment written on a blackboard'. It concluded that 'a substantial group of children has been left behind in education and has derived little from ten years at school', with the result that they 'join the industry with a sense of comparative failure and a lack of will to develop their abilities to the full'.[18]

A similar verdict was forthcoming from the Electricity Council. This was careful to explain that its experience was based largely on the 'better type' of SMS leaver, and that it included relatively few of their 'average' and even fewer of their 'below average' pupils. Even so, it had no doubts about 'criticising the standard reached by secondary school leavers in the basic subjects, as reflected in their performances on joining the industry', and it continued: 'In the considered judgement of the industry it would appear that this part of the education system judged by this test is not at the present time doing its job satisfactorily.' It added that poor performance in the three Rs was evident not only in the case of applicants for craft apprentices, 'who are necessarily "non-academic" types', but was also characteristic of clerical staff. The Electricity Council blamed this poor level of attainment not on the level of intelligence of its new recruits, but on the education system itself, especially since 'proper instruction' in the industry's workshops and attendance at training classes had the effect that, as it noted, 'the potential ability of newly recruited employees has been found to be better than at first appeared, and their standard of achievement has markedly improved'.[19]

A further criticism of the SMSs was that not only did they suffer in general from low standards, but they also exhibited a very wide range of standards of attainment. This extensive range of standards was commonly attributed to the practice of streaming classes in secondary schools. Mr D.A. Pidgeon, senior research officer at the National Foundation for Educational Research (NFER), was invited to explain this problem to a full meeting of the CAC in July 1962. He pointed out that in a recent comparative study of achievement of 13-year-olds in England and 11 other countries, England had shown the widest spread of results in all of the tests that had been used. Moreover, he suggested, this unusually wide spread of attainment results 'might lie partly in the practice of "streaming" in schools, and still more, in the teachers' attitude which commonly went with it'. Pupils in the C and D forms tended to be underestimated, and the effect of this attitude, rather than the effect of streaming itself, was to widen the gap between the abler and less able pupils as they got older. It was observed also that the most experienced teachers were usually assigned to the A streams, 'whereas teachers of very limited experience commonly took the C and D streams'.[20]

The dangers of streaming pupils were also emphasized in a number of submissions to the inquiry.[21] The Association of Teachers in Technical Institutions (ATTI), for example, was emphatic that streaming had a retrogressive effect by systematizing the pupils' experience of failure so that 'the main lesson learnt by many children in ten years of compulsory schooling is that they are educational failures'.[22] The Physical Education Association also expressed its opposition to streaming, on the grounds that pupils in C and D streams appeared to be 'bigger louts' in the gymnasium because the system of streaming 'has given them the reputation of dead-headedness and loutishness which they have to live up to'.[23] Perhaps the most arresting evidence on this topic, however, was amassed by one of the members of the committee, Alec Clegg, the chief education officer in the West Riding of Yorkshire (educated at Long Eaton Grammar School and Clare College, Cambridge), in the form of a collection of pupils' own reactions to streaming: 160 children in the C, D and E streams of SMSs in Clegg's own area were asked to write essays on the topic 'What I like and what I do not like about being in a C or D stream'. The main reasons given for liking the form in which they were placed were that they liked being with their form friends, that the work was easier, and that they were given more personal attention. The main reasons given for dislike were that they were neglected or too often blamed, that they felt inferior, that they would not be able to get a good job, and that they were given insufficient responsibility. Feelings of inferiority were expressed in one case as 'When you go in 2C people tease you about it and they say I'm in 2B and your in 2C your a dunce but I'm brainy.' Anxiety about the job market, meanwhile, was indicated by one boy who according to Clegg was 'at the very bottom of the ability range', in the following terms: 'I would santd a beter canst of get a good

job in a work whit you like but all 4R are good for is the pit filling tubs
and clevering roads why the B class get the top jobs'.[24]

The strong criticisms voiced about standards and the effects of streaming
in the SMSs served to increase doubts first as to whether these schools could
promote equality of opportunity, and second as to the quality of teachers
and teaching in them. So far as the issue of equality was concerned, for
example, a strong call for greater 'parity of opportunity' came from the
National Union of Teachers, which argued that only through such parity
could the Education Act (1944) be fully implemented. This meant in turn,
according to the NUT, that each child of secondary school age should have
teachers, buildings, playing fields, books and equipment adequate for their
needs and aptitudes.[25] The Workers' Educational Association defined the
problem in terms of a systematic 'wastage' of talent created because the large
proportion of pupils leaving school at the compulsory leaving age effectively
'cuts off the development of the majority of young people before its potential
is even identified'.[26] The way in which secondary education was organized
was held to be partly responsible for this situation. The Communist Party
also pointed out that many pupils of high ability were leaving school at 15,
and that the majority of this group came from 'the families of skilled, semi-
skilled and unskilled workers'. This meant, it concluded, that 'the children
of the bulk of the working-class' were being unfairly denied the facilities for
full education.[27] By now, such criticism was common currency across the
labour movement and the Labour Party also, and again intensified criticisms
of the role of the SMS.

The role of teachers in the SMSs also did not escape criticism. Newsom's
committee was alarmed to discover that very few trained teachers were
being prepared to teach in the SMSs, and it appeared that there was a
strong tendency for teachers in these schools to prefer working with the
most able pupils rather than with the 'ordinary child'. After visiting teacher
training colleges to find out the nature of training for SMS teachers, members of the committee reported their

> extreme concern [that] under present policies scarcely any of the work
> of the training colleges could have relevance for the C.A.C.'s inquiry,
> because the students – much to their own disappointment in many
> cases – were being directed away from work in the secondary modern
> schools.[28]

The 'knowledge' and 'experience' of the training colleges were being neglected, and their potential contribution wasted.[29] Clegg pointed out that
ministry policy was to direct training colleges to produce teachers for
primary schools, while the proportion of untrained graduates entering
teaching was rising. Trained graduates were still tending to take posts in
grammar schools, but the untrained graduates were often going into the
SMSs. Clegg concluded: 'It would appear, therefore, that untrained graduates

are tending to teach in schools where they teach children with abilities least like their own and where training is most needed.'[30]

The consequences of this were widely observed. According to the AEC, while many teachers were keen to take the A streams and some others preferred to work with the 'retarded pupils', the 'middle group' were 'probably being taught by the least enthusiastic members of the staff', and this helped to account for 'the group's failure to show ability or distinction in school, and for the low attainment of its members'.[31] The Association of Chief Education Officers (ACEO) also noted pointedly that 'Possibly the greatest need is to find teachers who can deal with ordinary boys and girls without patronage – without making them feel that they would rather be with the brighter ones!'[32] To some observers, such as Professor J.W. Tibble of Leicester University, this indicated that teachers were mainly concerned with trying to reproduce 'people like us', and perhaps that they were 'deliberately unwilling to share their culture with children from different backgrounds as a form of snobbery'.[33] Even in some SMSs, indeed, it was openly acknowledged that 'certain types of staff are unable to deal with C and D children, even though they are experienced, because they tend to patronise the children because they were fundamentally snobs and these teachers were the ones who had disciplinary problems with them'.[34]

All of these criticisms suggested that the SMS experiment was a failure. The SMSs had failed to resolve the idea of secondary education for all in relation to average and below average children. Their distinctive provision of a particular form of secondary education for working-class children was already discredited, but it appeared that they also failed to give sufficient access to more familiar and acceptable forms of secondary education. Their overall standards of attainment were very low. They did not produce equality of opportunity. Moreover, far from catering for the less academic pupils who were deemed unsuitable for grammar schools, as had been anticipated, there was evidence to suggest that such pupils were actually neglected in the SMSs.

If the SMSs had failed, as was apparent, the comprehensive schools were the most likely form of provision to eventually take their place, despite all the strenuous resistance that had been exhibited during the 1950s. In the mean time, attention was switched to concentrate on aspects of provision that might survive the collapse of the SMSs in order to maintain and develop approaches that would be suited to the 'ordinary child'. The focus of debate turned, therefore, to the nature of the curriculum and examinations.

## The secondary modern curriculum

Discussion of the kind of school curriculum that might be best suited to the needs of the 'ordinary child' tended to assume that this would be different in many respects from the curriculum of the academically able. It also suggested important differences in the kinds of curriculum that were appropriate for 'average' girls as opposed to those designed for 'average' boys. The Newsom committee in its deliberations attempted to define the nature of a secondary modern curriculum in a way that the SMSs themselves had failed to do.

The committee encountered some strong resistance to the idea that the curriculum of 'average' pupils should be differentiated from that of the 'more able'. In visits to SMSs that were apparently 'held in some esteem locally',[35] at the beginning of their investigation, members were told that such distinctions were not helpful. According to one teacher whose comments were recorded, 'It is a mistake and a source of division in the school and in society, to think that the education of the less able children should be radically different in approach from that of their more able contemporaries.' At another school, it was reported that

> The curriculum, which is of a conventional and somewhat academic type, is the same for all pupils. . . . The situation derives not from any lack of resources or deficiency of equipment, but from the conviction of the Headmaster that all children have the same basic educational needs.

It was quickly apparent that there were differences of principle, as well as of practical necessity, involved in the issue of differentiating the curriculum, and the secretary of the committee was led to inquire:

> Do we assume too uncritically that there must be 'differentiation' for the Cs and Ds, or is the conflict of principles over this more apparent than real? i.e. does acknowledging that the 'basic educational needs' of all children are the same preclude different presentations of educational experience?[36]

Nonetheless, the committee did not dwell long on this troubling thought, for it soon began to focus on appropriate methods of differentiating the curriculum.

An immediate issue in deciding this was how to ensure 'elementary literacy in the generalised sense of what is needed for mere maintenance for oneself in the world of today' for such pupils.[37] This also prompted the question of what more should be expected of such pupils, and members of the committee were alert to the implications of this, although they struggled to relate narrowly instrumental aims to more ambitious educational horizons. Withrington, the senior inspector for SMSs, pondered rather uncomfortably:

> If 'mere self-maintenance' is putting it low, what is the next stage? One has the criticism of the outside world, which is constantly saying, 'these people from modern schools do not know enough'. They need

elementary literacy in reading; numeracy; do they need some information of the kind of world that they are living in if they are to exercise their duties as citizens rather than 'just get by'?

Others insisted that 'we have got to go further than "keeping the people happy" which seems to be implied in this particular question'. Newsom himself noted that even in defining what literacy meant for such pupils, 'presumably we mean more than being able to get a job shoving a broom around', but he warned at the same time that if the committee failed to say 'what we mean by the minimum standard capable of achievement by our children' it would be 'accused of talking flannel and not getting down to brass tacks'.

It was eventually agreed that the curriculum should help to integrate such children into society both in the 'working sense' and in the 'social sense', but it remained unclear how to achieve this. Professor B.A. Fletcher, director of the Institute of Education at the University of Leeds and chair of the curriculum sub-committee, suggested what he viewed as a dichotomy between 'essential education' and 'individual development', and proposed that these might be considered 'in terms of a minimum target defined in terms of minimum literacy or essential knowledge, something that at least every child should have; and then all the rest on top of that'. However, Alec Clegg, an influential member of the committee, warned his colleagues against what such an approach might lead to: 'I hope we shall not do this, I hope we shall not say they have got to be able to do Arithmetic and to read and that is our minimum standard and then go on to try to list the subjects which then must be added to the curriculum.' Clegg preferred a different starting point, that children should be encouraged to have an 'alert mind', and to identify subjects that 'if properly handled, can contribute to that end'.[38]

Clegg had already sketched out some of his ideas on the curriculum in a separate memorandum for the committee. In this, he argued persuasively that in order to understand the purposes of the curriculum, it was important to

> make some attempt to define what we want our children to be as well as what we want them to know, and to think somewhat less in terms of skills to be mastered and knowledge to be gained and somewhat more in the terms of qualities to be acquired and developed through a variety of experience.

Such qualities, he added, should be identified in straightforward ways that could be accepted by parents, employers, the general public, teachers, and the pupils themselves. These consisted in particular of five aims with which the curriculum should be concerned. First, he emphasized 'sound attitudes and behaviour', which included 'not only self-respect and consideration for others but the development of diligence'. Second came the three Rs of reading, writing and arithmetic, including the ability to communicate in speech as well as writing. Third, he proposed 'alertness of mind' as a principal aim, 'and by this I mean such intellectual interest in the affairs of nature and men as ability and aptitude permit'. Fourth, he identified 'imagination', or 'the power to think and act creatively in a variety of fields according to ability and aptitude'. Fifth, he endorsed what he called the 'enjoyment of things designed to give pleasure', including art, music, literature, and a range of physical activities.[39]

In order to promote these aims, Clegg emphasized, schools would need a wide range of materials, including

> games and history, camps and mathematics, religious instruction and the dance, science and drama, geography and pictures, rural studies and gymnastics, school dinners and excursions, arts and crafts, the personal appearance of the head and his staff, their geniality, the decoration and general cleanliness of the school, etc.

They could be developed in different ways across the curriculum, although they would require good teaching, for example,

> The physical education teacher who encourages each child to compete against his own previous best effort is more likely to promote the enjoyment of physical activity than one who puts forty children over the same piece of apparatus so that the last few are humiliated by their failure.

The key to success, according to Clegg, was to define the purpose of teaching 'not in terms of an examination syllabus, but in terms of human development', which in turn implied emphasizing 'how much well-directed school activities can do for the children rather than stressing how little their limited abilities will enable them to achieve'. The curriculum itself would then be conceived 'not as a full bag of tricks from which an old one must be discarded before any new one is taken in', but as 'an array of tools from which the head can select those which in the circumstances in which he is working he deems appropriate to develop the desired qualities in the children concerned'.[40] Such ideas about the purposes of the curriculum for the 'ordinary child' suggested that it might be possible to define a curriculum that would be neither 'a watered-down version of what is given to the As and Bs, the latter itself deriving largely from the Grammar school's approach to acquiring knowledge',[41] nor a basic utilitarian approach involving no personal and social development or intellectual challenge.

## Gender and class

The issue of gender differences similarly raised difficult problems in terms of the purposes of the curriculum, and these were also strongly contested within the committee itself. Preconceptions about the proper role of women in society were highly influential in helping to shape the views of the committee about how to develop the SMS curriculum for girls. Catherine Avent, careers advisory officer for the London County Council youth employment service and a member of the Newsom committee, viewed some of her male colleagues on the committee as 'misogynists'. One, she recalls, was a 'total misogynist' who saw women as 'either caterers or secretaries – the idea of girls being engineers was anathema to him'.[42] A range of views were expressed about the nature of the SMS curriculum for 'average girls' that were based on gender as well as class based ideals.

Newsom himself had already articulated some firm views about the education of girls. In a book entitled *The Education of Girls*, published in 1948, he had insisted that secondary education for the majority of girls should be directed more clearly towards their future vocation in life, which he defined as being located in the home rather than in paid employment, in 'the business of home-making and the early nurture of children'. The secondary school curriculum of the less academic girls, he argued, should therefore emphasize 'home-making' and indeed 'how to grow into women and to re-learn the graces which so many have forgotten in the past thirty years'.[43]

Another member of the committee, Dr Kathleen Ollerenshaw, a Conservative member of Manchester City Council and a member of its education committee, also publicly announced her ideas on this topic. She was not as rigid on the 'home-making' ideal as Newsom had been, and emphasized that there was more to the education of girls than 'simply preparing them to be homemakers and workers'.[44] She accepted that the education of 'average' girls should not be the same as that of boys, although she suggested that it should 'look for all that is best in the education of boys, but with a different slant'.[45] Furthermore, she argued, women in particular required 'an education which stimulates their imaginations, develops their intellectual, artistic and practical talents, and leads them to greater awareness of the world around them and a lasting sense of service'.[46] There were clearly some unresolved tensions here as to the proper character and role of the SMS curriculum for girls, but the committee proceeded from the initial basis at least that for girls, much of the content in the ordinary subjects of the curriculum was 'vocational for them in their personal development and in their lives in their homes in the future'.[47]

The problems identified in relation to the SMS curriculum for girls were also based on an uncomfortable and often hostile image of the 'working-class girl'. Such girls, it was widely asserted, were generally rebellious, sexually promiscuous, and a danger to society. The National Association of Head Teachers (NAHT), in its evidence to the Newsom commission, argued that the majority of girls who left school as soon as possible had a 'strong desire to leave school'. These girls, it suggested, were motivated first by a desire for freedom, that is, 'to stay out late, to frequent dance halls, coffee bars, cinemas, etc.', second by a desire for money, 'to provide both the freedom and DRESS', and third because many 'unfortunately, have already entered the world of adult sex experience'. In these cases, according to the NAHT,

> Underlying this is a sense of needing to justify their place in society. It is a reject problem. Affection, approval, a sense of value is given by the attention of a boy-friend – hence the hot-pursuit. Underneath this is the conviction that the only real thing that the future holds for them is marriage.

Even more threatening, however, were girls with all of these problems who also lacked intelligence, had a greater sense of failure and rejection, and came from a 'generally poorer social background'. The NAHT argued, somewhat melodramatically, that

> From this group come the delinquent girls. Truancy is succeeded by dishonesty, immorality and the anti-social behaviour that ruins their lives. Such girls are able neither to help themselves, nor to be helped by their parents, and generally they are rejected by adult society. Girls in this category are rejected by the local Youth Centre, Organisation, Club, and even place of employment. They are, therefore, driven to their doom.

For these girls, it concluded, the SMS curriculum should involve a 'practical course' that would 'give these girls opportunities to be socially acceptable, and to behave socially in a way which, in any society, usually falls to the most able', while at the same time linking their work with 'their future hope – marriage'. On this scenario, the home, the family, the baby, and the growing children would be subjects for study, while mothercraft would become 'an essential subject if it is linked practically with real babies, nursery visits (one morning per week during the year) and other visits throughout the year'. Personal and household budgeting would take the place of arithmetic.[48]

Much of this approach was summed up more succinctly by the headmistress of Blenheim County Secondary School in Buswell, who noted that the aim of her SMS, an all-girls' school, was 'to make the clever girl cleverer and the less able girl nice'.[49] Its implications were stated somewhat more trenchantly in Richard Farley's treatise on 'secondary modern discipline', which suggested that girls tended on the whole to be 'more docile' and 'a little more civilised' than boys:

> Teaching a girls' class is often an uneventful affair; the girls write out notes, listen, look at the board and at the end of the lesson haven't much idea about the subject of the lesson. Their range of behaviour is narrower than that of a boys' class; one has less idiots and hooligans and less original thought.

However, he warned, 'when one has a really difficult girl, she can cause more trouble than half a dozen boys, and . . . this is a matter for a mature and experienced woman teacher and not a man'.[50] Interestingly, Farley's work was singled out as recommended reading at a meeting of the Central Advisory Council just after it began work on its inquiry into average and below average children in May 1961.[51]

These considerations tended to reinforce a prevailing preconception that 'craft' subjects like woodwork and handicraft were suitable for boys, while 'domestic subjects' were for girls. Such a notion was shared among SMS teachers, for example those involved in teaching housecraft. The stated policy of the Association of Teachers of Domestic Subjects (ATDS) was 'gradually to bring home to the girls all that is entailed in caring for and running a home so that the maximum amount of brightness, comfort, beauty and cleanliness may be obtained with the minimum expenditure of effort'. By the end of her school life, it continued, 'the girl should be cap-able of managing a home competently'.[52] Housecraft was championed as an 'integral part of the Secondary Modern schools round which all other subjects should revolve'.[53] It was viewed as being a subject that would educate in the same way as other subjects, cultivating the development of the mind, lucidity of thought, clarity of expression and the stimulation of creative impulses, while also encouraging 'special facilities' such as 'mind in co-ordination with hand, independent logical thought and planned action', together with greater 'social confidence'. At the same time, it was argued, housecraft would also satisfy the 'self respect' of girls by helping to foster qualities such as for example 'good diet and cooking, good looks and clothes, good surroundings so far as cleanliness and arrangement and design go, good use of leisure'.[54] So far as the Hotel and Catering Institute was concerned, however, such training gave only limited opportunities for girls after they left SMSs. Those who were obliged to seek employment at the age of 15, it noted, should be able to find it in 'Restaurants, Tea-shops, Hospitals, Schools Meals Kitchens or Industrial Canteens', and should also attend part-time classes at their nearest technical college.[55] It was anxious to see more courses developed for ex-SMS pupils because 'the Industry *does* urgently need Cooks and Chefs, Waiters and Waitresses'. However, such recruits would not generally be suitable for hotel bookkeeping or for the reception: 'We feel that the Grammar School type of girl is, generally speaking, the type required for Hotel Reception.' It conceded that some former SMS girls might prove equally suitable, but, it stressed, it was essential for such posts that 'the general educational standard should be good and that they should have, if possible, knowledge of at least one language other than English'.[56]

Such class and gender based overtones also permeated the discussions of the Newsom committee over subjects such as English for the 'ordinary' child. The English panel of HMIs advised the committee of its serious concerns about the current limitations of this subject in its application to pupils of average and less than average ability. The 'restrictions of home background' that affected many of these pupils seemed especially important in relation to English, because of the lack of what was described as 'spiritual energy' among 'subcultured groups', and also because of their poor command of language.[57] The recent research of Basil Bernstein of the University of London was cited to support the view that 'command of language is affected by social background and in turn affects educability, modes of communication and social relationships'. Therefore, it was argued,

> If the verbal equipment is lacking, these pupils simply cannot do justice to the ability which they do possess. The teacher who can help these children to achieve a greater command of language will be doing much for their development as human beings.

The difficulties of communicating the higher ideals of English such as 'creative expression' and the 'vision of greatness' to the 'weaker streams' was also emphasized. It was acknowledged that teachers should continue to attempt to communicate such ideals to the less able pupils, and not to 'think of the weaker boys and girls as living in a kind of nature reserve, debarred by lack of ability from the great things of our civilisation', since 'that way lies apartheid'. On the other hand, the HMI panel continued,

> Some teachers, including many who have never been trained for teaching English, give them a watered down version of what they remember from their own grammar school experiences. Much use is made of text books providing endless exercises in comprehension, composition and the like, but the sentences are seldom about anything really relevant to the pupil; after a surfeit of such books one begins to wonder whether 'the pen of my godfather's aunt', expelled long since from grammar school French, has not found final refuge here.

In these circumstances, it suggested, English might need to be presented in a less abstract way so as to be of greater 'potential importance' to the pupils.

The HMI panel also took pains to elaborate on the rival influences that were created by the pupils' backgrounds:

> His standards in speech, as in so much else, reflect those of his family. He has heard much about the outside world from older relatives already in jobs, as well as from the newspaper, the magazine, the cinema and the telly. The last appears particularly potent, if only because so many particularly of the less able pupils have imbibed so much of it.

Boys would be attracted by such things as pop records, clothes, cigarettes and motor cycles, while the girls would be mainly interested in 'dresses, shoes and make-up'. It was important, therefore, to try to relate to the particular background, experience and interests of such pupils in seeking to enhance their 'personal development' and 'social competence', especially through conversation and discussion. The major aim would be to go beyond a narrow focus on achieving literacy, and to attempt to communicate established cultural ideals, by seeking an approach to English that would be 'relevant and important to their needs as they see them'.[58] This outlook also proved to be attractive to the Newsom committee, which developed a longer list of possible topics to include in English for the ordinary child. For example, it was suggested, English could give advice of direct relevance for such pupils: 'Bread and butter use – how to apply for a job, read directions, write simple letters etc.' In particular, it was noted, ' "our" children are usually more interested in practical things than in abstractions; a successful teacher of English is more likely to succeed if he has one or two practical interests in common with them to provide topics for discussion'.[59]

Discussions about mathematics and science for the ordinary child reflected similar assumptions. The provision of mathematics and science for such pupils clearly differed in its amount from that in the grammar schools. From a survey of mathematics and science subjects in the SMSs, it was found that boys tended to have more time for mathematics and science than did girls, and that less time on the whole was given by both boys and girls to science and maths in C streams as opposed to A streams.[60] The nature of the mathematics and science that should be taught was also closely linked to the social purposes of the SMS curriculum. The secondary modern panel of HMIs pointed out that a 'more adult twist' could be given to the teaching of both mathematics and science, with the aim of dealing with matters of 'immediate concern' but also attempting to relate contemporary advances in scientific knowledge to broader moral issues.[61] Kathleen Ollerenshaw, whose specialist subject was mathematics, argued that the 'special needs' of girls should be given more attention, and that 'mathematics for girls' should also be emphasized 'in social studies, in biology, in art and architecture, in toy making and other crafts'.[62] She suggested that some mathematical work should be avoided for children of average and less than average ability, for example 'complicated division of fractions' and 'long columns of addition'. Instead, greater emphasis should be given to the kind of mathematics that would be of direct relevance in adult life, as she continued: 'Every young worker and adult should be able to add, subtract, multiply and do simple division of numbers and money, and handle simple fractions with complete accuracy given sufficient time.' Furthermore, what she called 'social arithmetic', dealing with gas and electricity accounts, rates and taxes, and 'how local and welfare services are paid for and their cost', should be included in the school curriculum of all pupils.[63]

The SMS curriculum for the 'ordinary child' was thus clearly marked off from that of the grammar school curriculum for the 'more able'. The social characteristics of the pupils involved were seen as being integral to the kind of curriculum best suited to them. A narrowly functional approach was discouraged, as was a 'watered down' version of the grammar school curriculum, as the Newsom committee tried to discern an alternative educational path for the SMS child. It is also interesting that ethnicity was not recognized explicitly as an important issue in this regard either in the evidence heard by the committee or in the committee's own work, despite the increasing immigration that was taking place during this period from other Commonwealth countries. By contrast, both gender and social class constituted key dimensions of curricular differentiation for the 'ordinary child'.

## The 'sub-GCE'

In the late 1950s, there was much resistance to the idea that SMS pupils should take external examinations, whether the GCE examinations that were taken in the grammar schools or another examination specifically designed for the 'ordinary' or 'average' child. Encouraging SMSs to take GCE examinations would mean imitating the curriculum of grammar schools even more than they did already, and would be inappropriate for many of their pupils. It might also devalue the qualification in the eyes of parents, universities and employers. Conversely, developing a new examination would risk associating the SMS with an inferior, second-class substitute for the GCE.

Sir David Eccles as minister of education was suspicious of the likely effects of a new examination, preferring as he did to expand the number of special courses in SMSs and thereby to encourage greater differences between schools.[64] He argued that a new examination of a lower standard than the GCE would confirm the differentiation of status between grammar schools and SMSs that was already apparent, and insisted that 'once the curriculum of a secondary modern school became geared to an external examination it would become classed as a second-rate grammar school'.[65] It might lead also to 'the "dilution" of the GCE', and to 'curbing and restricting the secondary modern school curriculum'.[66] Geoffrey Lloyd, later in the decade, had similar misgivings, and emphasized to John Lockwood, the chairman of the SSEC, that he was 'anxious not to encourage any developments that would, in the result, endanger the freedom of the Heads and their staffs to devise their own curriculum and teaching methods or impose on them a uniformity of aim or method'.[67] Despite this, the SSEC supported the idea, and so established its own sub-committee to be chaired by Robert Beloe, CEO for Surrey (himself educated at Winchester and Hertford College, Oxford), to explore the possibility. Beloe's committee duly proposed a new examination directed to the needs of 40 per cent of pupils, that is, a large middle group of pupils who were not academically suited to the GCE taken by the 'top' 20 per cent, but who might benefit from a record of their progress in school in a way that it was felt the 'bottom' 40 per cent would not. It was this proposal that was to eventuate in the Certificate of Secondary Education (CSE), which became established from 1965.[68] This provided a new means by which to differentiate between the 'able pupil' and the 'ordinary child'.

The issue of how the new examination should compare to the established GCE examination was acknowledged within the SSEC itself as a major problem for the future. It was agreed that if no clear relationship were established between the two examinations, 'borderline pupils' might be entered for both, or switched from one to the other. At the same time, it did not seem desirable that the new examination should become a 'pale imitation' of the Ordinary level GCE exam. Rather, it was hoped that the CSE examination would 'be accepted in its own right as being, at a given grade of pass, as good a predictor of success in continued education or training as a pass at Ordinary level of the GCE examination'.[69] This notion itself begged a number of questions, and in particular ignored the self-fulfilling character of alternative examination routes. Sir David Eccles, in his second term as minister of education in the early 1960s, was more realistic in this respect:

> I do not want a first eleven GCE, a second eleven Beloe and all the rest non-players. I find it doubtful whether the staff of say a comprehensive or a large secondary modern could cope fairly and adequately with three grades of children. I would think the bottom 60 per cent bound to suffer.[70]

The potential advantages and disadvantages of the new examination were soon apparent to local education officers. R.E. Hodd, CEO for Blackpool, recognized that it would need to relate to the distinctive kind of curriculum that was being developed for SMS pupils:

> I think we need to realise that the approach to many subjects for the kind of children who will be taking these examinations, needs to be through their concrete experience of the world about them. One of the most important needs of the secondary modern school is to make apparent to the pupil that what he is doing at school is relevant to living and livelihood, i.e. to become grown up (because this is precisely just what the early teenager wants to do).[71]

Such considerations were taken to mean that the new examination should be related more closely to local and regional differences, and that teachers should be more closely involved, than was the case with the GCE.

There remained, even so, a great deal of suspicion as to the implications of the new examination. Some, like J.M. Pullan in Bristol, objected to the increasing prominence of examinations which seemed to be 'rapidly taking a stranglehold on the whole educational system'.[72] Of more specific concern to the new proposal, J.K. Elliot, CEO in Manchester, warned D.A. Routh of the Ministry of Education that 'the term "sub-GCE" examination which you use' should not 'pass into general currency'.[73] Elliot continued:

> I can think of no term which would be more harmful in its implications. What is needed is not an inferior version, a second-best or pale imitation of the GCE but an examination which will not be afraid to strike out along new lines in seeking to meet the needs of a substantial group of pupils who deserve the best in their own field.[74]

Another CEO, Percy Lord in Lancashire, also made clear his opposition to the new development on the grounds that it would undermine the 'wide choice of examinations' which already existed, and would impose instead 'a specific examination of national character which will inevitably be the examination which almost every pupil in a Secondary Modern School will expect to take'.[75] In the end, he warned, it would 'inevitably' become 'to Secondary Modern Schools and (more important still) to the parents, what the GCE Ordinary level has become to Grammar Schools'.[76] To these critics, not only would the new examination create a new means of differentiation but also it would be inherently inferior to the GCE, and so would label the pupils who took it as second best.

These developments over the proposed new CSE examination placed Newsom's committee in some difficulty. In its early stages it had been expected that public examinations would not be an objective for the kinds of pupils that it was considering. The Beloe Report made it clear that the new examination would affect at least some of these pupils. At first, Newsom hoped that these effects could be minimized, and he suggested to his school curriculum sub-committee in October 1961 that 'If we said, for example, O.K., have it (the examination) but do not let it be a serious influence on "our" children, that might be something worth saying.'[77] It soon became evident that such advice would not be sufficient or even relevant. By May 1962, it was acknowledged that once the new examination had become established, 'local pressures would render it virtually impossible for an isolated school to have no part in examinations at all'.[78]

The development of this new examination was of great importance for provision for the 'ordinary child'. It meant that the earlier insistence of proponents of a distinctive 'working-class secondary education' on a curriculum unhindered by examination requirements had been overcome. It suggested that secondary schools should all be encouraged to develop examination courses for their pupils, and in this way further minimized the outward distinctions between different types of schools. At the same time, however, it served to reinforce differentiation between the grammar school curriculum and the SMS curriculum, on terms that were likely to reinforce status differences and divisions between academically able pupils and children of average and below average ability.

### 'An education that makes sense'

The final report of Newsom's committee avoided addressing what was the principal organizational issue facing secondary education, the respective merits of a bipartite or tripartite system as against comprehensive schooling. It did attempt to chart a way forward for a large group of pupils that it identified rather uncomfortably as 'our children', whatever form of organization might be developed for them. It also reflected fixed and pervasive assumptions about the future vocation of such pupils that had changed little if at all since the late nineteenth century.

Although it did not explicitly say so, Newsom's committee undoubtedly associated children of average and below average ability with those who were being educated in the SMSs. It was these that its members visited to inform the inquiry, despite the objections of one, Anne Godwin, who refused to accept that it was only children who were not 'the grammar school type' who should be defined as being average or below average in their ability.[79] By and large, too, the committee anticipated that children in its remit would eventually go on to take up the less rewarding positions in society. It was observed that teachers should guard against 'under-estimating the C and D stream pupil', and that there should be 'no "depressed class" within the school community', but even so, the pupils 'had at some time, preferably before they left school, to come to terms with their own limitations and capacities, and the school should help them to face this adjustment'.[80] The Newsom committee was concerned to explain the nature of these 'limitations and capacities', and to facilitate the necessary 'adjustment'.

Many of the witnesses revealed similar preconceptions in their evidence to the committee. The AEC, for example, noted that children of average and below average ability would tend in later life to be 'more governed than governing', although 'they will have the right in democracies to vote and because of their great number can considerably influence the society in which they live'.[81] The Association of Chief Education Officers assumed that such children 'prefer the immediate and tangible to what seems distant and abstract', and that they were 'most at home in a familiar environment'. It also had a clear notion of their social characteristics as distinct from those of their parents: 'They are very different from the children of earlier generations, having spent their lives in a world changed in almost every respect from the world that invented the elementary school (or even the senior school).' But despite all of these changes, at least one thing had apparently not changed, as the ACEO concluded without a hint of irony: 'Many of them grow up to do relatively routine jobs in society.'[82] The Institute of Personnel Management specified the kinds of post that would be most suitable in such cases: 'Unskilled and semiskilled factory jobs including some machine operating jobs; packaging; work in retail jobs; domestic duties; petrol pump attendants; agricultural labouring; laundry work; warehousing, etc, etc.'[83] Meanwhile, the National Association of Head Teachers emphasized the key priority in reconciling the new rights and privileges of such pupils with their ultimately circumscribed role in society. Since they were 'destined to become the "average" wage-earners and home-makers of the future', it opined, they 'must be given standards and values, a sense of responsibility to the community, tolerance and appreciation of others, and be trained in dependability and absolute honesty'.[84] These, then, were to be the essential goals of the education of the 'ordinary child'.

As the Newsom committee prepared to complete its report, some of its members attempted to challenge the direct correspondence that was being asserted between average and below average ability children and their future role in 'routine jobs', who would be 'more governed than governing'. David Winnard of the Trades Union Congress protested that the draft of the report 'implied that most of the pupils with whom it was concerned would take up manual work, whereas the proportion of manual workers in the population might in the future be substantially changed by technological developments'.[85] Furthermore, he added, 'the kind of vocational courses suggested, combined with a statement that most of the pupils were likely to be children of manual workers, might be misunderstood to imply that manual occupations would necessarily be occupied by manual workers' children'.[86] Footnotes and additions were incorporated in the draft to try to take account of this kind of intervention,[87] but overall the original assumptions of the architects of the report remained clear.

The Newsom Report was published in October 1963, six days before the Robbins Report on higher education, and its findings and significance were overshadowed in rather a symbolic fashion in the subsequent debate over the universities. It was concerned, as the members of the Newsom committee accepted, with 'half our future'.[88] It recommended that the school leaving age should be raised from 15 to 16 for all pupils entering the secondary schools from 1965 onwards, and that all full-time education up to the age of 16 should be based in schools. It recognized that many schools had what it called 'functional deficiencies' due to overcrowding or facilities, and that these needed to be overcome and that more research was needed on 'environmental and linguistic handicaps', and on teaching techniques for overcoming the learning difficulties created by these. It proposed an interdepartmental working party to be set up to deal with the general social problems, including education, that were encountered in 'slum areas'. It also emphasized the teaching of reading, writing and calculation, while noting that the value of the educational experience provided would be assessed 'in terms of its total impact on the pupils' skills, qualities and personal development, not by basic attainments alone'.[89] Several other recommendations were put forward to improve the accommodation and facilities that were provided for such pupils.

In many ways, however, the keynote of the Newsom Report was its attempt to articulate the nature of what it called 'an education that makes sense' for the pupils with which it was concerned. This education, it argued, should be practical, realistic and vocational, while also allowing opportunity for personal fulfilment. It would also encourage the pupils to become literate and to become able to perform simple calculations. Yet there would also be limits to what the schools could achieve. For example, it suggested, the degree to which such pupils could exercise 'mental ordering' was 'strictly limited' in some of the most important areas of modern knowledge, and so they would need to develop an awareness of such areas that lay within their own capacity:

> The abstract thinking of mathematics, and the concepts of the scientific method will be beyond their reach, but they can acquire a commonsense in figure handling and a reasoned application of scientific skills in particular conditions, such as the diagnosis of electrical faults or the correct installation of a hot-water system, which involve true selfconscious judgement and are thoroughly secondary in the sense in which we have used the word.[90]

It noted also that 'Many of our boys are going to work with their hands, whether in skilled or unskilled jobs.'[91] For this reason, it suggested, 'It would seem wholly sensible to plan courses for some of these boys centring round the use, perhaps the making, of tools; the handling and working of various types of materials; the operating and maintenance of machines.'[92] In the case of girls, marriage would constitute the 'most important vocational concern' for 'many, perhaps most of them', and although at the age of 14 or 15 this might be manifested mainly in terms of a 'preoccupation with personal appearance and boy friends', many were able to 'respond to work relating to the wider aspects of homemaking and family life and the care and upbringing of children'.[93]

The education of the 'ordinary child' conveyed in the Newsom Report was one that attempted to reconcile the contradictions of secondary education for all as they had been revealed over the previous 20 years especially through the failed experiment of the SMSs. It projected a way forward that would support the secondary education of a large group of pupils whose needs were not catered for in the grammar schools, nor in the grammar school curriculum. It did not depend on the device of separate schools for these pupils, as the SMSs that had developed for this purpose were now widely discredited. Instead, it looked to a distinctive SMS curriculum, and the examinations and assessment that would be associated with it, to maintain the needs and the limitations of such education in whatever kind of secondary school might be developed for the purpose. This task was to fall, at last, to the comprehensive schools.

# PART 3

## The legacy

For a majority of young people, education is of more variable benefit. The talents of many are not valued enough and not developed enough; and, once they start in work, the same is true in terms of training. In addition, an uncomfortably large minority of young people leaving school have trouble with literacy and numeracy and seem to have benefited all too little from their education.

(*Learning to Succeed*, 1993: 1)

# 9

# The comprehensive experience

After the election of a Labour government under Harold Wilson in 1964, there was a rapid shift in policy in favour of comprehensive schools. Circular 10/65, issued to LEAs the following year, requested them to submit plans for comprehensive education, although it did not require them to do so.[1] In the face of this new wave of reform, the SMSs could attract very few active supporters even among Conservatives, and most were soon reorganized or combined with other schools to become comprehensive schools. In terms of the outward organizational changes involved, this amounted to a massive and apparently unassailable victory for a fresh approach that emphasized equality of opportunity for all secondary school pupils, whatever their abilities and aptitudes. At the same time, there remained a strong tendency to differentiate between pupils in terms of their social backgrounds, and in particular a continuing legacy of the SMSs and of the distinctive tradition of working-class secondary education from which they derived.

## 'Save the secondary modern schools'?

The spread of the comprehensive schools was hailed by their supporters as a 'great experiment',[2] just as the SMSs had been envisaged only 20 years before. By contrast, the SMSs appeared to be completely discredited, and were widely rejected as an experiment that had patently failed to achieve the desired results. For Conservative opponents of comprehensive schools, the SMSs became a standing embarrassment that they usually preferred to gloss over while emphasizing the need to preserve the grammar schools. Some Conservatives were willing to give their support to the further development of comprehensive schools, but the principles and the practices involved remained strongly contested in many quarters.[3]

These tensions were evident in debates on secondary education that took place in the House of Commons during the months that followed Labour's narrow election victory. In November 1964, a Conservative motion was debated that referred only to the grammar schools and made no mention at all of the SMSs:

> That this House, while mindful of the need to ensure that the abilities and aptitudes of every child are developed to the fullest extent, and while recognising the importance of flexibility and variety in the organisation of secondary education including, in cases where appropriate, on educational grounds the comprehensive principle, would none-the-less deplore the wholesale abolition, whether by closure or radical alteration, of direct grant and maintained grammar schools.[4]

Alan Hopkins, Conservative MP for Bristol North West speaking on behalf of this motion, argued in favour of 'coexistence' between comprehensive schools, grammar schools and SMSs,[5] and he suggested that the spread of comprehensive schools in Bristol would harm the 'existing very good secondary modern schools'.[6]

Even so, the secretary of state for education and science, Michael Stewart (educated at Christ's Hospital and St John's College, Oxford), in his reply to the debate was able to exploit the evident lack of support for the SMSs, and also the incoherence that had developed since the 1950s in their general rationale. As Stewart wryly observed, the emphasis of the Conservative argument had been 'Save the grammar schools', but nobody had come forward to say 'Save the secondary modern schools'. Furthermore, he added, the SMS had failed to establish parity of esteem for itself, and in imitating the grammar schools was now left without a clear purpose: 'If the object of the policy is to narrow to a minimum the difference between secondary modern and grammar school, why go to the trouble of separating children and deciding which should go to which school in the first place?'[7] By contrast, Stewart insisted, comprehensive schools would provide 'a range of courses suited to the needs of all normal children', so that they could develop on equal terms. Indeed, he asserted,

> The essence of a comprehensive system is that one can say to every parent, 'We do not know what your child will prove himself to be fit for as time goes on', but no child will be put in a position of being sent to a school which is accepted from the start as not possessing as good facilities as some other schools for advanced academic education.[8]

This was an optimistic claim that would be thoroughly tested in the years that followed.

Battle was rejoined in a further debate in January 1965 on the 'comprehensive system and grammar schools'. This time it was Quintin Hogg, a senior figure and a former minister of education, himself educated at Eton and Christ Church Oxford, who put the Conservative case,

> That this House, conscious of the need to raise educational standards at all levels, endorses the recommendation of the Newsom Report that it would be premature to attempt a reasoned judgment of comprehensive and other types of secondary education, urges Her Majesty's Government to discourage local education authorities from adopting schemes of reorganisation at the expense of grammar schools and other existing schools of proved efficiency and value, and would deplore any proposal to impose a comprehensive system upon local authorities.[9]

Again, Hogg proved more comfortable discussing grammar schools than he was on the topic of SMSs, but he was willing to speak in defence of these latter schools. It was true, he acknowledged, that 'no one defends a secondary modern school which is put in old buildings, in an old all-age school', nor an SMS that did not make O level courses widely available. On the other hand,

> I can assure hon. Members opposite that if they would go to study what is now being done in good secondary modern schools, they would not find a lot of pupils biting their nails in frustration because they had failed their 11-plus. The pleasant noise of banging metal and sawing wood would greet their ears and a smell of cooking with rather expensive cooking equipment would come out of the front door to greet them. They would find that these boys and girls were getting an education tailor-made to their desires, their bents and their requirements. They would find that the best of them were getting their O levels with the equivalent degree of skill and ability of those who had been selected for grammar school education.[10]

In fact, he concluded, the Labour Party had not done a good service to education or to the children of the country 'by attacking that form of school, or seeking to denigrate it'.[11]

As in the earlier debate, Stewart responded by emphasizing the contradictions of the SMSs. His amendment to Hogg's motion also recognized the need to 'raise educational standards at all levels', but went on to add that, 'regretting that the realisation of this objective is impeded by the separation of children into different types of secondary schools', it noted with approval

> the efforts of local authorities to reorganise secondary education on comprehensive lines which will preserve all that is valuable in grammar school education for those children who now receive it and make it available to more children; recognises that the method and timing of such re-organisation should vary to meet local needs; and believes that the time is now ripe for a declaration of national policy.[12]

He poured scorn on Hogg's ideal of the SMSs, alleging that they were on his account 'full of hewers of wood and bangers of metal'. Stewart recognized that 'it is proper to provide a more manual content to education for some people than for others', which was itself a significant admission, but he contended that he was 'a little suspicious' when a SMS was described 'at first blush, as if this was its main feature'. At the same time, as in the previous debate, Stewart also highlighted the confusion underlying the development of examinations in the SMSs as he continued,

> we are bound to ask ourselves: what is the point of going through this 11-plus business in order to put the children into different schools, only to say, afterwards, 'We will put it right by making the two kinds of school as like each other as possible'?[13]

This proved to be Stewart's final direct contribution to the debate as he was transferred to the Foreign Office the following day, leaving the incoming minister, Anthony Crosland, with the task of completing comprehensive reorganization.

Subsequently there were relatively few die-hards who chose to defend the record of the SMSs in public. One such was Margaret Thatcher, who replaced the more conciliatory Edward Boyle as the Conservative spokesperson on education and science in 1969. Thatcher recalls in her memoirs that soon after her appointment she was invited to speak as a guest of education correspondents at a lunch at the Cumberland Hotel in London, and that she had chosen this occasion to support the work of the SMSs. As she explained,

> Those children who were not able to shine academically could in fact acquire responsibilities and respect at a separate secondary modern school, which they would never have done if in direct and continual competition and contact with the more academically gifted. I was perfectly prepared to see the 11-Plus replaced or modified by testing later in a child's career if that was what people wanted. I knew that it was quite possible for late developers at a secondary modern to be moved to the local grammar school so that their abilities could be properly stretched. I was sure that there were too many secondary modern schools which were providing a second-rate education – but this was something which should be remedied by bringing their standards up, rather than grammar school standards down.

To her surprise, Thatcher found herself isolated in her argument:

> Only two of those present at the Cumberland Hotel lunch seemed to agree. Otherwise I was met by a mixture of hostility and blank incomprehension. It was not just that they thought me wrong: they could not imagine that I could seriously believe such things.[14]

Although she had already been advised by some Conservative sympathizers such as Kathleen Ollerenshaw of Manchester, who had served on the Newsom committee, that the SMSs were a 'total disaster',[15] Thatcher inclined towards a different view: 'It opened my eyes to the dominance of socialist thinking among those whose task it was to provide the public with information about education.'[16]

By the end of the decade, comprehensive reorganization was well under way, with over 1300 comprehensive schools already in existence including nearly a third of secondary school age pupils, and many more being planned for the future.[17] Even though the Conservative Party was returned to office in 1970, with Margaret Thatcher as secretary of state for education and science, the process could not be reversed, and Thatcher found herself in the uncomfortable position of approving a further major spread of comprehensive schools over the following four years. The secondary modern schools could not be saved, while the comprehensive schools had triumphed in the most emphatic way.

## Poor relations

Despite the rapid movement towards comprehensive schools, strong misgivings about the new policy were expressed among officials at the new Department of Education and Science (DES). In some cases, these doubts indicated important limitations in the potential of comprehensive schools to achieve their hopes that were to become clearly apparent in later years. One official, the senior inspector J.J. Withrington, observed that some of the most acute dilemmas that faced secondary education would become increasingly difficult whatever form of organization was adopted, and that these problems would especially affect pupils of average and below average ability in urban schools. He noted that whereas 'abler pupils' were offered some choice of curriculum at age 14, the 'less able' often received 'what is called a general course – the mixture as before plus some element of preparation for leaving'.[18] The result, he acknowledged, was 'often that the last two or three years of the 15-year-old leaver's course tend to have an air of "Good-bye to education" about them'.

Moreover, according to Withrington, the position of what he called 'slum schools with multiple problems' was worsening rather than improving, particularly under the new pressures that he felt were being created through Commonwealth immigration in large urban centres:

> Just when the Newsom report has played down the stories of 'jungle schools', we could be entering a period when the nightmare could become a reality in a number of large towns. The most difficult cases are those where slum schools have also many nationalities represented among the pupils. Difficulties will increase if only because the majority

of immigrant children who have been in the primary schools are coming into the secondary schools in increasing numbers. To the natural
educational handicaps are added those of incomplete assimilation to
our society and a growing awareness on the part of the pupils that life
will not be easy for them when they leave.

To meet these difficulties, Withrington proposed a number of ways of
helping such 'immigrant children' to become more fully assimilated into
society, including 'more definite teaching' about 'the fundamentals of our
social and political order', and a special emphasis on 'some vocational skill or
knowledge' in order for them to be able to 'face the prospect of employment
with some confidence'. Above all, Withrington added, 'the teachers in these
schools are facing an almost superhuman task', since in addition to their
'grave problems of curriculum and method' they needed also to 'act as part-
time welfare workers as well'.[19] The Newsom Report had recognized many
of these problems, although it had failed to note the educational implications
of Commonwealth immigration. These implications were now becoming
increasingly evident, for example in a confidential socio-educational survey
conducted by the London County Council in north and east London in
1964, which raised fears that 'the size of the problem was most disturbing,
and that it was slowly but unmistakably becoming graver as the difficulties of recruiting staff increased'.[20] In these circumstances, the change from
SMSs to comprehensives could be regarded as somewhat superficial in
nature, virtually irrelevant to the scale of the challenge confronting the
schools, which continued to demand specific approaches to the needs of
their mass clientele.

The plans of the new Labour government were also received with some
scepticism among officials at the DES. One took pains to outline likely
objections to the proposed spread of comprehensive schools. In particular,
it was observed, comprehensive schools would be in the main 'neighbourhood schools', and would therefore be different in 'middle class areas' from
those in 'poor socially under-privileged areas'.[21] Thus, 'The schools in the
better areas will have a higher proportion of children who have benefitted
from being with better-educated parents who take more interest in their
development.' This would lead in turn to 'more social segregation than exists
now', especially as the more able children from the poorer areas would be
given very little opportunity to go to schools outside their own neighbourhood. As a result, this official concluded, 'It can be argued that the separatist
system gives the best opportunity to the able child from a poor home.' At
the same time, it was pointed out, separate grammar and modern schools
might be able to give a better education to all children because they were
attuned to different needs and aptitudes. On the one hand,

> The academic child benefits by being in a school which concentrates on
> intellectual achievement, which sets high standards of work and attainment

and in which the efforts of highly specialist academic teachers are devoted entirely to the kind of pupils they are best suited to deal with.

On the other,

> In the modern schools the children of middling ability are not discouraged by the presence of those of first class ability. They have a chance to become leaders and often blossom into success in various directions which they might never do in a school which included the most able. Similarly in modern schools, which can be much smaller than comprehensive schools the least able and the most difficult children – those with very poor home backgrounds – can have the benefit of direct personal supervision by teachers in a community which does not overwhelm them by its size.[22]

These comments, doubtless intended to be helpful, seemed to ignore the record of the SMSs over the previous two decades. They are significant even so in demonstrating the reservations that surrounded the new direction to which the government was committed.

Some of the doubts expressed at this time were not clearly or fully resolved, and indeed were acknowledged to be limitations in the new policy. This was especially the case in relation to the prospect of greater social differentiation between schools as they became identified with their own 'neighbourhoods'. During the preparation of the circular to LEAs to encourage comprehensive reorganization, this problem was repeatedly emphasized both within the DES and by the educational interest groups that were consulted. A draft of the circular attempted to explain the nature of the 'school community' that comprehensives would comprise, and also the nature of their relationship with their local neighbourhoods. In its early form, paragraph 40 of the circular read as follows:

> A comprehensive school aims at establishing a school community in which pupils over the whole normal ability range and with differing interests and backgrounds can be encouraged to mix with each other, gaining stimulus from the contacts and learning tolerance and understanding in the process. Particular comprehensive schools will reflect the characteristics of the neighbourhood in which they are situated. But schools in some areas will lack the stimulus and sparkle which other schools enjoy, because their community is less varied and fewer of the pupils come from home backgrounds which encourage educational interests. There is clearly a danger that such schools may come to be considered as 'poor relations'; and this can be cumulative in its effect. Great care needs to be taken, therefore, in determining catchment areas; it may be possible to link two different districts in a two-tier system, in which all pupils from both areas go to the same junior and senior comprehensive schools.[23]

This was a highly significant paragraph as it evoked both the potential and the limitations of the comprehensive schools in establishing a broad and fully inclusive social composition. The remark about some schools becoming 'poor relations', with the cumulative effects of such an impression, was an especially sharp and pertinent warning, which was actually omitted from the final version of Circular 10/65 as it was published in July 1965. During this stage of drafting and consultation, however, it attracted critical observations from a number of sources.

An early comment on this paragraph from an official within the DES highlighted the contradictions of the 'neighbourhood school'. It was observed that since children of all ranges of ability would normally have to go to the school that served their neighbourhoods, and since there would be substantial differences between schools according to the nature of their neighbourhoods, there would inevitably arise significant inequalities in educational opportunities between schools in different areas: 'Thus schools in a predominantly working-class neighbourhood will be less likely to provide good educational opportunities because of the attitude to school and learning of the generality of the pupils there than schools in a middle-class neighbourhood.'[24] These differences would probably be heightened by the greater difficulty in attracting 'good staff' to the schools in the 'less attractive areas'. The pupils who would suffer most as a result of this would be 'the able children in these "poor" neighbourhoods who, under the selective system, have been and still are sent to grammar schools'. Having posed the problem, this official observed that 'No way out of this dilemma suggests itself.' All likely expedients would meet local opposition or would be superficial in nature. Therefore, 'One is forced to the conclusion that there is no escape from the dilemma and that a comprehensive school pattern must involve some loss of educational opportunity for bright children in poor neighbourhoods.' Such a 'loss' would need to be 'entered as one of the items on the "loss" side in the profit and loss account in going comprehensive', the official concluded. However, it was noted, 'Many people regard it as a particularly serious one because it detracts from the main purpose of the policy, viz., counteracting the educational disadvantages arising from a poor social background.' It was this background that explained the 'rather feeble admonitions' in paragraph 40 of the draft circular.[25]

These were highly damaging comments as they made clear that comprehensive schools would in practice do little to reduce the social segregation that existed between schools in different areas, and might in some ways reinforce it further. There would be some schools in mainly working-class urban areas that would be working-class secondary schools, while others in mainly middle-class areas would be middle class in nature. Several educational interest groups also pointed out this issue during the consultation process. The National Association of Schoolmasters (NAS), for example, stressed the 'possible dangers' of 'neighbourhood comprehensive schools in poor and less-educated areas', which would be 'unlikely to include many children who wished to stay on beyond the age of compulsory schooling and would be less effective as a result'. This would lead, the NAS added, to 'particular disadvantages for their small proportion of more able children'.[26] Both the County Councils Association (CCA) and the Association of Municipal Corporations (AMC) also pointed out related problems. According to the CCA, the draft paragraph 'dismisses too lightly the problems of socially distinctive districts and catchment area problems',[27] while the AMC warned that 'artificial catchment areas' would do little to offset differentiation between schools and might actually undermine the development of a 'cohesive community' within them.[28] The Headmasters' Association predicted what it considered to be the likely result when it argued that the proposed safeguards of the draft circular would prove to be 'no permanent solution' and might 'even accentuate class distinctions which present schools blur':

> The truth is that parents who can afford to do so may seek accommodation in what they consider to be favoured areas; the aim of the linking will thereby be frustrated, and only house agents will have cause for joy.[29]

These were major criticisms, and they went unresolved. The DES official who analysed the results of the consultation was obliged to admit that it was 'not feasible to say more about these problems in the Circular'. Indeed, he conceded, 'Some will be fundamentally insoluble. In other cases piecemeal solutions will be possible; but these are essentially difficulties to be tackled on the ground.'[30] Inspectors were also aware of 'the problems that were likely to arise over catchment areas, staffing, the position of the voluntary schools, assessment in the primary schools and other related questions', and they were invited to

> urge upon their Authorities the early necessity for full and frank explanations to their local population about the nature of these schools, especially as regards the different courses they would contain, otherwise the Authorities were likely to create difficulties for themselves in a few years' time.[31]

It was on this basis that Circular 10/65 was published and distributed to LEAs in July 1965,[32] with the DES and major educational interest groups privately aware that comprehensive schools would embody social differentiation between schools. The secretary of state for education and science, Michael Stewart, had told the House of Commons in the education debate of January 1965 that 'no child will be put in a position of being sent to a school which is accepted from the start as not possessing as good facilities as some other schools for advanced academic education'. The promise was belied by the reality. Working-class secondary education, unrecognized in the ideals of the comprehensive schools, would live on in the secondary schools of urban working-class districts.


## Social relations in the comprehensive schools

As with social differentiation between schools, social differentiation within the schools also persisted in spite of the shift towards comprehensive education. A great deal of evidence on the processes of differentiation inside the schools was amassed over the following 20 years to demonstrate that they were similar in nature to those that had been evident within the SMSs and the grammar schools before them. The research of David Hargreaves in the 1960s revealed that the social system of SMSs, exemplified in 'Lumley Secondary Modern School for Boys', involved powerful informal processes of social differentiation among pupils that were strengthened further by streaming. Hargreaves also observed that although his research had been conducted at an SMS, the 'social processes' at work 'may be independent of, or little affected by, comprehensive reorganization'.[33] Colin Lacey's study of 'Hightown Grammar School' sought to explain the disappointing performance of working-class boys in grammar schools. He also emphasized that his study might help address the 'problem of the working-class pupil within the comprehensive system', in that the processes at work were 'in part the result of pressures emanating from society', and that the same pressures would affect the comprehensive schools.[34] Later research on the social relations within an SMS, 'Lowfield Secondary School', made a very similar point as its author observed that the status of the school 'was irrelevant to my concerns, its basic structures and processes being common among secondary schools generally'.[35] This view was borne out with respect to the social relations that operated in the comprehensive schools.

In schools that were reorganized from being SMSs to become comprehensives, the underlying continuities were often readily apparent, especially as the buildings, facilities, teachers and pupils were the same as before. They also retained their former reputation in the local community, and their previous status was often an encumbrance. Archway School in north London, for example, was reorganized from being an SMS for girls and an SMS for boys in two separate sites, to become a mixed comprehensive school. Even so, according to its headteacher, Frederick Fogg, 'Our worst problem is that the old secondary modern tag still sticks. As a comprehensive school, we don't rate as highly with parents as the new comprehensives or the ones that were originally grammar schools.'[36] Especially in districts where grammar schools were retained, such comprehensive schools were often simply the old SMS in a new guise. As recent research has made clear, the nature of the comprehensive school depended at least in part on whether it was a former grammar school or a former SMS, whether it was in an LEA with a largely manual or non-manual population, and whether it offered sixth form courses. Thus, according to Kerckhoff and his colleagues, 'Even after they were transferred into comprehensives, former grammar schools and former secondary schools were more often attended by students from non-manual backgrounds, and they were more likely to offer sixth-form courses.'[37] The change to comprehensives therefore embodied significant continuities of some features of the selective system.

Curriculum and assessment patterns were a key area in which continuity was a striking feature. The spread of external examinations that had already been evident in the 1950s and 1960s ensured that comprehensive schools generally adopted an established structure which strongly influenced their internal relationships and attitudes. The GCE O and A level examinations that had been associated with the grammar schools were assimilated within the comprehensive schools for the most 'able' pupils, while the more recently created CSE examinations were designed for the less able pupils. These separate examinations served distinct courses that echoed the old grammar–secondary modern divide. As Goodson observes,

> As in the tripartite system, so in the comprehensive system, academic subjects for able pupils are accorded the highest status and resources. The triple alliance between academic subjects, academic examinations and able pupils ensures that comprehensive schools provide similar patterns of success and failure to previous school systems.[38]

The provision of distinct courses for pupils of 'average' and 'below average' ability, as stipulated in the Newsom Report of 1963, reinforced these trends. The 'Newsom courses' were generally given lower esteem and poorer resources than were the examination oriented courses of the 'more able' pupils. Burgess's research in 'Bishop McGregor School', a coeducational, Roman Catholic comprehensive, found that, as he observed, 'Being a Newsom pupil carried a social stigma which was, in part, transferred to their courses and their teachers.'[39] Separate sets of expectations were built up that led to the development of an alternative form of schooling within the school, in such a way that 'the label "comprehensive" merely covered a number of diverse activities that took place on one site'.[40] Courses that became associated with low achievers, such as social studies, were largely ignored and often went into decline.[41] As Ball pointed out, the 'deep structures' of the comprehensive school system continued to reflect the basic assumptions of the tripartite system, so that practical and vocational subjects and CSE courses were 'reserved for those pupils who have failed in the traditional curriculum'.[42] The teachers involved were no less vulnerable, and tended to be marginalized and excluded from promotion and positions of power within the school.[43]

The ultimate effect, documented in Ball's study of a coeducational comprehensive school, 'Beachside Comprehensive', was a persistent pattern of low achievement on the part of working-class pupils, especially in the majority of schools where streaming of forms remained a potent factor. Ball found that selection on the basis of streaming continued to underlie social class differentials in educational opportunity.[44] The 'polarized' and 'unstable' social structure that resulted from this contrasted markedly with the optimistic claims that had been put forward by many of the earlier advocates of comprehensive schooling. Michael Stewart's aspirations for 'a range of courses suited to the needs of all normal children' did not in practice lead to the realization of the aim articulated in Circular 10/65, for 'a school community in which pupils over the whole ability range and with different interests and backgrounds can be encouraged to mix with each other'.

Jackson and Marsden, in their seminal study published in the 1960s entitled *Education and the Working Class*, concluded that continuity had triumphed over change: 'Comprehensive schools don't abolish grammar schools – they enclose them.'[45] They might equally have added that the comprehensive schools, although they had succeeded in discrediting and supplanting the secondary modern schools, did so not by abolishing them but by enclosing them also. The grammar school and the SMS were yoked together under a single label, but the resilient traditions of differentiation remained as active as ever, with the potential of renewing themselves in fresh and virulent forms.

# 10

## Choice and diversity

Under the Conservative governments of the 1980s and 1990s, led first by Margaret Thatcher and then by John Major, the issue of social differentiation that had been largely concealed by the spread of comprehensive schools again became starkly evident. In the pursuit of 'choice and diversity' as defined in the major White Paper published in 1992, differences both between schools and within schools were strongly emphasized. Differentiation between schools revived disputes that were reminiscent of those of the 1950s over the social divisions between grammar schools and secondary modern schools. Curriculum initiatives designed for particular groups of pupils also tended to promote the social distinctions inside the comprehensive schools that had already been apparent.

### A 'different educational world'

Some of the features that had symbolized most graphically the causes and effects of social differentiation in secondary education were less visible during this period than they had been hitherto. The record of the SMSs and the 11-plus examination was completely discredited. Non-selective comprehensive schools had become the main institutional form of secondary education in England and Wales, with only about 200 schools still officially designated as secondary moderns by the end of the 1980s. The GCE and CSE were abolished as separate examinations, to be replaced in 1985 by a single examination, the General Certificate of Secondary Education (GCSE). A National Curriculum was introduced under the Education Reform Act (1988) to provide a common curriculum framework for all children in state schools from the age of 5 to 16, supported by attainment targets to be examined at the ages of 7, 11, 14 and 16.

At the same time, schools were encouraged to improve through the more efficient use of their own resources, which it was argued could be a more important factor in determining success than the social conditions of the school or the background of its pupils. Many schools, including some former SMSs, demonstrated that it was possible for them to cater well for a wide range of pupils and to gain significant improvement in examination results despite the continuing problems posed by the school buildings and the local environment.[1] The Anglo-European School in Ingatestone, Essex, which had been due for closure as an SMS in 1973, was credited as the best comprehensive school in England and Wales in a survey in 1995.[2] Large urban comprehensives with a a diverse social and ethnic population often achieved success.[3] Different schools with similar circumstances and student intakes were shown in some cases to differ markedly in their examination performance.[4] Such findings seemed to undermine the straightforward correlation between social class and secondary education that had been so powerful throughout the twentieth century.

In spite of these changes, on the other hand, there were many underlying tensions that remained as acute as ever. The Conservative government was increasingly dissatisfied with the overall performance of the comprehensive schools, and actively searched for alternatives that would encourage greater specialization and selection. Kenneth Baker, secretary of state for education and science from 1986 to 1989 and responsible for the Education Reform Act (1988), was especially critical of the comprehensive schools. His insistence on radical reform of the education system was based largely on his view that it had 'lost its way in the 1960s', when the comprehensive schools had replaced the tripartite system: 'I had been amazed that Britain had decided to abandon the structure of its education system in this way, and as each year passed it became clearer that the high hopes of the comprehensive movement had not been fulfilled.'[5] He was therefore determined to 'modernize' the curriculum and the structure of secondary education in order to meet what he saw as the 'needs of twenty-first-century Britain'.[6]

The Technical and Vocational Education Initiative (TVEI) of the 1980s was an early example of the Conservatives' desire to instil greater diversity into the curriculum within the secondary schools. The potential attraction of the initiative for the large number of pupils who continued to be unsuccessful in the academic curriculum was emphasized. David Young, chairman of the Manpower Services Commission which was directly responsible for the scheme, suggested that it would be especially suited to the 'fifteen to eighty-five percentiles of the ability range'.[7] Sir Keith Joseph, secretary of state for education and science, argued that it would help to address the problems of an education system in which 'there really is inadequate provision for a very substantial minority'.[8] However, the initiative attracted strong criticism from educational groups on the basis that it would encourage the reconstruction of tripartite divisions in the comprehensive schools

themselves, with 'worker-pupils' being assigned to a technical and vocational curriculum.[9] As the TVEI became established in the schools, these
initial anxieties began to subside until a fresh initative sought to create a
new class of secondary schools, city technology colleges (CTCs). The CTCs,
announced by Kenneth Baker in 1986, would be new secondary schools
that were outside the influence of LEAs, designed specifically to offer a
'new choice of school' with a strong technological element in the curriculum.[10] The impact of the CTCs proved to be limited especially because of
difficulties of funding and the logistics of founding a new type of secondary school. More important was the overall thrust of government policy
that they came to symbolize, towards a greater emphasis on 'choice' and
'competition' between a diverse range of schools.

The White Paper *Choice and Diversity*, produced soon after the Conservatives' fourth successive general election victory in 1992, was a clear
expression of such aspirations. It envisaged the spread of grant-maintained
schools, self-governing but funded directly by a central agency, to promote
what it saw as the key themes of quality, diversity, parental choice, greater
autonomy for schools, and greater accountability. It argued that through such
means, it would become more possible for parents to choose the school 'best
suited to the particular interests and aptitude of their children'.[11] At the same
time, it was conscious of the parallels that might be drawn with the selective
system and the different types of schools of the 1940s and 1950s, and so
strove to distance the new scenario from this familiar spectre. It did so by
insisting that all schools would enjoy parity of esteem, especially because the
National Curriculum would be taught in all (state) schools. Thus, it declared,
'The Government is committed to parity of esteem between academic, technological and creative skills, with all children – whatever their aptitude and
in whatever type of school – being taught the National Curriculum to the
same high standard.' This would ensure that 'there are no tiers of schools
within the maintained system but rather parity of esteem between different
schools, in order to offer parents a wealth of choice'. By contrast, it argued,
the grammar schools and SMSs of the 1950s had inhabited a 'different
educational world'.[12]

The government's dependence on the idea of parity of esteem was itself
an indication that the educational world had not completely changed. The
idea of parity of esteem between different types of secondary schools, which
had been so influential in the 1940s, had been completely discredited as a
result of the failure of the SMSs, but returned to favour in the 1990s.[13]
This was also evident in a major review of the National Curriculum and its
assessment, which proposed reducing the amount of prescription in the
National Curriculum and increasing the scope for teachers' 'professional
judgement'. A 'margin' for the school to use at its own discretion, it
suggested, would improve the provision of education by creating 'scope for
the school to draw upon particular strengths in its teaching staff; to take

advantage of learning opportunities provided by the local environment; and to respond to the needs and enthusiasms of particular children'.[14] For students over 16 years of age, in particular, it recommended the development of 'three broad educational pathways', the 'craft' or 'occupational', the 'vocational', and the 'academic'.[15] However, it asserted, 'The Government is right to state that the alternative pathways must be of equal quality, leading to parity of esteem.'[16]

## Good enough for your child?

As has so often been the case over the past century, the practice contrasted with the theory. Parity of esteem was not achieved, either between different kinds of schools or between different types of curriculum. Instead, there were growing signs of inequality between the two distinct nations that had long been identified in the secondary education of England and Wales: on the one hand, the minority of academically able children whose interests were generally well served, and on the other, the majority of 'ordinary' or 'average' children who consistently underachieved. This basic disparity was clearly expressed in an independent report published in 1993 under the title *Learning to Succeed*. Produced by a National Commission on Education that had been established by the Paul Hamlyn Foundation, this report emphasized the continuing gulf between the academically able and the rest in secondary schools. For a 'minority of academically able young people', it noted, there was 'a good, if narrow, education and, for them, provision is well suited and well run'.[17] In international terms, 'those who are *academically* the most able fare well in the United Kingdom today (as they have in the past)'. A high proportion of young people became graduates compared to other nations, especially within Europe, and this proportion was rapidly increasing.

However, it pointed out, prospects were less attractive for a majority of pupils:

> For a majority of young people, education is of more variable benefit. The talents of many are not valued enough and not developed enough; and, once they start work, the same is true in terms of training. In addition, an uncomfortably large minority of young people leaving school have trouble with literacy and numeracy and seem to have benefitted all too little from their education.[18]

Overall, it claimed, the 'most serious shortcoming' of education was 'its failure to enable not just a minority but a large majority of young people to obtain as much from their education as they are capable of achieving'.[19] Comparable school qualifications were far lower on average in England at the ages of 16 and 18 plus than in Germany, France and Japan, and far fewer gained vocational qualifications. These tendencies were exacerbated, according to the report, by continuing differences between schools, and in particular the 'gulf in outcomes between our best schools and our worst', which was 'big, much bigger than in most countries'.[20] In secondary schools, it added, 'the design of the curriculum has been dominated by the needs of the minority who are being prepared for further study at an intensive academic level'.[21] Independent fee-paying schools continued to provide a higher level of resources and facilities for a small proportion of pupils, while many state schools especially in 'deprived areas' had the 'dice' loaded against them so that 'a cycle of failure may set in which is self-reinforcing; abler pupils and more active parents seek places elsewhere, resources decline as funds follow pupils away and good staff are increasingly hard to recruit'.[22] Large numbers of young people therefore left school as soon as they could, often without qualifications, and they were likely to become unemployed especially because of the large rise in structural unemployment that had taken place since the 1970s.

The trends identified in this report continued and even intensified in the following years. League tables of examination results introduced by the Conservative government demonstrated a widening gap between those pupils who performed best in GCSEs and those who performed worst. In 1995, the proportion that attained five A–C grades rose from 41.1 per cent two years before to 43.5 per cent, but the percentage that failed to obtain any passes at all rose from 7 per cent to 8.1 per cent over the same period. Critics pointed to a 'twelvefold gap between the top and bottom 20 per cent of GCSE results', and to a further lengthening of the 'long tail of underperformance'.[23] In 1996, this trend was maintained.[24] At the same time, it was widely recognized that a lack of funding was worsening provision in many state schools, as class sizes grew, school buildings fell into disrepair, and teaching posts were lost. Gillian Shephard, the secretary of state for education and employment, acknowledged in a confidential memorandum to the Cabinet that was leaked to the media that 'There is a perception that schools are under-funded and peace in the classroom is threatened.'[25] The annual report of the chief inspector of schools found that one in five secondary schools, 800 in all, suffered from poor accommodation, while 1000 secondary schools had an insufficient number of books.[26] Other surveys revealed widespread deterioration in school facilities and inadequate resources of a kind that had been familiar features in the SMSs of the 1950s.[27]

It was in this context that the SMSs returned to the centre of educational and political debate. Many comprehensive schools appeared to be simply SMSs in a new guise. A hierarchy of schools had developed in many local areas in which the comprehensive schools were left with few academically able children. Sir Peter Newsam, the former education officer of the Inner London Education Authority, pointed out that 'secondary education in inner

London is not, as a system, "comprehensive" and never has been; it is both diverse and highly selective'.[28] According to Newsam, a large number of secondary schools in inner London were effectively secondary modern schools so far as their pupil intake was concerned, despite their 'comprehensive' labels. Professor Peter Mortimore, director of the University of London Institute of Education, argued in similar vein that 'Some inner-city comprehensives are really secondary moderns.'[29] This was reflected in the standard of education, Mortimore suggested, so that there was 'underachievement in our average performance compared with that of the Germans or the Chinese'.[30] A headteacher in the London borough of Merton warned in graphic terms that 'the dogfight between local comprehensives that has emerged in recent years', encouraged by Conservative education policies, would mean that 'many of our comprehensives, situated in unattractive, deprived areas of our cities, will rapidly become the secondary moderns of yesteryear'.[31] In Watford, also, secondary schools differed widely in their admissions criteria and social composition, and what was described as a 'cut-throat competition for bright children' left the two remaining non-selective LEA comprehensives as '*de facto* secondary modern schools'.[32] Similar processes took place in many other urban areas as the theory of 'choice and diversity' promoted the practice of selection and differentiation. In Kent, one of the few local areas where grammar schools and SMSs had been left intact and where the 11-plus examination had been retained, the full effects in terms of 'underachievement in the system as a whole and the most inequality of educational opportunity' could still be witnessed.[33] The prospect elsewhere was of a reversion to type through the competition of the local marketplace.

### A grammar school in every town?

This prospect became increasingly likely as Conservative education policies placed even stronger emphasis on the merits of choice and diversity. John Major as prime minister favoured the return of grammar schools as centres of academic excellence, a notion symbolized in his desire for a 'grammar school in every town'. The impact that this would have on other secondary schools became a major issue in the debate that preceded the general election of 1997.

The government's aspirations were again clearly expressed in a new White Paper published in June 1996 under the title *Self-Government for Schools*. This emphasized the importance of promoting greater autonomy for schools and increasing the number of grant-maintained schools. It also supported the principles of 'choice, diversity and specialisation', on the grounds that children had 'different abilities, aptitudes, interests and needs' that 'cannot all be fully met by a single type of school, at least at secondary level'.[34] It therefore proposed to encourage the development of new grammar schools as well as other specialized schools, and 'as a matter of general policy, to look favourably on proposals for change which increase diversity in the local pattern of schools'.[35] However, it denied that this would recreate the familiar patterns of the 1950s:

> This pattern of diversity goes well beyond the outmoded division between grammar schools and secondary moderns. The aim is to encourage all schools to consider what special strengths they can develop to meet local needs, and so give more opportunities for young people to develop their varied talents to the full.[36]

This was again asserted in strong terms in chapter four of the White Paper, which repeated that the 'division between grammar schools for the few and secondary moderns for the rest' was 'outmoded'.[37]

Many critics of the White Paper doubted whether it would achieve its objectives,[38] but attention increasingly focused on the idea of 'grammar schools for the few and secondary moderns for the rest'. It was noted that 'Astute aspiring voters will be as aware as anyone else that while grammar schools may help some of their children, their siblings may get stuck in the secondary modern down the road.'[39] The failure to cater adequately for the large majority of pupils again seemed most apparent, as it was thoughtfully observed that

> The big failing in our school system is not primarily lack of diversity, lack of meritocratic opportunity, or lack of parental choice, though all of those things are important. It is our complete inability to provide an adequate education for large numbers of children who leave school without qualifications, and often without basic literacy and numeracy skills.[40]

The Labour Party leader, Tony Blair, was quick to condemn the government's policy of a 'return to the 11-plus' as 'a mistake of monumental proportions'. Blair argued that it would revive a 'grammar-school system [of] grammar schools for the minority, secondary moderns for the majority' that had catered for the needs of a 'vanished society which required a small educated class and a large number of manual workers'.[41] He was anxious to 'refine and redefine' the comprehensive schools, which his education and employment spokesperson David Blunkett had already criticized for their failure to change the established pattern of 'excellence at the top and chronic under-performance at the bottom',[42] but rejected the idea of 'the majority of children going to secondary moderns'.[43]

These exchanges set the terms of debate in the early months of 1997. The Conservative government introduced a new Education Bill, but with only a small working majority in the House of Commons it was obliged to abandon temporarily its plans for greater selection. Its aspirations were again to the fore in the general election campaign, when the Conservative Party became embroiled in controversy over proposals to introduce a programme costing £360 million that would allow up to 720 secondary schools to select pupils by aptitude or by academic ability.[44] It continued to advocate the development of new grammar schools,[45] and this again served to direct attention towards the spectre of the SMSs. Blair argued that such plans 'would mean secondary modern education for 80 per cent of pupils', which was 'the opposite of what is needed, turning the clock back when we need to turn it forward'.[46] In the last few days before the general election, he returned to this theme with an even more vigorous attack on what he described as a 'policy of rejection' that would mean 'selection for the few, rejection for the many'.[47] This was a stance that proved to be decisively vindicated on 1 May, when the Labour Party was returned to office at the general election for the first time in 18 years, with a commanding parliamentary majority of nearly 200 over all other parties.

The prominence of the secondary modern schools in the general election of 1997 might be taken as an ironic footnote to the debates of the previous generation. It was nevertheless more significant than such a view would imply. It reflected the enduring legacy of social differentiation in secondary education that had been preached in the doctrines of working-class secondary education, and that had reached its logical culmination in the secondary modern schools. Under the newly espoused theories of choice and diversity as promoted in the 1990s, the ambiguities that had been inherent in the comprehensive schools ever since their inception became increasingly evident, while the historic features of hierarchy and differentiation reasserted themselves in new and dynamic ways. The 'policy of rejection' that was promoted by the Conservative government was itself rejected, but the underlying pattern had already shown its resilience, and the legacy remained.

# 11

# Conclusions

Unlike earlier Labour governments, which have been criticized for 'a lack of political will, of strength of purpose' in their approach to education,[1] the new Labour government elected in May 1997 soon demonstrated its commitment to educational reform as a central feature of its social programme. The first White Paper produced by the government, in July 1997, set out its plans for education under the title of *Excellence in Schools*. This sought to redress the problems that in its view had been caused not only by 18 years of Conservative policies, but also by a century of neglect. The extent to which it would succeed where others had failed in promoting the needs of the 'ordinary child', especially in the secondary schools, remained to be seen.

In his foreword to the White Paper, the secretary of state for education and employment, David Blunkett, set the tone for the document as a whole by affirming the need to 'overcome economic and social disadvantage', and to 'make equality of opportunity a reality'. In order to achieve these goals, he argued, it was necessary to 'eliminate, and never excuse, underachievement in the most deprived parts of our country', which also involved overcoming what he called 'the spiral of disadvantage, in which alienation from, or failure within, the education system is passed from one generation to the next'.[2] In the six general principles that were identified as forming the basis for the government's educational approach, it was emphasized that policies would be 'designed to benefit the many, not just the few', and that there would be 'zero tolerance [of] underperformance'.[3] At the heart of the analysis presented by the White Paper was a conviction that 'too many of our children are failing to realise their potential',[4] a general failure that was highlighted in poor results in national tests and examinations at the ages of 11, 14 and 16, and which was also reflected in international comparisons.

The principal problem of the education system, according to *Excellence in Schools*, was its failure to cater in an adequate way for the 'majority of children'. Although there was excellence 'at the top', and there were 'some first-class schools', and 'our best students compare with the best in the world', still, it observed, 'by comparison with other industrialised countries, achievement by the average student is just not good enough'. It recognized the 'deep and historic roots' of this failure, suggesting that unlike competing nations such as France, Germany and the United States, Britain had 'failed to lay the foundations of a mass education system at the end of the 19th century'. Thus, while these other nations

> recognised that a strategy for national prosperity depended on well-developed primary and secondary education for all pupils, combined with effective systems of vocational training and extensive higher education [in Britain] mass education was neglected, and governments were content to rely on private schools to provide the elite entry to universities and the professions.[5]

Furthermore, it added, progress had remained slow during the twentieth century, as a mass system was not developed until after the Second World War, and the focus continued to be on 'selecting a small proportion of young people for university'.[6]

This historical perspective helped to form the basis for the White Paper's proposals for the future of secondary education. Although comprehensive schools had been intended to redress the inequalities of the past, it maintained, they had not succeeded in improving the prospects of the majority of pupils. This would be achieved by 'modernising the comprehensive principle' along lines suggested in Chapter 4 of the document. In particular, it insisted, 'We are not going back to the days of the 11-plus; but neither are we prepared to stand still and defend the failings of across-the-board mixed ability teaching.'[7] Comprehensive education would therefore be modernized 'to create inclusive schooling which provides a broad, flexible and motivating education that recognises the different talents of all children and delivers excellence for everyone'.[8] Prominent in this ambition was the aim to promote 'diversity', for all children to 'develop their diverse abilities', and for 'diversity within one campus'.[9] The White Paper set out a range of initiatives designed to encourage this. Setting, target-grouping, and accelerated learning, for example, would involve different kinds of methods, and should stimulate 'more flexible and successful approaches to the grouping of pupils'.[10] Education Action Zones would be introduced with a pilot programme phased in over two to three years, 'with a mix of underperforming schools and the highest levels of disadvantage', which would take priority for central funding, and which might allow additional flexibility in the approaches adopted for 'motivating young people in tough inner city areas'.[11] Specialist schools and families of schools would also 'encourage diversity, with schools developing their own distinctive identity and expertise',[12] while also helping to 'raise standards for all'.[13] A New National Grid for Learning was also proposed to enhance the potential for new technologies in schools, together with greater investment for research and development into schools of the future.

The analysis and recommendations set out in this White Paper directly addressed the problems of secondary education, but were limited in some important respects. Specifically, it did not fully appreciate the nature of the historical failure to cater for the 'ordinary child', nor did it take enough account of the resilience of social differentiation in secondary education. As this book has demonstrated, mass education was not simply 'neglected' in the late nineteenth and twentieth centuries; indeed it was often the focus of a great deal of activity and interest. The real problem was the nature of such activity. This began in the nineteenth century as the pursuit of a radical agenda, challenging the hegemony of elite institutions and entrenched forms of curriculum, but the alternative and distinctive approach that was developed never attained parity of esteem with established forms of schooling, and certainly failed to establish itself as a superior or more appropriate model. During the twentieth century, these initiatives on behalf of a distinct working-class secondary education tended to become increasingly conservative in their effects, emphasizing as they did the need for the education of working-class children to conform to a preordained social and industrial order. Even then, there were strongly expressed ideals that continued to support such an aim, especially in the 1940s through the supporters of the SMSs and again in the 1960s through the 'secondary modern curriculum' and the 'sub-GCE'. Overwhelmingly, however, the practice as embodied in the secondary modern schools contradicted and undermined the theory. Hence a key factor in the failure of educational reform over the past century has been the difference between *theory* and *practice*, as the well meaning and benevolent experiments directed at working-class children and the ordinary child served overall to limit their capacity to overcome their social disadvantages. It seems especially important for educational reforms of the present and future to draw on this historical experience and especially to note this persistent tendency for the practice to refute the theory.

Further to this, it is clear that social differentiation has been a major and resilient underlying influence in secondary education, from the efforts to bridge the divide between the secondary education associated with the middle classes and the elementary education of the working class that were characteristic of the late nineteenth century, to the establishment of the tripartite system that underpinned secondary education for all in the twentieth century. Division, hierarchy and social inequality have been basic continuities in educational provision. Teachers and schools have attempted in many cases to transcend even the most unpromising of circumstances, often with some success, but they have not been able on the whole to overcome the general pattern of provision. The nature of the class society did change in many important respects in the course of the century, from the stratified industrial society of the Victorian era to the Welfare State and affluent society of the 1950s and 1960s, through phases of structural unemployment and those of full employment, and through fundamental transformations in the nature of work for different groups in society. Nevertheless, the society of the late nineteenth and early twentieth centuries generated deep seated conflicts and contradictions that surrounded and infiltrated secondary education throughout subsequent educational reforms, and wider social change. The inherent tensions between secondary education for the working class and working-class secondary education that originated in the nineteenth century were evident throughout the twentieth century. Both approaches were products of and responses to social class antagonisms. Both could evoke sincerely expressed ideals, the one on behalf of upward social mobility for able children of the working class, the other for an authentic and respectable alternative to middle-class assumptions. In the end, neither offered an answer to the problems of secondary education.

Comprehensive schools offered an attractive alternative, but in practice suffered from the legacy of the past. Even from the 1960s, when the structures of comprehensive schools seemed to have triumphed over tripartite precepts, the implications of working-class secondary education remained potent and active within comprehensive education itself. During the 1980s and 1990s, the effects of this legacy became increasingly evident under the pressure of government policies designed to promote choice and diversity, to the extent that many comprehensive schools, especially in metropolitan areas, could be viewed simply as secondary modern schools in a new guise.

There are two lessons that deserve emphasis from this resilient tradition of social differentiation, one for the past and one for the present. The first, of a historical nature, is that Harold Dent was broadly correct when he argued in the 1950s that tripartism was 'a manifestation of the "tradition of the society", with long and deep historical roots, and should be treated as such'.[14] It has emerged in the current study as an integral aspect of the social history of secondary education in the nineteenth and twentieth centuries. Differentiated education for distinct social groups and classes has attracted committed educational reformers at local and national levels and of all political persuasions, and should not be blamed simply on an 'educational establishment' intent on maintaining its own social and educational advantages. That is, as Dent insists, it is unconvincing to portray tripartism either as 'the result of a modern passion for administrative tidiness', or as 'a sinister plot to deprive "working-class" children of the educational opportunities which are theirs by right',[15] and it is unconvincing because this kind of provision was based much more deeply in society and culture than these analyses imply. At the same time, it is also true that at different times administrative concerns and class interests and ideologies have served powerfully to reinforce this underlying and embedded approach. The 'tradition' was manipulated in ways that Dent did not concede so as to favour the continued dominance of grammar and public schools, and of the academic and liberal curriculum.

The lesson for the present, therefore, is that educational policies need to take clear account of this deep seated tendency in favour of social differentiation in secondary education. Class based provision has persisted through changing circumstances, surviving relatively unscathed the educational and social reforms of the twentieth century. John Major's vision of a grammar school in every town may have been thwarted, but the underlying contours of tripartism remain as resilient as ever within the structures and practices of secondary education. If comprehensive education is to be modernized, the recognition of these features seems a vital preliminary step, with initiatives designed to mitigate and undermine them as an important objective of policy.

In the light of this history, it is doubtful whether the diversity advocated in *Excellence in Schools* will achieve such an aim. Indeed, the goal of diversity has itself been of central importance in maintaining social differentiation over the past century. In the present instance, the theory speaks of 'inclusive schooling which provides a broad, flexible and motivating education that recognises the different talents of all children and delivers excellence for everyone'.[16] It entertains the prospects for 'diversity within one campus [with] schools developing their own distinctive identity and expertise'. There is a distinct possibility that these ideas will allow scope for social differentiation to reassert itself, and that the practice, once again, will contradict the theory.

Finally, what of the 'ordinary child'? They have indeed been failed, not so much by neglect as by the contradictions of class based provision and the illusions to which it gave rise. The experiment of the secondary modern schools symbolized this failure, most graphically in the case of the Stonehill Street schools. Thirty years on, secondary education has still not fully recovered from the effects of this failed experiment, and continues to be influenced by the theories that underlay it. It will be little surprise if in the twenty-first century new ways are devised for failing the ordinary child.

# Notes

## Chapter 1

1 C.P. Snow (1963) *The Two Cultures and a Second Look*. Cambridge: Cambridge University Press, p. 19.
2 National Commission on Education (1993) *Learning to Succeed*. London: NCE, p. 239.
3 Department for Education and Employment (1997) *Excellence in Schools*. London: HMSO, p. 11.
4 Ibid., p. 10.
5 Ibid.
6 *Independent* (1996) front page headline article, Schools have failed pupils says Blunkett: Labour to rewrite its comprehensive policy, 28 February.
7 e.g. *Independent* (1996) leading article, A painful lesson for Labour, 28 February; Colin Hughes (1996) A comprehensive failure, *Independent*, 25 January; *Observer* (1996) leading article, The need for comprehensive change, 28 January; *Sunday Times* (1997) leading article, Learning curves, 25 May.
8 *Independent* (1996) report, Comprehensive education failed my sons, says Bernie Grant, *Independent*, 25 January.
9 e.g. C. Benn and C. Chitty (1996) *Thirty Years On*. London: David Fulton; C. Benn and C. Chitty (1996) Propelled by the weight of history, *Times Educational Supplement* (*TES*), 10 May; *Observer* (1996) report, Comprehensive results prove critics wrong, 5 May; Roy Hattersley (1995) Labour's big, bad idea, *Independent*, 22 June.
10 Tony Blair (1996) Don't give idealism a bad name, *TES*, 14 June.
11 e.g. *Independent* (1992) leading article, Nostalgia is no solution, 28 February; *Independent* (1996) leading article, Social selection is bad for schools, 4 January; *Independent* (1996) feature, Is selection good for the kids?, 29 March.
12 *Independent* (1996) leading article, Major's class act, 21 March.

13 George Walden (1995) The school wall won't fall down, *Independent*, 31 July; Walden (1996) *We Should Know Better*. London: Fourth Estate.

14 See e.g. G. McCulloch (1991) *Philosophers and Kings*. Cambridge: Cambridge University Press; H. Silver (1983) The liberal and the vocational, in his *Education as History*. London: Methuen, pp. 153–71.

15 See G. McCulloch (1989) *The Secondary Technical School*. London: Falmer; M. Sanderson (1994) *The Missing Stratum*. London: Athlone Press.

16 See e.g. I. Goodson (1992) On curriculum form: notes toward a theory of curriculum. *Sociology of Education* 65: 66–75.

17 R.H. Tawney (1931) *Equality*. London: George Allen and Unwin (1964 edn), pp. 144–5.

18 R.H. Tawney to Fred Clarke, 30 September 1940 (Tawney papers, Institute of Education).

19 e.g. R. Pedley (1963) *The Comprehensive School*. Harmondsworth: Penguin; K. Fenwick (1976) *The Comprehensive School 1944–1970*. London: Methuen.

20 e.g. S. Ball (1981) *Beachside Comprehensive*. Cambridge: Cambridge University Press; J. Lawrence and M. Tucker (1988) *Norwood was a Difficult School*. London: Macmillan; J. Abraham (1995) *Divide and School*. London: Falmer.

21 e.g. S. Ball (ed.) (1984) *Comprehensive Education*. London: Falmer; A. Green and S. Ball (eds) (1988) *Progress and Inequality in Comprehensive Education*. London: Routledge; A. Weeks (1986) *Comprehensive Schools*. London: Methuen; B. Barker (1986) *Rescuing the Comprehensive Experience*. Milton Keynes: Open University Press; C. Chitty (ed.) (1987) *Redefining the Comprehensive Experience*. London: Bedford Way Papers; D. Hargreaves (1983) *The Challenge for the Comprehensive School*. London: Routledge and Kegan Paul; B. Moon (ed.) (1983) *Comprehensive Schools*. London: NFER-Nelson.

22 e.g. Benn and Chitty, *Thirty Years On*; A. Kerckhoff, K. Fogelman, D. Crook and D. Reeder (1996) *Going Comprehensive in England and Wales*. London: Woburn; R. Pring and G. Walford (eds) (1997) *Affirming the Comprehensive Ideal*. London: Falmer.

23 B. Simon (1997) A seismic change: process and interpretation, in Pring and Walford (eds) *Affirming the Comprehensive Ideal*, p. 15. See also e.g. B. Simon (1991) *Education and the Social Order, 1940–1990*. London: Lawrence and Wishart.

24 C. Benn (1997) Effective comprehensive education, in Pring and Walford (eds) *Affirming the Comprehensive Ideal*, p. 121.

25 W. Taylor (1963) *The Secondary Modern School*. London: Faber and Faber.

26 D. Hargreaves (1967) *Social Relations in a Secondary School*. London: Routledge and Kegan Paul, p. 1.

27 Ibid., p. 138.

28 See also G. McCulloch and L. Sobell (1994) Towards a social history of the secondary modern schools. *History of Education* 23(3): 275–86, on this broad project.

29 H. Dent (1954) *Growth in English Education: 1946–1952*. London: Routledge and Kegan Paul, p. 76. See also e.g. Dent (1949) *Secondary Education for All*. London: Routledge and Kegan Paul.

30 H. Dent (1952) *Change in English Education*. London: University of London Press, p. 93.

## Chapter 2

1  A. Green (1990) *Education and State Formation*. London: Macmillan.
2  Report of the Commissioners appointed to inquire into the state of popular education in England (Newcastle Report, 1861); Report of the Royal Commission on the Elementary Education Acts (Cross Report, 1888).
3  e.g. T.W. Bamford (1967) *Rise of the Public Schools*. London: Nelson; J. Chandos (1984) *Boys Together*. London: Hutchinson; J.R. de S. Honey (1977) *Tom Brown's Universe*. London: Millington; B. Simon and I. Bradley (eds) (1975) *The Victorian Public School*. London: Gill and Macmillan; J. Roach (1986) *A History of Secondary Education in England, 1800–1870*. London: Longman.
4  Report of Her Majesty's Commissioners appointed to inquire into the revenues and management of certain colleges and schools, and the studies pursued and instruction given therein (Clarendon Report, 1864).
5  Report of the Royal Commission known as the Schools Inquiry Commission (Taunton Report, 1868), ch. 7, p. 587.
6  Ibid.
7  Ibid.
8  See e.g. P. Searby (ed.) (1982) *Educating the Victorian Middle Class*. Leicester: History of Education Society; D. Allsobrook (1986) *Schools for the Shires*. Manchester: Manchester University Press.
9  H. Steedman (1987) Defining institutions: the endowed grammar schools and the systematisation of English secondary education, in D. Muller, F. Ringer and B. Simon (eds) *The Rise of the Modern Educational System*. Cambridge: Cambridge University Press, p. 133.
10 Report of the Commissioners appointed to inquire into the state of popular education in England (Newcastle Report, 1861).
11 R. Lowe (1867) Primary and classical education, in D. Reeder (ed.) (1980) *Educating our Masters*. Leicester: Leicester University Press, p. 106.
12 Ibid., p. 108.
13 Ibid., pp. 125–6.
14 Schools Inquiry (Taunton) Commission, minutes of evidence, Revd J.C. Bruce, p. 759.
15 Schools Inquiry Commission, minutes of evidence, Revd W.B. Garnett Botfield, p. 582.
16 Schools Inquiry Commission, minutes of evidence, Rt Hon. Earl Fortescue, p. 301.
17 Schools Inquiry Commission, minutes of evidence, C.W. Hankin, pp. 466, 468.
18 Schools Inquiry Commission, minutes of evidence, Hon. and Revd Samuel Best, p. 702.
19 Schools Inquiry Commission, minutes of evidence, Revd J.S. Howson, p. 263.
20 Schools Inquiry Commission, Mr Green's Report, p. 180.
21 Ibid., p. 179.
22 Ibid.
23 Schools Inquiry Commission, Mr Bryce's Report, p. 792.
24 Schools Inquiry Commission, minutes of evidence, W. Gilpin, p. 754.
25 Schools Inquiry Commission, Final Report, 1868, p. 593.

26  Ibid., p. 594.

27  Ibid., p. 596.

28  Ibid.

29  B. Simon (1974) *Education and the Labour Movement, 1870–1920.* London: Lawrence and Wishart, p. 112.

30  Royal Commission on the Elementary Acts (Cross Commission), minutes of evidence, Lord Lingen, p. 526.

31  Ibid., p. 535.

32  Ibid.

33  Cross Commission, minutes of evidence, Revd D.J. Stewart, p. 133.

34  Ibid., p. 138.

35  Cross Commission, minutes of evidence, Sir Philip Magnus, p. 468.

36  Ibid., p. 470.

37  Ibid., p. 473.

38  Cross Commission, minutes of evidence, Revd Dr. H.W. Crosskey, p. 550.

39  Cross Commission, minutes of evidence, Mr J. Scotson, p. 266.

40  Ibid., p. 270.

41  See M. Vlaeminke (1990) The subordination of technical education in secondary schools, 1870–1914, in P. Summerfield and E. Evans (eds) *Technical Education and the State.* Manchester: Manchester University Press, pp. 51–76; also e.g. W. Robinson (1990) 'Breaking the elementary mould: a study of nine higher grade girls' schools under the London school board, 1882–1904', unpublished MA thesis. University of London.

42  Royal Commission on Secondary Education (1895) (Bryce Commission), minutes of evidence, Bishop of London, p. 362.

43  Ibid., p. 364.

44  Ibid., p. 370.

45  Ibid.

46  Bryce Commission, minutes of evidence, Sir John Donnelly, p. 131.

47  Bryce Commission, minutes of evidence, Hon. E.L. Stanley, p. 466.

48  Revd M.G. Glazebrook, answers received to a circular from the Bryce Commissioners, pp. 456–7.

49  Clara E. Collet, Memorandum on the education of working girls, for the Bryce Commission, pp. 380–1.

50  J.G. Fitch, Memorandum to Bryce Commission, The relations which should subsist between primary and secondary schools, p. 91.

51  Ibid.

52  Ibid., p. 93.

53  Bryce Commission, minutes of evidence, J.G. Fitch, p. 265.

54  Trades and Labour Councils, memorandum to the Bryce Commission, p. 494.

55  Ibid., p. 496.

56  Bryce Commission, minutes of evidence, G.W. Kekewich, p. 114.

57  Bryce Commission, minutes of evidence, Revd F.E. Anthony, p. 381.

58  Bryce Commission, minutes of evidence, C.A. Buckmaster and Gilbert R. Redgrave, p. 356.

59  Frances A. Kitchener, Report on secondary education in the County Palatine of Lancaster, Bryce Commission, p. 281.

60  Ibid., p. 289.

61 John Brown Paton, Secondary education for the industrial classes of England, memorandum prepared by request of the Council of the Recreative Evening Schools Association for the Bryce Commission, 1894, p. 3.

62 Ibid., p. 3.

63 Ibid., p. 7.

64 Ibid.

65 e.g. Bryce Commission, minutes of evidence, Mr R. Halstead and Mr F. Peaker on behalf of the Education Committee of the Cooperative Union, p. 412.

66 Royal Commission on Secondary Education, vol. 1, Report of the Commissioners (Bryce Report). London: HMSO, 1895, p. 41.

67 Ibid., p. 53.

68 Ibid., p. 77.

69 Ibid., p. 136.

70 Ibid., p. 63.

71 Sir John Gorst to G. Kekewich (Secretary of the Board of Education), 3 February 1901 (Board of Education papers, ED.24/40).

72 Board of Education (1906) *Report of the Consultative Committee upon Higher Elementary Schools*. London: HMSO. See also Simon, *Education and the Labour Movement*, pp. 264–8.

73 J.H. Brittain to A. Mansbridge, 28 April 1907 (Albert Mansbridge papers, file 65346).

74 G.R. Searle (1971) *The Quest for National Efficiency*. Oxford: Basil Blackwell, p. 79.

75 S. Webb to G. Wallas, 6 September 1900, quoted by Searle, *The Quest for National Efficiency*, p. 80. See also E.J.T. Brennan (1959) 'The influence of Sidney and Beatrice Webb on English education, 1892–1903', unpublished MA thesis. University of Sheffield; A.V. Judges (1961) The educational influence of the Webbs. *British Journal of Educational Studies* 10: 33–48.

## Chapter 3

1 W.F. Connell (1980) *A History of Education in the Twentieth Century World*. Canberra: Curriculum Development Centre, pp. 33–47.

2 Board of Education (1938) *Secondary Education with Special Reference to Grammar Schools and Technical High Schools* (Spens Report). London: HMSO, p. 73.

3 Board of Education (1926) *The Education of the Adolescent* (Hadow Report). London: HMSO, p. 46.

4 See e.g. I. Goodson (1994) *School Subjects and Curriculum Change*, 3rd edn. London: Falmer, esp. chs 2 and 3; C. Manthorpe (1986) Science or domestic science? The struggle to define an appropriate science education for girls in early twentieth century England. *History of Education* 15(3): 195–213.

5 J. Roach (1979) Examinations and the secondary schools, 1900–1945. *History of Education* 8(1): 58.

6 See e.g. G. Sutherland (1984) *Ability, Merit and Measurement*. Oxford: Clarendon Press; B. Simon (1970) Classification and streaming: a study of

grouping in English schools, 1860–1960, in P. Nash (ed.) *History and Education*. New York: Random House, pp. 115–59.

7  D. Reeder (1987) The reconstruction of secondary education in England, 1869–1920, in D. Muller, F. Ringer and B. Simon (eds) *The Rise of the Modern Educational System*. Cambridge: Cambridge University Press, p. 150.

8  D.W. Dean (1971) Conservatism and the national education system, 1922–40. *Journal of Contemporary History* 6: 151–65; G. Savage (1983) Social class and educational policy: the civil service and secondary education in England during the interwar period. *Journal of Contemporary History* 18: 261–80.

9  E. Percy (1958) *Some Memories*. London: Eyre and Spottiswoode, p. 95.

10  e.g. R.H. Tawney (1909) The economics of boy labour. *Economic Journal*, December: 517–37. See also R. Szreter (1990) A note on R.H. Tawney's early interest in juvenile employment and misemployment. *History of Education* 19(4): 375–82.

11  See also K. Lindsay (1926) *Social Progress and Educational Waste*. London: Routledge.

12  See Labour Party (1922) *Secondary Education for All*. London; also e.g. R. Barker (1972) *Education and Politics 1900–1951*. Oxford: Clarendon Press, esp. ch. 3; C. Griggs (1983) *The Trades Union Congress and the Struggle for Education, 1868–1925*. London: Falmer; J.R. Brooks (1994) Labour and educational reconstruction, 1916–1926: a case study in the evolution of policy. *History of Education*. 20(3): 245–59.

13  *School Government Chronicle*, 25 December 1909, report of LCC Education Committee meeting held on 22 December (Board of Education papers, ED.97/206).

14  Ibid.

15  *School Government Chronicle*, 16 October 1911, LCC deputation to Board of Education.

16  Ibid.

17  S. King (1990) Technical and vocational education for girls: a study of the central schools of London, 1918–1939, in P. Summerfield and E. Evans (eds) *Technical Education and the State since 1850*. Manchester: Manchester University Press, p. 78.

18  See D.W. Thoms (1975) The emergence and failure of the day continuation school experiment. *History of Education* 4(1): 36–50.

19  Labour Party Education Advisory Committee on Education (1918) *Continued Education under the New Education Act*, quoted in Barker, *Education and Politics 1900–1951*, p. 41.

20  W. Silto (1993) 'Compulsory day continuation schools: their origins, objectives, and development, with special reference to H.A.L. Fisher's 1918 experiment', unpublished PhD thesis. Institute of Education, University of London.

21  See also e.g. K. Brehony (1994) The 'school masters' parliament': the origins and formation of the Consultative Committee of the Board of Education, 1868–1916. *History of Education* 23(2): 171–93; B. Swinnerton (1996) The 1931 Report of the Consultative Committee on the primary school: tensions and contradictions. *History of Education* 25(1): 73–90; G. McCulloch (1993) 'Spens v. Norwood': contesting the educational state? *History of Education* 22(2): 163–80.

22 Note of deputation from Consultative Committee (Sir Henry Hadow, Percy Jackson, Ernest Barker, J.A. White) to Board of Education, 23 November 1923 (Board of Education papers, ED.24/1386).
23 Ibid.
24 Ibid. See also Simon's (1974) account of this delegation in his *The Politics of Educational Reform, 1920–1940*. London: Lawrence and Wishart, pp. 75–8.
25 Board of Education (1926) *The Education of the Adolescent* (Hadow Report). London: HMSO, p. iv.
26 H.M. Richards, oral evidence to Consultative Committee, 22 May 1928 (Board of Education papers, ED.10/147).
27 Ibid.
28 James Graham, memo to Consultative Committee, n.d. (Board of Education papers, ED.10/47).
29 J.L. Paton (1909) The secondary education of the working classes, in C. Norwood and A. Hope (eds) *The Higher Education of Boys in England*. London: John Murray, pp. 544–54.
30 J.L. Paton, oral evidence to Consultative Committee, 27 June 1924 (Board of Education papers, ED.10/147).
31 Ibid.
32 P. Nunn (1920) *Education: Its Data and First Principles*. London: Edward Arnold.
33 Professor P. Nunn, oral evidence to Consultative Committee, 26 February 1925 (Board of Education papers, ED.10/147).
34 Ibid.
35 Board of Education, *The Education of the Adolescent*, p. xix.
36 Ibid., p. 35.
37 Ibid., p. 42.
38 Ibid., p. 52.
39 Ibid., p. xxi.
40 Ibid., pp. xxi–xxii.
41 Ibid., p. xxiii.
42 Ibid.
43 Ibid., p. 84.
44 Ibid.
45 Ibid., p. 85.
46 Ibid.
47 Ibid., p. 86.
48 Ibid., p. 153
49 Ibid., p. 77.
50 Ibid., p. 99.
51 *TES* (1927), leading article, Secondary schools for all, 1 January.
52 Sir E. Phipps, note, 16 May 1927 (Board of Education papers, ED.24/1264).
53 Ibid.
54 H.J. Simmonds, note, 18 May 1927 (Board of Education papers, ED.24/1264).
55 Ibid.
56 Note (by Mr Watkins?) to Sir E. Phipps, 1 June 1927 (Board of Education papers, ED.24/1264).
57 Sir E. Phipps, note, 'The Consultative Committee Report: "Modern Schools"', 24 May 1927 (Board of Education papers, ED.24/1264).

58 Ibid.
59 Note of officials' meeting on modern schools, Wednesday 25 May [1927?] (Board of Education papers, ED.24/1264).
60 Ibid.
61 G. St L. Carson to Mr Richards (Board of Education), 8 October 1927 (Board of Education papers, ED.24/1264).
62 See also G. McCulloch (1991) *Philosophers and Kings*. Cambridge: Cambridge University Press, esp. chs 3 and 4.
63 Cyril Norwood, memo, The School Certificate (n.d.; January 1928?) (Board of Education papers, ED.12/255).
64 Ibid. See also F. Hunt (1991) *Gender and Policy in English Secondary Education, 1880–1940*. Sussex: Harvester.
65 W.R. Richardson, note, 26 March 1928 (Board of Education papers, ED.12/255).
66 Ibid.
67 F.B. Stead, note, 16 May 1928 (Board of Education papers, ED.12/255).
68 *TES* (1928) report, Examinations for central schools, 27 October.
69 Ibid.
70 Board of Education (1928) *The New Prospect in Education*, educational pamphlet no. 60. London: HMSO, p. 3.
71 Ibid., p. 4.
72 Ibid., p. 6.
73 Ibid., p. 7.

## Chapter 4

1 See e.g. T. Husen, A. Tuijnman and W. Halls (eds) (1992) *Schooling in Modern European Society*. Oxford: Pergamon Press; C. Brock and W. Tulasiewicz (eds) (1994) *Education in a Single Europe*. London: Routledge.
2 See e.g. A. Hearnden (1974) *Education in the Two Germanies*. Oxford: Basil Blackwell.
3 D. Philips (ed.) (1995) *Education in Germany*. London: Routledge.
4 e.g. J.E. Talbott (1969) *The Politics of Educational Reform in France, 1918–1940*. Princeton, NJ: Princeton University Press.
5 See e.g. D. Labaree (1989) *The Making of an American High School*. New Haven, CT: Yale University Press; W. Reese (1995) *The Origins of the American High School*. New Haven, CT: Yale University Press.
6 See e.g. J. Herbst (1996) *The Once and Future School*. London: Routledge, esp. ch. 12.
7 See e.g. J. Spring (1986) *The American School, 1642–1985*. London: Longman, esp. ch. 4.
8 e.g. R. Ueda (1987) *Avenues to Adulthood*. Cambridge: Cambridge University Press.
9 e.g. R.D. Anderson (1983) *Education and Opportunity in Victorian Scotland*. Oxford: Clarendon Press.
10 e.g. G. McCulloch (1988) Imperial and colonial designs: the case of Auckland Grammar School. *History of Education* 17(4): 257–67.
11 e.g. L.S. Hearnshaw (1979) *Cyril Burt, Psychologist*. London: Hodder and Stoughton; A. Wooldridge (1994) *Measuring the Mind*. Cambridge: Cambridge University Press.

12 Plato (1955 edn) *The Republic*.
13 See R. Crossman (1937) *Plato Today*. London: George Allen and Unwin; J. Dancy (1965) Technology in a liberal education. *Advancement of Science*, October: 379–87.
14 Sir R. Livingstone (1944) *Plato and Modern Education*. Cambridge: Cambridge University Press.
15 Ibid., p. 13.
16 J. Harris (1992) Political thought and the Welfare State 1870–1940: an intellectual framework for British social policy. *Past and Present*. 135: 142.
17 Ibid., p. 127.
18 Ibid., pp. 127–8.
19 See G. McCulloch (1996) Educating the public: Tawney, the *Manchester Guardian* and educational reform, in R. Aldrich (ed.) *In History and in Education*. London: Woburn, pp. 116–37; B. Simon (1974) *The Politics of Educational Reform, 1920–1940*. London: Lawrence and Wishart; R. Barker (1972) *Education and Politics 1900–1951*. Oxford: Clarendon Press, esp. chs 2–3.
20 See P. Gordon and J. White (1979) *Philosophers as Educational Reformers*. London: George Allen and Unwin; A. Vincent and R. Plant (1984) *Philosophy, Politics and Citizenship*. Oxford: Blackwell.
21 R.H. Tawney (1907) Schools and scholars: labour and culture. *Morning Post*, 16 August.
22 A. Mansbridge (1918) Education and the working classes. *Contemporary Review*, June.
23 R.H. Tawney (1920) A valuable Report. *Manchester Guardian*, 16 November; Tawney (1924) The new direction in education: preparing the next advance. *Manchester Guardian*, 6 May.
24 Labour Party (1922) *Secondary Education for All*, p. 7. See also on the background of these proposals, J.R. Brooks (1977) 'Secondary education for all' reconsidered. *Durham Research Review* 38: 1–8; N. Haslewood (1981) Tawney, the Labour Party and educational policy in the 1920s: a reappraisal, in R. Lowe (ed.) *Labour and Education*. Leicester: History of Education Society, pp. 51–62; J.R. Brooks (1991) Labour and educational reconstruction, 1916–1926. *History of Education* 20(3): 245–59.
25 Labour Party, *Secondary Education for All*, p. 11.
26 Ibid., p. 33.
27 Ibid.
28 Ibid., p. 28.
29 Ibid., p. 29.
30 Ibid., p. 30.
31 Ibid., p. 78.
32 R.H. Tawney, Memo on Labour education policy (n.d.) (Tawney papers, British Library of Political and Economic Science, 22/8).
33 R.H. Tawney to F. Clarke, 30 September 1940 (Tawney papers, Institute of Education).
34 R.H. Tawney to D. Miller, 30 January 1943; R.H. Tawney to R.A. Butler, 1 August 1943 (Tawney papers, Institute of Education).
35 *Manchester Guardian* (1942) leading article, Educational pillars, 16 December.
36 On Clarke's career in education, see F.W. Mitchell (1967) *Sir Fred Clarke, Master Teacher, 1880–1952*. London: Longman. Aspects of the development of

his educational ideas during his time in South Africa are discussed in P. Kallaway (1996) Fred Clarke and the politics of vocational education in South Africa, 1911–29. *History of Education* 25(4): 353–62.

37 F. Clarke (1940) *Education and Social Change*. London: Sheldon Press.
38 F. Clarke to R.H. Tawney, 5 October 1940 (Tawney papers, Institute of Education).
39 F. Clarke (1993) Some reflections on secondary education. *University of Toronto Quarterly* 3(1): 74.
40 Ibid., p. 75.
41 Ibid.
42 Ibid., p. 76.
43 Ibid., p. 85.
44 Ibid., p. 86.
45 See W. Taylor (1996) Education and the Moot, in R. Aldrich (ed.) *In History and in Education*. London: Woburn, pp. 159–86, on the nature of Clarke's discussions during the war.
46 F. Clarke, Notes on secondary education in England, 22 February 1942 (Clarke papers, BA1/CLA/24).
47 Ibid.
48 M.F. Young (secretary to Spens committee) to Lady Simon, 26 February 1936 (Lady Simon papers, M14/2/2/3).
49 R.H. Tawney to Lady Simon, 26 February 1936 (Lady Simon papers, M14/2/2/ 4).
50 R.H. Tawney to Lady Simon, 2 January 1937 (Lady Simon papers, M14/2/2/4).
51 Board of Education (1938) *Secondary Education with Special Reference to Grammar Schools and Technical High Schools* (Spens Report). London: HMSO, p. xxxv.
52 Ibid., p. 292.
53 Ibid., p. 293.
54 Ibid., p. 371.
55 R.S. Wood, memo, 30 July 1937 (Board of Education papers, ED.10/273).
56 Ibid.
57 R.S. Wood, further note (n.d.; 1937) (Board of Education papers, ED.10/273).
58 C. Norwood (1929) *The English Tradition Of Education*. London: John Murray.
59 Minutes of the 1st meeting of the Norwood committee, 18 October 1941, minute 2, Statement by the Chairman (Board of Education papers, ED.136/ 681).
60 Ibid.
61 A note on the grammar school, n.d. [January 1942] (Board of Education papers, ED.136/681).
62 Minutes of the 3rd meeting of the Norwood committee, 5–7 January 1942, minute 4 (IAAM papers, E1/1 file 3).
63 Norwood Committee, 'Detailed agenda for meetings', January 1942, IIv (IAAM papers, E1/1/file 3).
64 Third meeting of Norwood committee, 5–7 January 1942, minute 4 (IAAM papers, E1/1/file 3).
65 Board of Education (1943) *Curriculum and Examinations in Secondary Schools* (Norwood Report). London: HMSO, p. 2.
66 Ibid.

67 Ibid., p. 4.
68 Ibid., p. 7.
69 Ibid., p. 4.
70 Ibid., p. 3.
71 Ibid., p. 4.
72 Board of Education (1943) *Educational Reconstruction*. London: HMSO, p. 3.
73 Ibid., p. 9.
74 Ibid.

## Chapter 5

1 Ministry of Education, 'Secondary modern schools in England and Wales', June 1956 (Ministry of Education papers, ED.147/639).
2 City of Leeds (1947) *Development Plan* (1947); *City of Manchester Plan 1945*; City of Sheffield Education Committee (1947) *Development Plan*.
3 County Borough of Brighton (1946) *Development Plan for Primary and Secondary Schools*; Leicestershire County Council (1949) *Development Plan*; County Borough of Merthyr Tydfil (1947) *Development Plan*.
4 Darlington County Borough Education Committee (1946) *The Future of Education in Darlington*.
5 London County Council (1947) *London School Plan*.
6 See G. McCulloch (1989) *The Secondary Technical School*. London: Falmer, esp. chs 3–4.
7 See A.C. Kerckhoff, K. Fogelman, D. Crook and D. Reeder (1996) *Going Comprehensive in England and Wales*. London: Woburn.
8 *TES* (1945), leading article, The great adventure, 3 March.
9 Ministry of Education (1945) *The Nation's Schools*. London: HMSO, p. 3.
10 Ibid., p. 12.
11 Ibid., p. 20.
12 Ibid., p. 21.
13 Ibid.
14 Ibid., p. 22.
15 W.P. Alexander (1945) 'The Nation's Schools' – II: A Critical Examination. *Education* 8 June: 829.
16 *Journal of Education*, July 1945, 77 (912), review of *The Nation's Schools*, p. 334.
17 Sir R. Wood, minute, 15 April 1946 (Ministry of Education papers, ED.136/787).
18 See e.g. B. Vernon (1983) *Ellen Wilkinson 1891–1947*. London: Croom Helm, esp. ch. 10; B. Hughes (1979) In defence of Ellen Wilkinson, *History Workshop* 7: 156–69; D. Bourn (1995) Equality of opportunity? The Labour Government and schools, in J. Fyrth (ed.) *Labour's Promised Land?* London: Lawrence and Wishart, pp. 163–77; M. Francis (1997) *Ideas and Politics under Labour, 1945–51*. Manchester: Manchester University Press, ch. 6.
19 E. Wilkinson, note (n.d.; 1946) (Ministry of Education papers, ED. 136/788).
20 E. Wilkinson, 'Minister's view on "Modern" pamphlet', (n.d.; August 1946) (Ministry of Education papers, ED.136/788).
21 *Education* (1945), report, Miss Wilkinson and grammar schools, 9 November, p. 333.

22 Ibid.
23 *Education* (1946), report, Miss Wilkinson at Labour Conference, 21 June, p. 1055; *Labour Party Conference Report*, 1946, p. 195.
24 *Education* (1946), report, Miss Wilkinson at AEC meeting, 21 June, p. 1061.
25 *Education* (1946) report, Education in parliament, 12 July, p. 60.
26 D.R. Hardman, memo to Minister of Education, n.d. (1946) (Ministry of Education papers, ED.136/788).
27 Ibid.
28 D.R. Hardman, memo to Minister, 19 March 1946 (Ministry of Education papers, ED.136/788).
29 See H. Ree (1973) *Educator Extraordinary*. London: Longman.
30 Hardman, memo to Minister, 19 March 1946.
31 *Education* (1946) report, The modern secondary school, 17 May, p. 857.
32 *Education* (1946) report, Education in parliament: estimates debate, 12 July, pp. 64–5.
33 Ibid.
34 *Education* (1946) report, The new secondary education, 18 October, p. 635.
35 Ministry of Education (1947) *The New Secondary Education*, pamphlet no. 9. London: HMSO, p. 28.
36 Ibid., p. 29.
37 Ibid.
38 Ibid., p. 30.
39 Ibid.
40 Ibid., pp. 46–7.
41 Ibid., p. 47.
42 Wood, minute, 15 April 1946.
43 Ibid.
44 R.H. Charles, Comments on draft prepared by Mr Lester Smith and Mr Morris, 12 September 1945 (Ministry of Education papers, ED.146/13).
45 Memorandum prepared by the AEC for the CAC for Education (England) (n.d.; 1945) (Ministry of Education papers, ED.146/12).
46 Association of Municipal Authorities, written evidence to the CAC for Education (n.d.; 1945) (Ministry of Education papers, ED.146/12).
47 National Association of Class Teachers, written evidence to the CAC for Education (n.d.; 1945) (Ministry of Education papers, ED.146/12).
48 CCA, written evidence to the CAC for Education, Appendix D (n.d.; 1945) (Ministry of Education papers, ED.146/12).
49 Association of Teachers in Colleges and Departments of Education, Memorandum for the CAC for Education (England), January 1946 (Ministry of Education papers, ED.146/12).
50 WEA, written evidence to the CAC for Education (n.d.; 1945) (Ministry of Education papers, ED.146/12).
51 'Suggested selection of points to shape the Council's immediate inquiry: what exists now' (n.d.) (Ministry of Education papers, ED.146/13).
52 'Survey of the field of enquiry', IV. Choice of school (n.d.) (Ministry of Education papers, ED.146/13).
53 'School and life after school: the field of coincidence', IV. School education as a factor affecting British industry (n.d.) (Ministry of Education papers, ED.146/13).

54 Ibid., V. 'Adaptation of life at school to life after school', a. the curriculum.

55 Sir F. Clarke, 'Educational objectives: draft statement by the Chairman' (n.d.) (Ministry of Education papers, ED.146/13).

56 Ministry of Education (1945) *The Nation's Schools*, p. 21.

57 'Current criticisms of the proposed triad of secondary school types' (n.d.) (Ministry of Education papers, ED.146/13).

58 Draft report, ch. 1, 'The contrast between theory and practice', 10 May 1946 (Ministry of Education papers, ED.146/13).

59 Ministry of Education (1947) *School and Life*. London: HMSO, p. 15.

60 Ibid.

61 Ministry of Education (1945) *Organisation of Secondary Schools*, Circular 73. London: HMSO.

62 HMI G. Auty, memo on Manchester development plan, 26 January 1948 (Ministry of Education papers, ED.152/328).

63 Darlington County Borough Education Committee (1946) *The Future of Education in Darlington*, pp. 25–6.

64 See G.E. Jones (1990) 1944 and all that. *History of Education* 19(3): 235–50; also G.E. Jones (1997) *The Education of a Nation*. Cardiff: University of Wales Press, esp. ch. 8.

65 T.B. Tilley, 'Preliminary draft development plan and alternative plan', 12 April 1948 (Ministry of Education papers, ED.152/36).

66 Ibid.

67 J.F. Embley, memo to Mr Lasky, 20 December 1946 (Ministry of Education papers, ED.152/36).

68 Central Division of Durham Education Committee, minute 19, 13 July 1949 (Ministry of Education papers, ED.152/42).

69 W.G. Stone (director of education) to Miss K.A. Kennedy (Ministry of Education), 16 May 1949 (Ministry of Education papers, ED.152/42).

70 Ibid.

71 Miss K.A. Kennedy, memo, 30 May 1949; HMI R. Field, note, 1 June 1949 (Ministry of Education papers, ED.152/238).

72 Hertfordshire County Development Plan, June 1949; J.T.R. Graves, memo, 17 September 1949 (Ministry of Education papers, ED.152/57).

73 G.A.C. Witheridge (Ministry of Education), comments in interview with E.W. Woodhead (chief education officer, Kent), 28 April 1948 (Ministry of Education papers, ED.152/74).

74 Mr Howlitt (Ministry of Education), minute to Mr Burrows, 9 July 1946 (Ministry of Education papers, ED.152/81).

75 Lancashire development plan, interview memorandum, meeting between LEA and the Ministry, 22 July 1948 (Ministry of Education papers, ED.152/82).

76 A.L. Binns, report to Lancashire education committee, 'The future of the modern school', 11 November 1946 (Lancashire education committee papers).

77 Ibid.

78 G.F. Maw (1945) The future of the secondary modern school. *Journal of Education* 77(914): 431.

79 S.C. Mason to R.H. Charles (Ministry of Education), 5 March 1946 (Ministry of Education papers, ED.147/133).

80 Ibid.

81 W. Alexander (1940) *The Educational Needs of Democracy*. London: University of London Press, p. 17.

82 City of Sheffield education committee, 'Report on postwar reconstruction in education', May 1942, p. 7 (Sheffield Education Department papers).

83 Ibid., p. 8.

84 Ibid., p. 10.

85 Report of the special sub-committee on postwar reconstruction in education, 11 September 1944 (Sheffield Education Department papers).

86 City of Sheffield education committee (1947) *Development Plan for Primary and Secondary Schools*.

87 HMI T.H. Brewerton, comments on Sheffield development plan, 6 December 1947 (Ministry of Education papers, ED.152/374).

88 Ibid.

89 G.A.P. Witheridge, note to Mr Brewerton, 21 April 1948 (Ministry of Education papers, ED.152/374).

## Chapter 6

1 A.H. Halsey and L. Gardner (1953) Selection for secondary education and achievement in four grammar schools. *British Journal of Sociology* 4: 60–75.

2 Ibid., p. 66. See also e.g. H.T. Himmelweit, A.H. Halsey and A.N. Oppenheim (1952) The views of adolescents on some aspects of the social class structure. *British Journal of Sociology* 3: 148–72.

3 H.T. Himmelweit (1954) Social status and secondary education since the 1944 Act: some data for London, in D.V. Glass (ed.) *Social Mobility in Britain*. London: Routledge and Kegan Paul, p. 141.

4 See e.g. O. Banks (1955) *Parity and Prestige in English Secondary Education*. London: Routledge and Kegan Paul.

5 A.H. Halsey, A.F. Heath and J.M. Ridge (1980) *Origins and Destinations*. Oxford: Clarendon Press, p. 70.

6 Ibid.

7 M.P. Carter (1962) *Home, School and Work*. Oxford: Pergamon Press, p. 4.

8 Ibid., p. 6.

9 Ibid., p. 9.

10 Ibid., p. 51.

11 Ibid., p. 10.

12 Ibid., p. 59.

13 H.C. Dent (1958) *Secondary Modern Schools*. London: Routledge and Kegan Paul, p. 29.

14 Ibid., p. 33.

15 Ibid., p. 35.

16 J.B. Mays (1962) *Education and the Urban Child*. Liverpool: Liverpool University Press, p. 93.

17 Ibid., p. 154.

18 Ibid., p. 155.

19 Ibid., p. 156.

20 Ibid.

21 Ibid., pp. 85–6.

22 Ibid., pp. 151–2.

23 Ibid., p. 181.

24 Higher Openshaw County Secondary School, Manchester, HMI inspection report, 5–7 May 1954 (Ministry of Education papers, ED.109/8913).

25 New Moston County Secondary School, Manchester, HMI inspection report, 30 March to 1 April 1955 (Ministry of Education papers, ED.109/8913).

26 Birley County Secondary School for Girls, Manchester, HMI inspection report, 17–19 January 1956 (Ministry of Education papers, ED.109/9400); Birley County Secondary School for Boys, HMI inspection report, 7–9 February 1956 (Ministry of Education papers, ED.109/9400).

27 Harper Green County Secondary Girls' School, Farnworth, HMI inspection report, 12–14 November 1957 (Ministry of Education papers, ED.109/9322).

28 Hyndburn Park County Secondary School, Lancashire, HMI inspection report, 9–11 June 1958 (Ministry of Education papers, ED.109/9322).

29 Oakfield County Secondary School for Boys, Penge, Kent, HMI inspection report, 20–2 October 1947 (Ministry of Education papers, ED.109/8873).

30 Stacey County Secondary School, Cardiff, HMI inspection report, 8–10 May 1956 (Ministry of Education papers, ED.109/9451).

31 Ibid.

32 Newsom committee, visits to schools in South Wales, 22–5 October 1962: Splotlands County Secondary School for Boys, Cardiff (Ministry of Education papers, ED.146/52).

33 Splotlands County Secondary Boys' School, Cardiff, HMI inspection report, 6–8 December 1960 (Ministry of Education papers, ED.109/9451).

34 Ibid.

35 Harehills County Secondary School for Boys, Leeds, HMI inspection report, 5–8 February 1960 (Ministry of Education papers, ED.109/9229).

36 Ibid.

37 Roseville County Secondary School, Leeds, HMI inspection report, 16–18 June 1953.

38 Summer Lane County Modern School, Birmingham, HMI inspection report, 28–9 November 1955 (Ministry of Education papers, ED.109/9363).

39 Slade Boys' County Modern School, Birmingham, HMI inspection report, 28 February to 1 March 1956 (Ministry of Education papers, ED.109/9363).

40 Chillingham Road County Secondary School for Boys, Newcastle, HMI inspection report, 22–4 March 1955 (Ministry of Education papers, ED.109/9024).

41 Sharston Secondary School, Manchester, HMI inspection report, June 1946 (Ministry of Education papers, ED.109/8914).

42 Hatfield House Lane County Secondary School, Sheffield, HMI inspection report, 6–19 February 1953 (Ministry of Education papers, ED.109/9238).

Tretherras County Secondary School, Newquay, HMI inspection report (Ministry of Education papers, ED.109/9301).

Bitterne Park County Secondary School, Southampton, HMI inspection report, 6–9 March 1956 (Ministry of Education papers, ED.109/9418).

45 Hynburn Park County Secondary School, Lancashire, HMI inspection report, 9–11 June 1958 (Ministry of Education papers, ED.109/9322).

46 Hynburn Park County Secondary School, Lancashire, record of HMI inspection meeting with school governors, 11 June 1958 (Ministry of Education papers, ED.109/9322).
47 Lea Village County Modern School for Girls, Birmingham, HMI inspection report, 21–3 February 1956 (Ministry of Education papers, ED.109/9363).
48 Manor Park County Modern School for Girls, Birmingham, HMI inspection report, 28 February to 1 March 1956 (Ministry of Education papers, ED.109/9363).
49 Ibid.
50 Newsom committee, visits to schools in South Wales, 22–5 October 1962 (Ministry of Education papers, ED.146/52).
51 Newsom committee, visits to schools in South Wales, 22–5 October 1962: Splotlands County Secondary School for Boys, Cardiff (Ministry of Education papers, ED.146/52).
52 Splotlands County Secondary Boys' School, Cardiff, HMI inspection report, 6–8 December 1960 (Ministry of Education papers, ED.109/9451).
53 Ibid.
54 Central County Secondary Boys' School, Southampton, HMI inspection report, 2–5 July 1956 (Ministry of Education papers, ED.109/9418).
55 Ibid.
56 Belle Vue County Secondary School for Girls, Leeds, HMI inspection report, 31 January to 1 February 1956 (Ministry of Education papers, ED.109/9396).
57 Ibid.
58 Woodhouse County Secondary School, Leeds, HMI inspection report, 20–1 February 1956 (Ministry of Education papers, ED.109/9396).
59 Cambridge St County Secondary School, Newcastle, HMI inspection report, 6–8 March 1951 (Ministry of Education papers, ED.109/9024).
60 Ibid. Report of HMI inspection meeting with school governing body, 8 March 1951.
61 Bow County Secondary School for Boys, London, HMI inspection report, 10–13 December 1956 (Ministry of Education papers, ED.109/9329).
62 CAC for Education (England), notes on a visit to Bow Secondary School for Boys, London, E.1., Wednesday 5 July 1961 (Ministry of Education papers, ED.146/59).
63 Ibid.
64 Bow County Secondary School HMI inspection report, 10–13 December 1956 (Ministry of Education papers, ED.109/9329).
65 Ibid.
66 CAC for Education (England), notes on visit to Bow Secondary School, 5 July 1961.
67 Ibid.
68 E. Blishen (1955) *Roaring Boys: A Schoolmaster's Agony*. London: Thames and Hudson, p. 7.
69 Ibid.
70 Ibid., p. 19.
71 Ibid., p. 42.
72 Ibid.
73 Ibid., p. 59.

74 Ibid., p. 42.
75 Ibid.
76 Ibid., Foreword.
77 Edward Blishen, interview with the author, 26 October 1994.
78 See L. Spolton (1962) The secondary school in post-war fiction. *British Journal of Educational Studies* 9: 125–41.
79 E. Blishen (1957) The task of the secondary modern school. *The Listener*, 21 February, p. 303.
80 See M. Lawn (1995) Encouraging license and insolence in the classroom: imagining a pedagogic shift. *Curriculum Studies* 3(3): 245–61.
81 R. Farley (1960) *Secondary Modern Discipline*. London: Adam and Charles Black, p. 20.
82 Ibid., p. 59.
83 Ibid., p. 98.
84 Ibid., p. 99.
85 CAC for Education (England), interim analysis of questionnaire, 16 December 1961 (Ministry of Education papers, ED.146/46).
86 CAC for Education (England), Modern schools survey: phase 1 (n.d.; 1961) (Ministry of Education papers, ED.146/46).

## Chapter 7

1 H. Spearman to R.H. Tawney, 5 December 1951 (Tawney papers, Institute of Education).
2 *Manchester Guardian* (1953) report, Miss Horsbrugh's faith in the 'modern' school: characteristic British contribution, 2 July.
3 Ibid.
4 Sir D. Eccles to A. Eden, 14 April 1955 (Ministry of Education papers, ED.136/861).
5 e.g. B. Simon (1955) *The Common Secondary School*. London: Lawrence and Wishart. Apologias for the 11-plus examination included e.g. J.J.B. Dempster (1954) *Selection for Secondary Education*. London: Methuen.
6 Eccles to Eden, 14 April 1955.
7 See Chapter 5.
8 Sir D. Eccles, note, ' "The New Secondary Education", 1947', 3 January 1955 (Ministry of Education papers, ED.147/207).
9 Sir D. Eccles, note to secretary, 17 January 1955 (Ministry of Education papers, ED.147/639).
10 Ibid.
11 Eccles, note, ' "The New Secondary Education", 1947'.
12 Minute to Minister, ' "The New Secondary Education", 1947', n.d. [January 1955] (Ministry of Education papers, ED.147/207).
13 Eccles, note to secretary, 17 January 1955.
14 Ibid.
15 Sir D. Eccles, note to secretary, 'Secondary technical schools', 20 December 1954 (Ministry of Education papers, ED.147/207).

16 Ibid.
17 Sir D. Eccles, note, 'Our meeting on secondary education', 22 February 1955 (Ministry of Education papers, ED.147/206).
18 Sir D. Eccles, note to secretary, 'Secondary technical schools', 24 January 1955 (Ministry of Education papers, ED.147/207).
19 Ibid.
20 Eccles, note, 'Our meeting on secondary education', 22 February 1955.
21 Eccles, note, 'Secondary technical schools', 24 January 1955.
22 Eccles, note to secretary, 17 January 1955.
23 Eccles, note, 'Secondary technical schools', 24 January 1955.
24 Ibid.
25 T.R. Weaver, 'Background notes for a speech, or other publicity or action, on THE SECONDARY SCHOOL BULGE' (based on a discussion in the Minister's room, 24 April 1956), 26 April 1956 (Ministry of Education papers, ED.147/639).
26 Sir D. Eccles, memo, 'Secondary education', 18 September 1956 (Ministry of Education papers, ED.147/636).
27 Ibid.
28 R.H. Heaton, memo, 'Secondary education', 2 October 1956 (Ministry of Education papers, ED.147/636).
29 M.P. Roseveare, note, 'Secondary education', 21 September 1956 (Ministry of Education papers, ED.147/636).
30 Interview memo, Dr R. Pedley with Minister of Education, 16 October 1956 (Ministry of Education papers, ED.147/636).
31 Ibid.
32 G. Lloyd to R.A. Butler, 12 March 1958 (Ministry of Education papers, ED.136/945).
33 Ibid.
34 G.N. Flemming, draft paper for Minister of Education, 21 February 1958, long term educational programme: draft paper for the Ministerial Committee on Higher Education (Ministry of Education papers, ED.136/945).
35 Ibid.
36 *Hansard*, House of Commons Debates, 20 March 1958, cols 1464–5.
37 Ibid., col. 1465.
38 Ibid.
39 Ibid., col. 1466.
40 Ministry of Education (1958) *Secondary Education for All* (Cmnd 604). London: HMSO, p. 4.
41 Ibid., p. 4.
42 Ibid., p. 7.
43 Ibid., p. 5.
44 Ibid., p. 6.
45 B. Simon (1991), *Education and the Social Order, 1940–1990*. London: Lawrence and Wishart, p. 204.
46 W.R. Elliott, memo, 'Notes on various forms of secondary school organisation', 10 December 1960 (Ministry of Education papers, ED.147/641). See also G. McCulloch (1989) *The Secondary Technical School*. London: Falmer, esp. chs 4 and 5, on the failure of the secondary technical schools.

47 Elliott, 'Notes on various forms of secondary school organisation', 10 December 1960.
48 Ministry of Education secondary modern sub-panel, 11–12 April 1956 (Ministry of Education papers, ED.147/639).
49 Ibid.
50 HM Inspectorate, secondary education panel, meeting, 24 April 1959, minute 4(c) (Ministry of Education papers, ED.158/20).
51 Ibid.
52 Secondary modern sub-panel, meeting, 11–12 April 1956 (Ministry of Education papers, ED.147/639).
53 Ibid.
54 HMI secondary education panel, 25 April 1960 (Ministry of Education papers, ED.158/20).
55 HMI report, Greaves Council School, 13 February 1908 (Greaves School Lancaster log book).
56 HMI report, Greaves Council School, 11 April 1921 (Greaves School Lancaster log book).
57 Greaves School Lancaster log book, 26 March 1926.
58 HMI report, Greaves Central School, 13–16 February 1932 (Greaves School Lancaster log book).
59 e.g. Greaves Central School log book 22 November 1933, visit by Mr Vernon Love of Stockport LEA; and log book 2 October 1935, visit by the Parliamentary Secretary of the Board of Education, Mr H. Ramsbotham MP.
60 *The Greavesan, magazine of the Greaves School Lancaster*, vol. 1 (July 1949), p. 4.
61 Interview with Mrs J. Nicholson, 14 September 1993.
62 Interview with Haldane Webb, 6 October 1993; interview with Michael Worth, 15 September 1993.
63 *The Greavesan*, vol. 1 (July 1949), p. 4.
64 Ibid., p. 5.
65 Ibid., p. 7.
66 J.H. Sutton (1953) Editor's introduction, *Bulletin* of the Association of Headmasters and Headmistresses of Lancashire County Secondary Modern Schools, vol. 1, no. 1, June.
67 J.H. Sutton (1956) A mixed school, *Bulletin* of the Association of Headmasters and Headmistresses of Lancashire County SMSs, no. 4, June, p. 6.
68 Ibid.
69 Ibid., p. 8.
70 J.H. Sutton (1963) The headteacher, *Bulletin* of the Association of Headmasters and Headmistresses of Lancashire County SMSs, no. 8, September, p. 4.
71 Interview with Michael Worth, 15 September 1993.
72 Greaves SMS log book, 26 June 1957, 30 July 1957.
73 Interview with Michael Worth, 15 September 1993.
74 See e.g. *Lancaster Guardian and Observer* (1952) report, Staff and students are like one big happy family: Greaves SMS has fine traditions, 7 March, p. 5.
75 Greaves SMS log book, 5 November 1954; 24 January 1958.
76 Greaves SMS log book, 17 April 1958.
77 Greaves SMS log book, 13 June 1960.

78 CAC for Education (England), 'Visit to Greaves County Secondary School, Lancaster', 20 June 1961 (Ministry of Education papers, ED.146/59).
79 Ibid.
80 HMI inspection report, Campions County Secondary School, 5–8 June 1962.
81 Interview with Janet Clark (née Holman), 14 April 1994.
82 On Hertfordshire's school building programme, see J.S. Maclure (1984) *Educational Development and School Building*. London: Longman.
83 Miss Dickinson's speech, official opening of Campions School, 9 March 1956 (Janet Clark papers).
84 Ibid.
85 HMI inspection report, Campions County Secondary School, 5–8 June 1962.
86 J.H. Newsom (1950) *The Child at School*. Harmondsworth: Penguin, p. 65.
87 Ibid., p. 76.
88 Ibid.
89 J. Newsom to J. Holman, 14 June 1955 (Clark papers).
90 Conference with heads of SMSs at Hatfield Technical College, 12 July 1955: headings for discussion (Clark papers).
91 Ibid.
92 J. Holman, speech at Speech Day, autumn 1957 (Clark papers).
93 Ibid.
94 J. Holman, speech at Speech Day, autumn 1958 (Clark papers).
95 Ibid.
96 J. Holman, speech at Speech Day, autumn 1960 (Clark papers).
97 J. Holman, speech at Speech Day, autumn 1961 (Clark papers).
98 Ibid.
99 J. Holman, speech at Speech Day, autumn 1962 (Clark papers).
100 Ibid.
101 J. Holman to Sir R. Gould, n.d. (September 1961) (Clark papers).
102 J. Holman, speech at Speech Day, autumn 1962 (Clark papers).
103 HMI report, Campions County Secondary School, 5–8 June 1962.

## Chapter 8

1 Ministry of Education (1959) *15 to 18* (Crowther Report). London: HMSO, p. 87.
2 Ibid.
3 Ibid., pp. 87–8.
4 Ibid., p. 93.
5 Ibid., p. 94.
6 A. Rowe (1959) *The Education of the Average Child*. London: Harrap, p. 12.
7 Ibid.
8 Ibid., p. 13.
9 Paper prepared by the secondary modern sub-panel for the Central Advisory Council, n.d. [1962] (Ministry of Education papers, ED.146/51).
10 Ibid.
11 CAC for Education, Visits to schools in S. Wales, 22–5 October 1962 (Ministry of Education papers, ED.146/52).

12 Sub-committee 1, School curriculum, Paper 1/61 [n.d.] (Ministry of Education papers, ED.146/53).

13 Ministry of Education (1947) *The New Secondary Education*, pamphlet no. 9. London: HMSO, p. 29.

14 D.B. Bartlett, 'Some aspects of education in the Netherlands' [n.d.] (Ministry of Education papers, ED.146/46).

15 CAC for Education (England), sub-committee 3, School and work, minutes of 3rd meeting, 23 January 1962, item 6, 'The employer's view of the school leaver', (a) (Ministry of Education papers, ED.146/56).

16 BEC, written submission to Newsom inquiry, no. 28 [n.d.] (Ministry of Education papers, ED.146/47).

17 Ibid.

18 NCB, written submission to Newsom inquiry, no. 38 [n.d.] (Ministry of Education papers, ED.146/48).

19 Electricity Council, written evidence to Newsom inquiry, no. 41 [n.d.] (Ministry of Education papers, ED.146/48).

20 CAC for Education (England), minutes of 133rd meeting, 24–5 July 1962, 1(c) (Ministry of Education papers, ED.146/45).

21 This evidence was summarized by the committee's secretary, Miss M.J. Marshall HMI, in 'Streaming in the secondary school', October 1962, CAC paper 135/2/62 (Ministry of Education papers, ED.146/46).

22 ATTI, written submission to Newsom inquiry, no. 11 [n.d.] (Ministry of Education papers, ED.146/47).

23 Physical Education Association, written submission to Newsom inquiry [n.d.] (Ministry of Education papers, ED.146/48).

24 A.B. Clegg, '"Streaming" in primary and secondary schools', July 1962, CAC paper 133/6/62 (Ministry of Education papers, ED.146/46).

25 NUT, written submission to Newsom committee, no. 8 (Ministry of Education papers, ED.146/47).

26 WEA, written submission to Newsom committee, no. 27 (Ministry of Education papers, ED.146/47).

27 Executive Committee of the Communist Party, written submission to Newsom committee, no. 78 (Ministry of Education papers, ED.146/49).

28 CAC for Education (England), meeting 22–3 January 1963, minute 62 (Ministry of Education papers, ED.146/45).

29 Ibid.

30 A.B. Clegg, 'The training of teachers for the slow learner', 12 December 1961, CAC paper 128/2/61 (Ministry of Education papers, ED.146/46).

31 'A summary of evidence on teacher training and recruitment, and the deployment of staff in schools', CAC paper 131/4/62 (Ministry of Education papers, ED.146/46).

32 ACEO, written submission to Newsom committee [n.d.] (Ministry of Education papers, ED.146/47).

33 CAC, visit to Leicester University School of Education, points made by principals and staff, Inf. 71/63 [n.d.] (Ministry of Education papers, ED.146/60).

34 CAC, reports on visits June–July 1961, visit 11B(b), Blenheim County Secondary School, Bulwell (Ministry of Education papers, ED.146/59).

35 Reports on the visits to schools made in June and July 1961 (Ministry of Education papers, ED.146/59).

36  Ibid.
37  Sub-committee I (school curriculum), 18 October 1961, minute 2(a) (Ministry of Education papers, ED.146/54).
38  Ibid.
39  A.B. Clegg, 'A possible way of dealing with curricular and extra-curricular matters', 25 April 1961 (Ministry of Education papers, ED.146/46).
40  Ibid.
41  J. Newsom, memo, 'Some key issues for the Report' [n.d.; 1961] (Ministry of Education papers, ED.146/46).
42  Catherine Avent, interview, 14 January 1994.
43  J. Newsom (1948) *The Education of Girls*. London: Faber, p. 109.
44  K. Ollerenshaw (1961) *Education for Girls*. London: Faber, p. 18.
45  Ibid., p. 195.
46  Ibid.
47  School Curriculum sub-committee, paper 1/61 [n.d.; 1961] (Ministry of Education papers, ED.146/53).
48  NAHT, memo to Newsom commission, 'The education of the average and below-average pupils of 13–16 years: some thoughts and findings relating to GIRLS ONLY' [n.d.] (Ministry of Education papers, ED.146/47).
49  CAC for Education (England), visit XI(ii), 4 July 1961, Blenheim County Secondary School, Bulwell (Ministry of Education papers, ED.146/59).
50  R. Farley (1960) *Secondary Modern Discipline*. London: Adam and Charles Black, p. 63.
51  CAC for Education (England), 125th meeting, May 1961 (Ministry of Education papers, ED.146/45).
52  ATDS, 'Policy for teaching housecraft in secondary modern schools' [n.d.] (ATDS papers, 177/3/2/4).
53  Miss M. Marshall (Truro Secondary Modern Girls' School), 'Report on handicraft in modern schools' [n.d.] (ATDS papers, 177/3/2/4).
54  Ibid.
55  B.C. Edwards (Hotel and Catering Institute) to Miss E.I. Harper (secretary, ATDS), 23 March 1950 (ATDS papers, 177/3/2/5).
56  Ibid.
57  English panel of HMIs, 'English for pupils of average or less than average ability between the ages 13–16' (Ministry of Education papers, ED.146/51).
58  Ibid.
59  D. Ayerst, issues paper, 'The English subjects and the teaching of English', January 1962 (Ministry of Education papers, ED.146/53).
60  Issues paper for sub-committee 1 on mathematics and science [n.d.; 1962] (Ministry of Education papers, ED.146/53).
61  Paper prepared by the secondary modern sub-panel of HMIs [n.d.] (Ministry of Education papers, ED.146/51).
62  K. Ollerenshaw, memorandum submitted to the curriculum sub-committee, 'Mathematics for 13–16 year olds of average and less than average ability', 7 February 1962 (Ministry of Education papers, ED.146/53).
63  Ibid.
64  Sir D. Eccles, note to Secretary, 7 February 1955 (Ministry of Education papers, ED.147/303).

65 Note of a meeting between the Minister and the Chairman of the SSEC on 17 March [1955] (Ministry of Education papers, ED.147/303).
66 Meeting on secondary school examinations, 4 May 1955 (Ministry of Education papers, ED.147/303).
67 G. Lloyd to J. Lockwood, 17 June 1958 (Ministry of Education papers, ED.147/304).
68 SSEC (1960) *Secondary School Examinations other than the GCE* (Beloe Report). London: HMSO; see also e.g. P. Fisher (1982) *External Examinations in Secondary Schools in England and Wales, 1944–1964*. Leeds: University of Leeds.
69 SSEC, CSE Standing Committee, paper no. 19, 'A project to compare the ability of candidates for GCE and CSE' [n.d.] (Ministry of Education papers, ED.147/776).
70 M. Smieton to T.R. Weaver, 4 July 1961 (Ministry of Education papers, ED.147/310).
71 R.E. Hodd to D.A. Routh (Ministry of Education), n.d. [1961] (Ministry of Education papers, ED.147/679).
72 J.M. Pullan to HMI Mr Staton, 4 June 1962 (Ministry of Education papers, ED.147/756).
73 J.K. Elliot to D.A. Routh (Ministry of Education), 22 December 1961 (Ministry of Education papers, ED.147/679).
74 Ibid.
75 P. Lord to D.A. Routh, 21 December 1961 (Ministry of Education papers, ED.147/679).
76 Ibid.
77 Minutes of meeting of sub-committee 1 (school curriculum), 18 October 1961, discussion on examinations (Ministry of Education papers, ED.146/54).
78 CAC for Education, minutes of weekend conference, 18–20 May 1962, item 34, Examinations and assessments (Ministry of Education papers, ED.146/45).
79 A. Godwin to Lord Amory, 25 April 1961 (Ministry of Education papers, ED.146/46).
80 CAC meeting, 16–17 October 1962, item 47, discussion on streaming, part 3 (Ministry of Education papers, ED.146/45).
81 AEC, evidence to Newsom committee, no. 1 [n.d.] (Ministry of Education papers, ED.146/47).
82 ACEO, evidence to Newsom committee, no. 5 [n.d.] (Ministry of Education papers, ED.146/47).
83 Institute of Personnel Management, evidence to Newsom committee, no. 35 [n.d.] (Ministry of Education papers, ED.146/47).
84 NAHT, evidence to Newsom committee, no. 13 [n.d.] (Ministry of Education papers, ED.146/47).
85 CAC meeting, 17–19 June 1963 (Ministry of Education papers, ED.146/45).
86 Ibid; also paper 145/2/63 (Ministry of Education papers, ED.146/46).
87 CAC meeting, 9–10 July 1963, item 77(d) (Ministry of Education papers, ED.146/45).
88 CAC meeting, 7–9 June 1963, minute 1 (Ministry of Education papers, ED.146/45).
89 Ministry of Education (1963) *Half our Future* (Newsom Report). London: HMSO, p. 31.

90  Ibid., p. 113.
91  Ibid., p. 36. The earlier draft criticized by Winnard had begun: 'Most of our boys are going to work with their hands, whether in skilled or unskilled jobs.'
92  Ibid.
93  Ibid., p. 37.

## Chapter 9

1  See B. Simon (1992) The politics of comprehensive reorganization: a retrospective analysis. *History of Education* 21(4): 355–62.
2  *Daily Mirror* (1965) feature, The great experiment, 19 May.
3  See e.g. D. Crook (1993) Edward Boyle: Conservative champion of comprehensives? *History of Education* 22(1): 49–62; C. Knight (1990) *The Making of Tory Education Policy in Post War Britain, 1950–1986*. London: Falmer.
4  *Hansard*, House of Commons Debates, 27 November 1964, col. 1705.
5  Ibid., col. 1707.
6  Ibid., col. 1710.
7  Ibid., col. 1780.
8  Ibid., col. 1781.
9  *Hansard*, House of Commons Debates, 21 January 1965, col. 413.
10  Ibid., cols 423–4.
11  Ibid., col. 424.
12  Ibid., col. 429.
13  Ibid., cols 439–40.
14  M. Thatcher (1995) *The Path to Power*. London: HarperCollins, p. 159.
15  Kathleen Ollerenshaw, interview, 17 September 1993.
16  Thatcher, *The Path to Power*, p. 159.
17  C. Benn and B. Simon (1972) *Half Way There*, 2nd edn. Harmondsworth: Penguin, p. 101.
18  J.J. Withrington, note, 24 June 1964 (Ministry of Education papers, ED.147/642).
19  Ibid.
20  Inspectorate, secondary education panel, meeting, 7–8 October 1964, minute 4(f) (DES papers, ED.158/21). On educational responses to Commonwealth immigration in the 1960s, see also I. Grosvenor (1994) 'Education, history and the making of racialised identities in post-1945 Britain', unpublished PhD thesis. University of Birmingham; L. Chessum (1997) 'Sit down you haven't reached that stage yet': African Caribbean children in Leicester schools 1960–74. *History of Education* 26(4): 409–29.
21  Miss W. Harte, 'Comments on Secretary of State's draft Paper on comprehensive education dated 29.12.64' (DES papers, ED.147/827A).
22  Ibid.
23  Fourth draft of circular on the reorganisation of secondary education, 14 March 1965, paragraph 40 (DES papers, ED.147/827B).
24  'Secondary reorganization: commentary on the draft circular. Additional comment on paragraph 40 of the Draft' (n.d.; March 1965?) (DES papers, ED.147/827A).

25  Ibid.

26  NAS, meeting with secretary of state, 25 May 1965, minute 14(ii) (DES papers, ED.147/827B).

27  CCA, 'Observations on the draft circular by the Department of Education and Science on "The organisation of secondary education"', 11 June 1965 (DES papers, ED.147/827B).

28  AMC, 'Department of Education and Science draft circular entitled "The Organisation of Secondary Education": comments of the Education Committee of the Association', 3 June 1965 (DES papers, ED.147/827B).

29  Headmasters' Association, 'Observations on the draft circular from the Department of Education and Science on the organisation of secondary education', March 1965 (DES papers, ED.147/827C).

30  M.L. James, 'Draft circular on the organisation of secondary education: results of consultation with bodies outside the Department', 18 June 1965 (DES papers, ED.147/827C).

31  Inspectorate, secondary education panel, 28–9 April 1965, minute 7 (DES papers, ED.158/21).

32  DES (1965) The organisation of secondary education, Circular 10/65, 12 July.

33  D. Hargreaves (1967) *Social Relations in a Secondary School*. Routledge and Kegan Paul, London: p. ix.

34  C. Lacey (1969) *Hightown Grammar*. Manchester: Manchester University Press, pp. xi–xii.

35  P. Woods (1979) *The Divided School*. London: Routledge and Kegan Paul.

36  *Daily Mirror* (1965) feature, The great experiment, 19 May.

37  A. Kerckhoff, K. Fogelman, D. Crook and D. Reeder (1996) *Going Comprehensive in England and Wales*. London: Woburn, p. 210.

38  I. Goodson (1992) *The Making of Curriculum*, 2nd edn. London: Falmer, pp. 140–1. See also e.g. I. Goodson (1987) *School Subjects and Curriculum Change*, 2nd edn. London: Falmer; I. Goodson (1984) Defining a subject for the comprehensive school: a case-study, in S. Ball (ed.) *Comprehensive Schooling*. London: Falmer, pp. 177–99; I. Goodson (1992) On curriculum form: notes towards a theory of curriculum. *Sociology of Education* 65(1): 66–75.

39  R.G. Burgess (1983) *Experiencing Comprehensive Education*. London: Methuen, p. 129.

40  Ibid., p. 240.

41  See e.g. G. Whitty (1985) Social studies and political education in England since 1945, in I. Goodson (ed.) *Social Histories of the Secondary Curriculum*. London: Falmer, pp. 269–88; Goodson, *School Subjects and Curriculum Change*, esp. ch. 8; A. Hargreaves (1986) *Two Cultures of Schooling*. London: Falmer, esp. ch. 8.

42  S. Ball (1984) Introduction: comprehensives in crisis?, in Ball (ed.) *Comprehensive Schooling*, pp. 1–26.

43  See e.g. G.F. Riseborough (1981) Teacher careers and comprehensive schooling: an empirical study. *Sociology* 15(3): 352–80; P.J. Sikes (1984) Teacher careers in the comprehensive school, in Ball (ed.) *Comprehensive Schooling*, pp. 247–71.

44  S. Ball (1981) *Beachside Comprehensive*. Cambridge: Cambridge University Press, p. 34.

45 B. Jackson and D. Marsden (1966) *Education and the Working Class*, 2nd edn. Harmondsworth: Penguin, p. 250.

**Chapter 10**

1 See e.g. J. Lawrence and M. Tucker (1988) *Norwood was a Difficult School*. London: Macmillan.
2 *Independent* (1995) report, Reprieved school heads A-level table, 18 August.
3 See e.g. National Commission on Education (1996) *Success Against the Odds: Effective Schools in Disadvantaged Areas*. London: Routledge; *TES* (1997) report, The pile 'em high club, 21 February.
4 e.g. *Sunday Times* (1992) report, Life at the bottom, 22 November; *Observer* (1997) report, Yes, location matters, but teaching matters more, 16 March.
5 K. Baker (1993) *The Turbulent Years*. London: Faber and Faber, p. 165.
6 Ibid., p. 169.
7 *Education* (1982) report, Mailed fist and velvet glove from Mr David Young, 19 November.
8 *TES* (1983) report, Good enough for your child?, 25 February.
9 See e.g. G. McCulloch (1987) History and policy: the politics of the TVEI, in D. Gleeson (ed.) *TVEI and Secondary Education*. Milton Keynes: Open University Press, pp. 13–37.
10 See e.g. G. McCulloch (1989) City technology colleges: an old choice of school? *British Journal of Educational Studies* 37(1): 30–43.
11 Department for Education (1992) *Choice and Diversity*. London: HMSO, p. 10.
12 Ibid.
13 See also G. McCulloch (1995) The power of three: 'parity of esteem' and the social history of tripartism, in E. Jenkins (ed.) *Studies in the History of Education*. Leeds: University of Leeds Press, pp. 113–32.
14 R. Dearing (1994) *The National Curriculum and its Assessment*. London: SCAA, p. 21.
15 Ibid., p. 19.
16 Ibid., p. 20.
17 National Commission on Education (1993) *Learning to Succeed*. London: Heinemann, p. 1.
18 Ibid.
19 Ibid., p. 2.
20 Ibid., p. 6.
21 Ibid., p. 7.
22 Ibid.
23 *Independent* (1995) report, Best and worst in schools grow further apart, 21 November.
24 *Independent* (1996) report, Gulf between best and worst still growing, 20 November.
25 *Independent* (1995) front page report, Shephard paper admits schools are short of cash, 15 September; *Observer* (1995) front page report, Parents in revolt over school cuts, 15 September.

26 *Independent* (1996) report, School report: cramped and short of books, 6 February.
27 *Observer* (1996) report, Schools of shame, 3 March.
28 P. Newsam (1996) Take the terminology to task, *TES*, 22 March.
29 J. Judd (1996) The great comprehensive debate: pass or fail? *Independent*, 7 March.
30 Ibid.
31 T. Mooney (1996) Is selection good for the kids? *Independent*, 29 March.
32 *TES* (1996) report, Appalled by some unnatural selection, 22 March.
33 J. Caperon (1996) This sickening see-saw of success, *TES*, 9 February.
34 Department for Education and Employment (DfEE) (1996) *Self-Government for Schools*. London: HMSO, p. 2.
35 Ibid., p. 3.
36 Ibid.
37 Ibid., p. 37.
38 e.g. *TES* (1996) report, Dream on Mr Major . . . , 28 June.
39 *Independent* (1996) leading article, A playground punch-up that misses the point, 26 June.
40 Ibid.
41 T. Blair (1996) Don't give idealism a bad name, *TES*, 14 June.
42 *Independent* (1996) front page report, Schools have failed pupils says Blunkett, 28 February.
43 T. Blair (1996) Don't give idealism a bad name, *TES*, 14 June.
44 *Independent* (1997) front page report, 'Go grammar' lure for schools, 14 April.
45 *Guardian* (1997) report, Tories offer infant grammars, 22 April.
46 *Independent* (1997) report, Blair pledges 21-point plan for education, 15 April.
47 *Independent* (1997) report, Blair attacks Tory 'policy of rejection', 28 April.

## Chapter 11

1 B. Simon (1992) The politics of comprehensive reorganization: a retrospective analysis. *History of Education* 21(4): 302.
2 DfEE (1997) *Excellence In Schools*. London: HMSO, p. 3.
3 Ibid., p. 5.
4 Ibid., p. 10.
5 Ibid.
6 Ibid., p. 11.
7 Ibid., pp. 37–8.
8 Ibid., p. 38.
9 Ibid.
10 Ibid., p. 39.
11 Ibid., pp. 39–40.
12 Ibid., p. 40.
13 Ibid., p. 41.
14 H. Dent (1952) *Change in English Education*. London: University of London Press, p. 93.
15 Ibid.
16 DfEE, *Excellence in Schools*, p. 38.

# Bibliography

## Unpublished sources

Association of Teachers of Domestic Subjects (ATDS) – University of Warwick Modern Records Centre.
Board of Education – Public Record Office, Kew.
Clark, J. (Campions School) – private collection.
Clarke, F. – Institute of Education, London.
Department of Education and Science – Public Record Office, Kew.
Greaves School, Lancaster – held by the school.
Incorporated Association of Assistant Masters (IAAM) – Institute of Education, London.
Lancashire education committee – Lancashire local records office, Preston.
Mansbridge, A. – British Museum, London, Add. Mss 65253.
Ministry of Education – Public Record Office, Kew.
Sheffield Education Department – Sheffield local records office, Sheffield.
Simon, Lady Shena – Manchester Central Library.
Tawney, R.H. – British Library of Political and Economic Science, London; and Institute of Education, London.

## Interviews

C. Avent, 14 January 1994
E. Blishen, 26 October 1994
Mrs J. Clark (née Holman), 14 April 1994
Mrs J. Nicholson, 14 September 1994
Dame K. Ollerenshaw, 17 September 1993
H. Webb, 6 October 1993
M. Worth, 15 September 1993

## Newspapers and periodicals

*Contemporary Review*
*Daily Mirror*
*Education*
*Journal of Education*
*The Guardian*
*Independent*
*Lancaster Guardian and Observer*
*The Listener*
*Manchester Guardian*
*Morning Post*
*Observer*
*School Government Chronicle*
*Sunday Times*

## Official policy reports and records of proceedings

Board of Education (1906) *Report of the Consultative Committee Upon Higher Elementary Schools*. London: HMSO.

Board of Education (1926) *The Education of the Adolescent* (Hadow Report). London: HMSO.

Board of Education (1928) *The New Prospect in Education*, educational pamphlet no. 60. London: HMSO.

Board of Education (1938) *Secondary Education with Special Reference to Grammar Schools and Technical High Schools* (Spens Report). London: HMSO.

Board of Education (1943a) *Curriculum and Examinations in Secondary Schools* (Norwood Report). London: HMSO.

Board of Education (1943b) *Educational Reconstruction* (Cmd 6458). London: HMSO.

Dearing, R. (1994) *The National Curriculum and its Assessment* (Dearing Report). London: School Curriculum and Assessment Authority.

Department for Education (1992) *Choice and Diversity: A New Framework for Schools* (Cm 2021). London: HMSO.

Department for Education and Employment (1996) *Self-Government for Schools* (Cm 3315). London: HMSO.

Department for Education and Employment (1997) *Excellence in Schools* (Cm 3681). London: HMSO.

Department of Education and Science (1965) *The Organisation of Secondary Education*, Circular 10/65. London: HMSO.

*Hansard* – House of Commons Debates.

Labour Party (1922) *Secondary Education for All: A Policy for Labour*. London: Labour Party.

*Labour Party Conference Reports*.

Local development plans – Brighton, Darlington, Durham, Hertfordshire, Lancashire, Leeds, Leicestershire, London, Manchester, Merthyr Tydfil, Sheffield, Swansea.

Ministry of Education (1945) *Organisation of Secondary Schools, circular* no. 73. London: HMSO.

Ministry of Education (1945) *The Nation's Schools: Their Plan and Purpose.* London: HMSO.

Ministry of Education (1947a) *The New Secondary Education,* pamphlet no. 9. London: HMSO.

Ministry of Education (1947b) *School and Life.* London: HMSO.

Ministry of Education (1958) *Secondary Education for All: A New Drive* (Cmnd 604). London: HMSO.

Ministry of Education (1959) *15 to 18* (Crowther Report). London: HMSO.

Ministry of Education (1963) *Half Our Future* (Newsom Report). London: HMSO.

National Commission on Education (1993) *Learning to Succeed.* London: NCE.

National Commission on Education (1996) *Success Against the Odds: Effective Schools in Disadvantaged Areas.* London: Routledge.

Report of Her Majesty's Commissioners appointed to inquire into the revenues and management of certain colleges and schools, and the studies pursued and instruction given in them (1864) (Clarendon Report).

Report of the Commissioners appointed to inquire into the state of popular education in England (1861) (Newcastle Report).

Report of the Royal Commission known as the Schools Inquiry Commission (1868) (Taunton Report), with minutes of evidence.

Report of the Royal Commission on the Elementary Education Acts (1888) (Cross Report).

Royal Commission on Secondary Education (1895) (Bryce Commission) *Report of the Commissioners.* London: HMSO, with minutes of evidence.

Secondary Schools Examinations Council (1960) *Secondary School Examinations other than the GCE* (Beloe Report). London: HMSO.

## Published works

Abraham, J. (1995) *Divide and School: Gender Dynamics in Comprehensive Education.* London: Falmer.

Allsobrook, D. (1986) *Schools for the Shires: The Reform of Middle-Class Education in Mid-Victorian England.* Manchester: Manchester University Press.

Anderson, R.D. (1983) *Education and Opportunity in Victorian Scotland: Schools and Universities.* Oxford: Clarendon Press.

Baker, K. (1993) *The Turbulent Years: My Life in Politics.* London: Faber and Faber.

Ball, S. (1981) *Beachside Comprehensive: A Case Study of Comprehensive Education.* Cambridge: Cambridge University Press.

Ball, S. (1984a) Introduction: comprehensives in crisis?, in S. Ball (ed.) *Comprehensive Education: A Reader.* London: Falmer, pp. 1–26.

Bamford, T.W. (1967) *Rise of the Public Schools: A Study of Boys' Public Boarding Schools in England and Wales from 1837 to the Present Day.* London: Nelson.

Banks, O. (1955) *Parity and Prestige in English Secondary Education: A Study in Educational Sociology.* London: Routledge and Kegan Paul.

Barker, B. (1986) *Rescuing the Comprehensive Experience.* Milton Keynes: Open University Press.

Barker, R. (1972) *Education and Politics 1900–1951: A Study of the Labour Party*. Oxford: Clarendon Press.

Benn, C. (1997) Effective comprehensive education, in R. Pring and G. Walford (eds) *Affirming the Comprehensive Ideal*. London: Falmer, pp. 121–36.

Benn, C. and Chitty, C. (1996) *Thirty Years On: Are Comprehensives Alive and Well or Struggling to Survive?* London: David Fulton / Penguin.

Benn, C. and Simon, B. (1972) *Half Way There*. 2nd edn, Harmondsworth: Penguin.

Blishen, E. (1955) *Roaring Boys: A Schoolmaster's Agony*. London: Thames and Hudson.

Bourn, D. (1995) Equality of opportunity? The Labour government and schools, in J. Fyrth (ed.) *Labour's Promised Land? Culture and Politics in Labour Britain*. London: Lawrence and Wishart, pp. 163–77.

Brehony, K. (1994) The 'school masters' parliament': the origins and function of the Consultative Committee of the Board of Education, 1868–1916. *History of Education*, 23(2): 171–93.

Brennan, E.J.T. (1959) 'The influence of Sidney and Beatrice Webb in English education, 1892–1903', unpublished MA thesis. University of Sheffield.

Brock, C. and Tulasiewitz, W. (eds) (1994) *Education in a Single Europe*. London: Routledge.

Brooks, J.R. (1977) 'Secondary education for all' reconsidered. *Durham Research Review*, 38: 1–8.

Brooks, J.R. (1991) Labour and educational reconstruction, 1916–1926: a case study in the evolution of policy. *History of Education* 20(3): 245–59.

Burgess, R. (1983) *Experiencing Comprehensive Education: A Study of Bishop McGregor School*. London: Methuen.

Carter, M.P. (1962) *Home, School and Work: A Study of the Education and Employment of Young People in Britain*. Oxford: Pergamon Press.

Chandos, J. (1984) *Boys Together: English Public Schools 1800–1864*. London: Hutchinson.

Chessum, L. (1997) 'Sit down you haven't reached that stage yet': African Caribbean children in Leicester schools, 1960–74. *History of Education* 26(4): 409–29.

Chitty, C. (ed.) (1987) *Redefining the Comprehensive Experience*. London: Bedford Way Papers.

Clarke, F. (1933) Some reflections on secondary education. *University of Toronto Quarterly* 3(1): 74–86.

Clarke, F. (1940) *Education and Social Change: An English Interpretation*. London: Sheldon Press.

Connell, W.F. (1980) *A History of Education in the Twentieth Century World*. Canberra: Curriculum Development Centre.

Crook, D. (1993) Edward Boyle: Conservative champion of comprehensives? *History of Education* 22(1): 49–62.

Crossman, R. (1937) *Plato Today*. London: George Allen and Unwin.

Dancy, J. (1965) Technology in a liberal education. *Advancement of Science* October: 379–87.

Dean, D.W. (1971) Conservatism and the national education system, 1922–40. *Journal of Contemporary History* 6: 151–65.

Dempster, J.J.B. (1954) *Selection for Secondary Education: A Survey.* London: Methuen.

Dent, H. (1949) *Secondary Education for All.* London: Routledge and Kegan Paul.

Dent, H. (1952) *Change in English Education: A Historical Survey.* London: University of London Press.

Dent, H. (1954) *Growth in English Education: 1946–1952.* London: Routledge and Kegan Paul.

Dent, H.C. (1958) *Secondary Modern Schools: An Interim Report.* London: Routledge and Kegan Paul.

Farley, R. (1960) *Secondary Modern Discipline: With Special Reference to the 'Difficult' Adolescent in Socially Deprived Industrial Areas.* London: Adam and Charles Black.

Fenwick, K. (1976) *The Comprehensive School 1944–1970.* London: Methuen.

Fisher, P. (1982) *External Examinations in Secondary Schools in England and Wales, 1944–1964.* Leeds: University of Leeds.

Francis, M. (1997) *Ideas and Policies under Labour, 1945–51: Building a New Britain.* Manchester: Manchester University Press.

Goodson, I. (1984) Defining a subject for the comprehensive school: a case-study, in S. Ball (ed.) *Comprehensive Education: A Reader.* London: Falmer, pp. 177–99.

Goodson, I. (1992a) *The Making of Curriculum: Collected Essays,* 2nd edn. London: Falmer.

Goodson, I. (1992b) On curriculum form: notes towards a theory of curriculum. *Sociology of Education* 65: 66–75.

Goodson, I. (1994) *School Subjects and Curriculum Change,* 3rd edn. London: Falmer.

Gordon, P. and White, J. (1979) *Philosophers as Educational Reformers.* London: George Allen and Unwin.

Green, A. (1990) *Education and State Formation: The Rise of Education Systems in England, France and the USA.* London: Macmillan.

Green, A. and Ball, S. (eds) (1988) *Progress and Inequality in Comprehensive Education.* London: Routledge.

Griggs, C. (1983) *The Trades Union Congress and the Struggle for Education, 1868–1925.* London: Falmer.

Grosvenor, I. (1994) 'Education, history and the making of racialised identities in post-1945 Britain', unpublished PhD thesis. University of Birmingham.

Halsey, A.H. and Gardner, L. (1953) Selection for secondary education and achievement in four grammar schools. *British Journal of Sociology* 4: 60–75.

Halsey, A.H., Heath, A.F. and Ridge, J.M. (1980) *Origins and Destinations: Family, Class, and Education in Modern Britain.* Oxford: Clarendon Press.

Hargreaves, A. (1986) *Two Cultures of Schooling: The Case of Middle Schools.* London: Falmer.

Hargreaves, D. (1967) *Social Relations in a Secondary School.* London: Routledge and Kegan Paul.

Hargreaves, D. (1983) *The Challenge for the Comprehensive School: Culture, Curriculum and Community.* London: Routledge and Kegan Paul.

Harris, J. (1992) Political thought and the Welfare State 1870–1940: an intellectual framework for British social policy. *Past and Present* 135: 116–41.

Haslewood, N. (1981) Tawney, the Labour Party and educational policy in the 1920s: a reappraisal, in R. Lowe (ed.) *Labour and Education: Some Twentieth Century Studies*. Leicester: History of Education Society, pp. 51–62.

Hearnden, A. (1974) *Education in the Two Germanies*. Oxford: Basil Blackwell.

Hearnshaw, L.S. (1979) *Cyril Burt, Psychologist*. London: Hodder and Stoughton.

Herbst, J. (1996) *The Once and Future School: 350 Years of American Secondary Education*. London: Routledge.

Himmelweit, H.T. (1954) Social status and secondary education since the 1944 Act: some data for London, in D.V. Glass (ed.) *Social Mobility in Britain*. London: Routledge and Kegan Paul, pp. 141–59.

Himmelweit, H.T., Halsey, A.H. and Oppenheim, A.N. (1952) The views of adolescents on some aspects of the social class structure. *British Journal of Sociology* 3: 148–72.

Honey, J.R. de S. (1977) *Tom Brown's Universe: The Development of the English Public School in the Nineteenth Century*. London: Millington.

Hughes, B. (1979) In defence of Ellen Wilkinson. *History Workshop* 7: 156–69.

Hunt, F. (1991) *Gender and Policy in English Secondary Education, 1880–1940*. Sussex: Harvester.

Husen, T., Tuijman, A. and Halls, W. (eds) (1992) *Schooling in Modern European Society: A Report of the Academia Europaea*. Oxford: Pergamon.

Jackson, B. and Marsden, D. (1966) *Education and the Working Class*, 2nd edn. Harmondsworth: Penguin.

Jones, G.E. (1990) 1944 and all that. *History of Education* 19(3): 235–50.

Jones, G.E. (1997) *The Education of a Nation*. Cardiff: University of Wales Press.

Judges, A.V. (1961) The educational influence of the Webbs. *British Journal of Educational Studies* 10: 33–48.

Kallaway, P. (1996) Fred Clarke and the politics of vocational education in South Africa, 1911–29. *History of Education* 25(4): 353–62.

Kerckhoff, A., Fogelman, K., Crook, D. and Reeder, D. (1996) *Going Comprehensive in England and Wales: A Study of Uneven Change*. London: Woburn.

King, S. (1990) Technical and vocational education for girls: a study of the central schools of London, 1918–1939, in P. Summerfield and E. Evans (eds) *Technical Education and the State*. Manchester: Manchester University Press, pp. 77–96.

Knight, C. (1990) *The Making of Tory Education Policy in Post-War Britain, 1950–1986*. London: Falmer.

Labaree, D. (1989) *The Making of an American High School*. New Haven, CT: Yale University Press.

Lacey, C. (1969) *Hightown Grammar: The School as a Social System*. Manchester: Manchester University Press.

Lawn, M. (1995) Encouraging license and insolence in the classroom: imagining a pedagogic shift. *Curriculum Studies* 3(3): 245–61.

Lawrence, J. and Tucker, M. (1988) *Norwood was a Difficult School*. London: Macmillan.

Lindsay, K. (1926) *Social Progress and Educational Waste*. London: Routledge.

Livingstone, R. (1944) *Plato and Modern Education*. Cambridge: Cambridge University Press.

McCulloch, G. (1987) History and policy: the politics of the TVEI, in D. Gleeson (ed.) *TVEI and Secondary Education*. Milton Keynes: Open University Press.

McCulloch, G. (1988) Imperial and colonial designs: the case of Auckland Grammar School. *History of Education* 17(4): 257–67.

McCulloch, G. (1989a) City technology colleges: an old choice of school? *British Journal of Educational Studies* 37(1): 30–43.

McCulloch, G. (1989b) *The Secondary Technical School: A Usable Past?* London: Falmer.

McCulloch, G. (1991) *Philosophers and Kings: Education for Leadership in Modern England.* Cambridge: Cambridge University Press.

McCulloch, G. (1993) 'Spens v. Norwood': contesting the educational state? *History of Education* 22(2): 163–80.

McCulloch, G. (1995) The power of three: 'parity of esteem' and the social history of tripartism, in E. Jenkins (ed.) *Studies in the History of Education.* Leeds: University of Leeds Press, pp. 113–32.

McCulloch, G. (1996) Educating the public: Tawney, the *Manchester Guardian* and educational reform, in R. Aldrich (ed.) *In History and in Education.* London: Woburn, pp. 116–37.

McCulloch, G. and Sobell, L. (1994) Towards a social history of the secondary modern schools. *History of Education* 23(3): 275–86.

Maclure, S. (1984) *Educational Development and School Building: Aspects of Public Policy 1945 to 1973.* London: Longman.

Manthorpe, C. (1986) Science or domestic science? The struggle to define an appropriate science education for girls in early twentieth century England. *History of Education* 15(3): 195–213.

Mays, J.B. (1962) *Education and the Urban Child.* Liverpool: Liverpool University Press.

Mitchell, F.W. (1967) *Sir Fred Clarke, Master Teacher, 1880–1952.* London: Longman.

Moon, B. (ed.) (1983) *Comprehensive Schools: Challenge and Change.* London: NFER-Nelson.

Muller, D., Ringer, F. and Simon, B. (eds) (1987) *The Rise of the Modern Educational System.* Cambridge: Cambridge University Press.

Newsom, J. (1948) *The Education of Girls.* London: Faber and Faber.

Newsom, J. (1950) *The Child at School.* Harmondsworth: Penguin.

Norwood, C. (1929) *The English Tradition of Education.* London: John Murray.

Norwood, C. and Hope, A. (eds) (1909) *The Higher Education of Boys in England.* London: John Murray.

Nunn, P. ( 1920) *Education: Its Data and First Principles.* London: Edward Arnold.

Ollerenshaw, K. (1961) *Education for Girls.* London: Faber and Faber.

Paton, J.L. (1909) The secondary education of the working classes, in C. Norwood and A. Hope (eds) *The Higher Education of Boys in England.* London: John Murray, pp. 544–54.

Pedley, R. (1963) *The Comprehensive School.* Harmondsworth: Penguin.

Percy, E. (1958) *Some Memories.* London: Eyre and Spottiswoode.

Philips, D. (ed.) (1995) *Education in Germany: Tradition and Reform in Historical Context.* London: Routledge.

Plato ( 1955 edn) *The Republic,* translated by H.P.D. Lee. Harmondsworth: Penguin.

Pring, R. and Walford, G. (eds) (1997) *Affirming the Comprehensive Ideal.* London: Falmer.

Ree, H. (1973) *Educator Extraordinary: The Life and Achievements of Henry Morris, 1889–1961*. London: Longman.

Reeder, D. (1987) The reconstruction of secondary education in England, 1869–1920, in D. Muller, F. Ringer and B. Simon (eds) *The Rise of the Modern Educational System*. Cambridge: Cambridge University Press, pp. 135–50

Reeder, D. (ed.) (1986) *Educating our Masters*. Leicester: Leicester University Press.

Reese, W. (1995) *The Origins of the American High School*. New Haven, CT: Yale University Press.

Riseborough, G. (1981) Teacher careers and comprehensive schooling: an empirical study. *Sociology* 15(3): 352–80.

Roach, J. (1979) Examinations and the secondary schools, 1900–1945. *History of Education* 8(1): 45–58.

Roach, J. (1986) *A History of Secondary Education in England, 1800–1870*. London: Longman.

Robinson, W. (1990) 'Breaking the elementary mould: a study of nine higher grade girls' schools under the London School Board, 1882–1904', unpublished MA thesis. University of London.

Rowe, A. (1959) *The Education of the Average Child*. London: Harrap.

Sanderson, M. (1994) *The Missing Stratum: Technical School Education in England, 1900–1990s*. London: Athlone Press.

Savage, G. (1983) Social class and educational policy: the civil service and secondary education in England during the interwar period. *Journal of Contemporary History* 6: 151–65.

Searby, P. (ed.) (1982) *Educating the Victorian Middle Class*. Leicester: History of Education Society.

Searle, G.R. (1971) *The Quest for National Efficiency: A Study in British Politics and Political Thought, 1899–1914*. Oxford: Basil Blackwell.

Sikes, P. (1984) Teacher careers in the comprehensive school, in S. Ball (ed.) *Comprehensive Education: A Reader*. London: Falmer, pp. 247–71.

Silto, W. (1993) 'Compulsory day continuation schools: their origins, objectives, and development, with special reference to H.A.L. Fisher's 1918 experiment', unpublished PhD thesis. Institute of Education, London.

Silver, H. (1983) The liberal and the vocational, in his *Education as History*. London: Methuen, pp. 153–71.

Simon, B. (1955) *The Common Secondary School*. London: Lawrence and Wishart.

Simon, B. (1965) *Education and the Labour Movement, 1870–1920*. London: Lawrence and Wishart.

Simon, B. (1970) Classification and streaming: a study of grouping in English schools, 1860–1960, in P. Nash (ed.) *History and Education: The Educational Uses of the Past*. New York: Random House, pp. 115–59.

Simon, B. (1974) *The Politics of Educational Reform, 1920–1940*. London: Lawrence and Wishart.

Simon, B. (1991) *Education and the Social Order, 1940–1990*. London: Lawrence and Wishart.

Simon, B. (1992) The politics of comprehensive reorganization: a retrospective analysis. *History of Education* 21(4): 315–62.

Simon, B. (1997) A seismic change: process and interpretation, in R. Pring and G. Walford (eds) *Affirming the Comprehensive Ideal*. London: Falmer, pp. 13–28.

Simon, B. and Bradley, I. (eds) (1975) *The Victorian Public School*. London: Gill and Macmillan.

Snow, C.P. (1963) *The Two Cultures and a Second Look*. Cambridge: Cambridge University Press.

Spolton, L. (1962) The secondary school in post-war fiction. *British Journal of Educational Studies* 9: 125–41.

Spring, J. (1986) *The American School, 1642–1985*. London: Longman.

Steedman, H. (1987) Defining institutions: the endowed grammar schools and the systematisation of English secondary education, in D. Muller, F. Ringer and B. Simon (eds) *The Rise of the Modern Educational System*. Cambridge: Cambridge University Press, pp. 111–34.

Summerfield, P. and Evans, E. (eds) (1990) *Technical Education and the State Since 1850: Historical and Contemporary Perspectives*. Manchester: Manchester University Press.

Sutherland, G. (1984) *Ability, Merit and Measurement: Mental Testing and English Education, 1880–1940*. Oxford: Clarendon Press.

Swinnerton, B. (1996) The 1931 Report of the Consultative Committee on the primary school: tensions and antecedents. *History of Education* 25(1): 73–90.

Szreter, R. (1990) A note on R.H. Tawney's early interest in juvenile employment and misemployment. *History of Education* 19(4): 375–82.

Talbott, J.E. (1969) *The Politics of Educational Reform in France, 1918–1940*. Princeton, NJ: Princeton University Press.

Tawney, R.H. (1909) The economics of boy labour. *Economic Journal* December: 517–37.

Tawney, R.H. (1931) *Equality* (1964 edn). London: George Allen and Unwin.

Taylor, W. (1963) *The Secondary Modern School*. London: Faber and Faber.

Taylor, W. (1996) Education and the Moot, in R. Aldrich (ed.) *In History and in Education*. London: Woburn, pp. 159–86.

Thatcher, M. (1995) *The Path to Power*. London: HarperCollins.

Thoms, D.W. (1975) The emergence and failure of the day continuation school experiment. *History of Education* 4(1): 36–50.

Ueda, R. (1987) *Avenues to Adulthood: The Origins of the High School and Social Mobility in an American Suburb*. Cambridge: Cambridge University Press.

Vernon, B. (1983) *Ellen Wilkinson, 1891–1947*. London: Croom Helm.

Vincent, A. and Plant, R. (1984) *Philosophy, Politics and Citizenship: The Life and Thought of British Idealists*. Oxford: Blackwell.

Vlaeminke, M. (1990) The subordination of technical education in secondary schools, 1870–1914, in P. Summerfield and E. Evans (eds) *Technical Education and the State*. Manchester: Manchester University Press, pp. 55–76.

Walden, G. (1996) *We Should Know Better: Solving the Education Crisis*. London: Fourth Estate.

Weeks, A. (1986) *Comprehensive Schools: Past, Present and Future*. London: Methuen.

Whitty, G. (1985) Social studies and political education in England since 1945, in I. Goodson (ed.) *Social Histories of the Secondary Curriculum*. London: Falmer, pp. 269–88.

Woods, P. (1979) *The Divided School*. London: Routledge and Kegan Paul.

Wooldridge, A. (1994) *Measuring the Mind: Education and Psychology in England c.1860–c.1990*. Cambridge: Cambridge University Press.

# Index